Henry Parry Liddon

Sermons Preached before the University of Oxford

Second Series (1868-1879)

Henry Parry Liddon

Sermons Preached before the University of Oxford
Second Series (1868-1879)

ISBN/EAN: 9783744742672

Printed in Europe, USA, Canada, Australia, Japan

Cover: Foto ©Lupo / pixelio.de

More available books at **www.hansebooks.com**

SERMONS

PREACHED BEFORE

The University of Oxford

(SECOND SERIES)

1868—1879

RIVINGTONS

London..*Waterloo Place*
Oxford...*Magdalen Street*
Cambridge..*Trinity Street*

SERMONS

PREACHED BEFORE

The University of Oxford

BY

H.^y P. LIDDON, D.D.

CANON RESIDENTIARY OF ST. PAUL'S, AND IRELAND PROFESSOR

SECOND SERIES
1868—1879

New York
E. P. DUTTON AND COMPANY
MDCCCLXXX

TO

JOHN ARCHIBALD SHAW STEWART, Esq. M.A.

BURSAR OF KEBLE COLLEGE,

IN WHOSE LIFE OF PRACTICAL BENEVOLENCE

HIS OXFORD CONTEMPORARIES HAVE BEEN WONT TO TRACE

THE POWER AND BEAUTY

OF A CLEAR AND CONSISTENT FAITH.

Advertisement.

OF the Sermons contained in this volume nine[1] were preached by the appointment of successive Vice-Chancellors, and the remainder in the author's turns as Select Preacher.

Two of the Sermons[2] have been published singly, and they differ somewhat in complexion from the rest. Recent discussions in Convocation have seemed to make it a duty to reprint that on "The Life of Faith and the Athanasian Creed."[3] And the Sermon on "Christ and Human Law"[4] will possess an interest, at least for a great many persons, distinct in degree and kind from that which any others in the volume could command. It was preached at the suggestion of Dr. Hamilton, the late Bishop of Salisbury, who was at the time lying on what proved to be his deathbed, and in whose hopes and fears respecting subjects that lay nearest to his heart the writer was permitted to share. The opinions which are embodied in the Sermon are substantially those of this revered and lamented prelate, while the author is alone responsible for any faults of treatment or expression.

[1] Sermons II., V., VI., XI., XII., XIII., XIV., XV., XVI.
[2] Sermons VII., XVI.   [3] Sermon VII.   [4] Sermon XVI.

3 AMEN COURT, E.C.,
    Michaelmas 1879.

CONTENTS.

SERMON I.

PREJUDICE AND EXPERIENCE.

ST. JOHN i. 46.

Nathanael said unto him, Can there any good thing come out of Nazareth? Philip saith unto him, Come and see . . . 1

Preached at St. Mary's on the Nineteenth Sunday after Trinity, Oct. 23, 1870.

SERMON II.

HUMILITY AND TRUTH.

1 COR. iv. 7.

Who maketh thee to differ from another? And what hast thou that thou hast not received? Now, if thou didst receive it, why dost thou glory, as if thou hadst not received it? 18

Preached at St. Mary's on Quinquagesima Sunday, Feb. 19, 1871.

SERMON III.

IMPORT OF FAITH IN A CREATOR.

GEN. i. 1.

In the beginning God created the heaven and the earth . . . 38

Preached at St. Mary's on Septuagesima Sunday, Feb. 5, 1871.

SERMON IV.

WORTH OF FAITH IN A LIFE TO COME.

Rev. vii. 9, 10.

I beheld, and lo, a great multitude, which no man could number, of all nations, and kindreds, and people, and tongues, stood before the throne, and before the Lamb, clothed with white robes, and palms in their hands; and cried with a loud voice, saying, Salvation to our God Which sitteth upon the throne, and unto the Lamb . . 55

Preached at St. Mary's on the Twenty-first Sunday after Trinity, Nov. 10, 1878.

SERMON V.

INFLUENCES OF THE HOLY SPIRIT.

St. John iii. 8.

The wind bloweth where it listeth, and thou hearest the sound thereof, but canst not tell whence it cometh, and whither it goeth . . 78

Preached at St. Mary's on Whitsun Day, June 4, 1876.

SERMON VI.

GROWTH IN THE APPREHENSION OF TRUTH.

Heb. vi. 1.

Therefore leaving the principles of the doctrine of Christ, let us go on unto perfection 98

Preached at St. Mary's on the First Sunday after Trinity (Act Sunday), June 15, 1879.

SERMON VII.

THE LIFE OF FAITH AND THE ATHANASIAN CREED.

St. John iii. 36.

He that believeth on the Son hath everlasting life; and he that believeth not the Son shall not see life; but the wrath of God abideth on him 119

Preached at St. Mary's on the Twenty-first Sunday after Trinity, Oct. 20, 1872.

SERMON VIII.

CHRIST'S SERVICE AND PUBLIC OPINION.

GAL. i. 10.

If I yet pleased men, I should not be a servant of Christ . . . 144

Preached at St. Mary's on the Twenty-fifth Sunday after Trinity, Nov. 18, 1877.

SERMON IX.

CHRIST IN THE STORM.

ST. MARK iv. 38.

And He was in the hinder part of the ship, asleep upon a pillow; and they awake Him, and say unto Him, Master, carest Thou not that we perish? 165

Preached at St. Mary's on the Twenty-third Sunday after Trinity, Nov. 12, 1871.

SERMON X.

SACERDOTALISM.

2 COR. v. 18.

But all things are of God, Who hath reconciled us unto Himself, through Jesus Christ, and hath given unto us the ministry of The Reconciliation: to wit, that God was in Christ, reconciling the world unto Himself, not imputing their trespasses unto them; and hath given unto us the word of The Reconciliation 183

Preached at St. Mary's on Sexagesima Sunday, Jan. 31, 1875.

SERMON XI.

THE PROPHECY OF THE MAGNIFICAT.

ST. LUKE i. 51-53.

He hath shewed strength with His arm: He hath scattered the proud in the imagination of their hearts. He hath put down the mighty from their seats, and exalted them of low degree. He hath filled the hungry with good things; and the rich He hath sent empty away 203

Preached at St. Mary's on the Twenty-fifth Sunday after Trinity, Nov. 22, 1874.

SERMON XII.

THE FALL OF JERICHO.

Heb. xi. 30.

By faith the walls of Jericho fell down, after they were compassed about seven days 222

Preached at St. Mary's on Trinity Sunday, June 8, 1873 (Ramsden Sermon).

SERMON XIII.

THE COURAGE OF FAITH.

Rom. i. 16.

I am not ashamed of the Gospel of Christ; for it is the power of God unto salvation to every one that believeth 242

Preached at St. Mary's on Trinity Sunday, May 25, 1877 (Ramsden Sermon).

SERMON XIV.

THE CURSE ON MEROZ.

Judges v. 23.

Curse ye Meroz, said the angel of the Lord, curse ye bitterly the inhabitants thereof; because they came not to the help of the Lord, to the help of the Lord against the mighty 264

Preached at St. Mary's on the Second Sunday after Trinity (Act Sunday), June 9, 1872.

SERMON XV.

THE GOSPEL AND THE POOR.

St. Luke iv. 18.

The Spirit of the Lord is upon Me, because He hath anointed Me to preach the Gospel to the poor 281

Preached at St. Mary's on Whitsun Day, June 9, 1878.

SERMON XVI.

CHRIST AND HUMAN LAW.

St. John xix. 10, 11.

PAGE

Then saith Pilate unto Him, Speakest Thou not unto me? knowest Thou not that I have power to crucify Thee, and have power to release Thee? Jesus answered, Thou couldest have no power at all against Me, except it were given thee from above: therefore he that delivered Me unto thee hath the greater sin 300

Preached at St. Mary's on the Third Sunday in Lent, Feb. 28, 1869 (Assize Sermon).

SERMON I.

PREJUDICE AND EXPERIENCE.

ST. JOHN i. 46.

Nathanael said unto him, Can there any good thing come out of Nazareth? Philip saith unto him, Come and see.

THE main purpose of the fourth Evangelist was to show, by a careful selection from our Lord's words and works, what was the full and momentous truth respecting His Divine Person.[1] But subordinate to this object there were others; and among these it was of importance to dispose of an objection, which would have been urged often and earnestly at the close of the Apostolical age. If the miracles of Christ were such as the earlier Evangelists had described, how was it, men asked, that they did not produce a more general conviction of His Divine Mission among His countrymen and contemporaries? The answer which the fourth Gospel gives to this question is in effect, that the conduct and temper of the Jews furnishes a sufficient explanation of their insensibility to the real value of the miracles of Christ. The picture of the Jews which is presented by the fourth Evangelist offers some undeniable points of contrast to that which meets us in the first three Gospels. The first three Gospels describe several individual Jews with marked lights and shadows of personal character; the fourth Gospel refers to them as a class with

[1] St. John xx. 31.

an average habit of thought and feeling. There is no inconsistency between these representations; and here, as elsewhere, St. John says enough to serve his immediate purpose, without at all implying that it is exhaustive, or more than a selection from the rich materials before him. "The Jews," as he describes them, are morally and spiritually, rather than intellectually, deficient and dull; they are at no loss for ingeniously captious arguments, but they are deaf to the persuasive eloquence of spiritual beauty. Face to face with the Light of the World, Who, as the Evangelist is persuaded, has only to be contemplated steadily by the true spirit's eye in order to be forthwith adored, the Jews arm themselves with the weapons of a petty dialectic, which betrays a warp and narrowness in the moral sympathies, even more than any intellectual wrongheadedness or religious ignorance. Thus the dialogues of the Gospel are an illustration of the thesis that "the Light shineth in darkness, and the darkness comprehended it not;"[1] they show us how it was that the Incarnate Word came unto the people which was, in virtue of its past history, especially His own, and which, although His own, did not receive Him.[2]

One great misery of this Jewish temper was that it kept men at a distance from our Lord. Physically, indeed, the Jews were close to Him; but spiritually they lived in another sphere of being. As they heard His language with the outward ear, and then set themselves to confute it; so they beheld His works with the bodily eye, but saw in them nothing higher than a skill which eluded detection. The reason was, according to the Evangelist, because both the words and works could only be placed in their true perspective by souls who were already in some sort of willing contact, however tentative and provisional, with the Person of the Speaker and Worker. St. John, indeed, does not

[1] St. John i. 5.   [2] St. John i. 11.

depreciate the evidential force of the miracles to which our Lord Himself appealed:[1] each of the seven miracles which the Evangelist describes is in some way pre-eminent, and the greatest of all the recorded miracles of Christ is described by St. John alone.[2] But the tendency of his narrative is to discourage exaggerated expectations as to the power of miracles by themselves to create faith; he does not allow us to suppose that they will enforce a conviction by sheer intellectual constraint in the case of those who are morally and spiritually indisposed to embrace it. Even the most startling miracle was not meant to stand unaided and alone: in the design of Providence it was to co-operate with the attractive power of a Faultless Character, appealing persuasively to the moral sense. When the moral sense was paralysed, a miracle naturally appeared to the understanding only in the light of an unusual or unwelcome occurrence, for which it was presumed some explanation, natural or artificial, must be forthcoming. A miracle becomes an intellectual challenge which irritates, where it is not the accompaniment of a moral influence which wins. To be in intimate contact with the Person of Christ, the Word Incarnate, manifesting forth His Glory; to gaze upon Him, not fitfully, but constantly, earnestly, penetratingly; to learn at length to see in His words and works the harmonious product of His superhuman Personality, a perpetual radiation from the Life of the All-Perfect Being: this was what St. John desired for his countrymen, as being what he had experienced himself. But it was precisely this for which the leading moral features of their peculiar temper so seriously indisposed the Jews: and the result is exhibited in St. John's narrative. He leads us on step by step to a double climax, in which the evidence for Christ's claims and His rejection by the Jews alike reach the

---

[1] St. John x. 38. St. Matt. xi. 4, 5. Cf. Heb. ii. 4.
[2] St. John xi.

highest point conceivable. On the one hand, Lazarus is raised from the dead: on the other, the Son of God is crucified.

If the fourth Gospel thus sets itself to explain why it was that the Jews did not receive the Light of the World manifested among them, it naturally completes this explanation by showing, in the way of contrast, how it was that the disciples did receive Him. The disciples, too, had had their difficulties in the way of faith: they came of the same stock as their unbelieving contemporaries; they breathed the same intellectual and originally the same moral atmosphere; they were fed by the same truths and warped by the same prejudices. But they placed themselves morally and spiritually in contact with the Person of Christ, the Incarnate Word, and from Him there streamed forth upon their souls a power which made them His. This is the Evangelist's inner sense when he tells us, as if incidentally, that the two disciples of the Baptist came and saw where Jesus dwelt;[1] or that Andrew brings his own brother Simon to Jesus;[2] or that St. Philip meets Nathanael's *à priori* objection to the prophetic or spiritual associations of Nazareth by the simple invitation, "Come and see."[3]

I.

Nathanael comes before our Lord as the victim and exponent of a popular prejudice. It was one of several irrational prejudices which went to make up the dull or passionate hostility shown towards Jesus Christ by the Jewish opinion of the time. When Philip, in his eager enthusiasm, announces that in Jesus from Nazareth was to be found the fulfilment of all the choicest hopes with which the Mosaic and prophetical writings had inspired the noblest souls in Israel, Nathanael bluntly asks whether any good thing can come out of Nazareth.

[1] St. John i. 39.   [2] *Ibid.* 42.   [3] *Ibid.* 46.

Why should no good come out of Nazareth? What was the nature of this presumption against Nazareth? Did it rest on some political or social feeling, the exact ground of which may have been guessed at by later tradition, but the true reason of which is lost? Or was its motive theocratic? Does "good" in Nathanael's mouth mean that specific good which in the judgment of every religious Israelite lay in the fulfilment of the Messianic promise? Is it his meaning that if the new Prophet announced Himself as from Nazareth, the case against Him must be decisive; because while Nazareth is not so much as named in the Jewish Scriptures, every Israelite knows that the Messianic King is to be born in Bethlehem, little indeed among the cities of Judah, yet "not the least," considering its theocratic rank, and the extraordinary honour that awaited it?[1] Or is Nathanael swayed by some popular saying, which altogether warps his judgment; and which, whatever may have been its historical origin, has placed the Galilean village under a religious ban, so that any disposition to expect from it a message of truth or an effort of virtue at once incurs rebuke or even ridicule?

Decide this question as we may, there can be no doubt about the strength of Nathanael's prejudice against Nazareth. Nor, let us remark, was he, as yet, morally the worse for entertaining it. Himself a native of Galilee, he had heard Nazareth depreciated all his life, and he simply gave expression to a conviction which it had not occurred to him to question. He held it, together with his other opinions and beliefs, with honest tenacity. If the intellectual furniture of our several minds could be examined and catalogued, it would probably be found that we are most, if not all of us, to a certain extent in Nathanael's condition: we have received from our elders an assortment of prepossessions which combine with the highest of

[1] Micah v. 2. St. Matt. ii. 5, 6.

truths the least tenable of assumptions. Most of us who think at all are engaged throughout our lives in revising at least some portion of this hereditary mental stock. Some men, it may be feared, only succeed in ridding themselves of priceless truths, while they cling on uninquiringly to stupid superstitions; as was his case who had no faith in the truth of Christ's Resurrection, but would on no account forget to turn his money in his pocket at the sight of the new moon.

Now, so long as an untenable prejudice lies dormant in the mind, and its holder has not been called upon to consider its worth, he is not necessarily the worse for holding it. Nathanael's prejudice against Nazareth was quite without foundation. Yet we know on the highest authority that he was an Israelite indeed, in whom was no guile.[1] Although the victim of a serious misapprehension, he had not trifled with his sense of truth, and the consequence was that his mistake did not permanently injure him. Nathanael is the type of that simple goodness in union with narrow prejudice which is sometimes in our day branded as "Philistinism." Brethren, it is well to be large-minded; but there are worse things in the moral world than "Philistinism." It is better to be cramped and narrowed by unexamined prejudice, than to hold no one conviction with the earnestness which would prompt you to make sacrifices for it. It is better to be making the most of some onesided or imperfect creed, which is a local or temporary compound of truth and error, than to pass through life with a feeble interest in all religions; an interest so comprehensive and so diluted as to involve conviction of the truth of none:—

> "Sitting apart, holding no form of creed,
> But contemplating all."

Nathanael was wrong about Nazareth; but he was near

[1] St. John i. 47.

to the Truth and Wisdom with which, throughout all time, Nazareth is associated.

And yet, although a man may hold to a misapprehension with such entire honesty of purpose that his moral nature is quite intact, the misapprehension is undoubtedly a misfortune. It is some disaster for any mind to hold any one thing for truth that is untrue, however insignificant it be, or however honestly it be held. It is a greater disaster when the false prejudice bars the way to some truth behind it, which, but for it, would find an entrance to the soul; and the greatness of the disaster will in this case be measured by the importance of the excluded truth. There are false prejudices which shut out no truth, and which lead to no error. If it is better to be without them, they may be tolerated without much difficulty. But a prejudice which keeps us from knowing a good man, or from recognising a great truth, is to be seriously deplored. What would Nathanael be thinking of his prejudice against Nazareth now, if it had really kept him back from discipleship to the Lord of Life?

In the sub-apostolic age, there was a persuasion abroad in heathen society that the Christians devoured little children. This misapprehension was doubtless traceable to the current language employed by the first Christians on the subject of the Eucharist; their true meaning would never have occurred to a pagan who chanced to hear them. Yet how complete a barrier, not to say against conversion, but against any contact whatever with the "*exitiabilis superstitio*," must have been erected by a real belief that Christians were guilty of so inhuman a crime! How many souls may not such a prepossession have kept back, only too effectually, from all that Christ's Gospel had to give them!

Observe St. Philip's way of dealing with Nathanael. Philip might have argued, either that the prejudice against Nazareth rested on no sure foundation, or that, whatever its truth, Jesus belonged to Nazareth in so limited and temporary a sense, that the reputation of the place did not touch Him or His claim to fulfil the Messianic prophecies. This, perhaps, would have been our modern plan of meeting the objection. Philip takes a shorter course. His object is not to put himself argumentatively in the right by vindicating Nazareth, or by showing that it does not stand in his way: he only wants to bring Nathanael into the Presence, ay, close to the Person of the Son of God. He is convinced that if Nathanael can only see Him, speak with Him, breathe the atmosphere that surrounds Him, feel the Divine majesty and tenderness which had already won himself, the prejudice against Nazareth will simply be forgotten. "Philip saith unto him, Come and see." The objection might be discussed at another time; but the immediate value of the objection might be settled at once by the simple process of contact with Him to Whose claims it was apparently fatal.

II.

St. Philip's invitation has, obviously enough, a very wide range of applicability. There is no department of the kingdom of truth whose representatives may not echo the "Come and see" of the Apostle. Scientific, historical, moral, as well as theological truth, may and must proclaim, in such terms as these, their anxiety to be approached and examined. Nor would such applications of the text involve an overstraining of it; since, properly speaking, all truth is in one sense religious truth. It leads ultimately up to God; it is what it is by His Will and authority. As all true virtue, wherever found, is a ray of the life of the All-Holy; so all solid knowledge, all really accurate thought, descends from the Eternal Reason, and ought, when we apprehend it, to guide us upwards to Him. This was a consideration upon which the teachers of the great Christian School of Alexandria were wont to dwell. By means of it they bridged over chasms between much of what was true in the Platonic philosophy, representing as it did the most active speculation of the time, and the Revelation of God in Christ. All truth is indeed the inheritance of the Church of Christ, although she may be long in entering upon some portions of her patrimony, or may even, here or there, through the mistakes of those who act on her behalf, depreciate and for a while disown her share in it. "All things are yours," said an Apostle to his children in the faith;[1] and his words are not less true of the treasures of knowledge than of the treasures of Grace.

To create the sense of this—the unity and the magnificence of truth—is one purpose of an University. The Universities of Europe were creations of the Christian Church. They sprang from her effort to realize the unity of all districts of existing human knowledge, as in harmony with and under the presidency of the knowledge of God revealed in Christ. Faith in the real and ultimately discoverable harmony of all truth is the faith upon which this University was built; and as a result of this faith, it must aim at encouraging a spirit of generous sympathy between the representatives of and workers in the various departments of knowledge which it has brought together and fosters.

The intellectual value of such a spirit as this need not be insisted on. It is the crowning grace of a liberal education. When the fields of human knowledge are so various and so vast as is the case in our day, the utmost that can be done by single minds not of encyclopedic range, is to master one subject or branch of a subject as thoroughly as possible, and to rest content with knowing that others are working in regions where neither time nor strength will permit us to

---

[1] 1 Cor. iii. 21.

enter, but where we can at least follow them with interest and respect. To know at least the outline of what may be known; to know accurately the real frontier of his own narrow knowledge;—this is more distinctively the attribute of an educated man, than the accumulation of any number of facts and figures. It carries with it the power of estimating what is known philosophically; of placing it in something like its true relation to conterminous fields of knowledge; of anticipating, at least tentatively and partially, that day of cloudless light, when all truth, the highest and the lowest, will be seen in its absolute unity.

Nor does the moral and religious value of this spirit rank below the intellectual. In a place like this, the good to be gained by intercourse with character is at least as great as the good to be gained by the appropriation and mastery of thought; the vastness and variety of the moral world around us, if we have eyes to see it, is not inferior to that of the world of knowledge. Each man whom we know has probably at least some one moral beauty in nature or from grace; while different studies beget their characteristic moral excellences and deficiencies: so that as classes of students, no less than as individuals, we have much to learn from each other. One study demands intellectual integrity, another reverence, another patience, another nerve and determination; and when mixing with their different representatives, we may learn, if not all the truth they severally have to teach, at least the specific moral excellence which is developed in attaining it.

If this be the intellectual and moral value of University life, it is too precious to be imperilled by the temptation to think that no truth or goodness is to be looked for at the hands of certain men, or in the pursuit of certain studies. Have we in Oxford altogether escaped this temptation? Have those, whom a strong and lofty faith should have rendered generous, always and altogether succeeded in escaping it? Have we never pointed to the Nazareth of the physical sciences; of some one of them, it may be, which a vagrant materialist has for awhile dishonoured, but which cannot reasonably or justly be so credited with his error, as to warrant us in supposing that no good thing can come out of the laboratories in which it is pursued? Have we never banned the Nazareth of criticism; too readily supposing that, because some teachers of Heidelberg or Tubingen have mistaken wild imagination for history in their treatment of the Holy Gospels, no good thing can be expected to come from any critical school? The loyalty to Revelation which animates our prejudice does not justify it; the great Alexandrians who baptized the Platonic philosophy, would have bidden us of to-day welcome, and christen the critical and scientific spirit. We might be assured that, whatever its exaggerations, we have much to learn from it, and that in the long run it must do the work of Him Whom we adore.

Men who hold a large and exacting creed with earnestness, have no doubt, from their very sincerity, to guard against a tendency to narrow judgments. And it is easy for others who have no positive faith whatever to enlarge on deficiencies, the temptation to which, unhappily for themselves, they have never known; just as the famishing poor of our great cities are naturally and keenly alive to abuses of property on the part of the wealthy classes. But is there then no liability to narrow prejudices in any sections of the "liberal" world? Is it never thought or whispered that from the Nazareth of Orthodoxy, with its cherished traditions and sympathies, with its passionate attachment to the past of Christendom, with its undeniable adherence to a fixed body of truths as stamped with Divine and therefore unerring authority, no good can be expected to come; no real additions to our spiritual and intellectual wealth, no new development or enrichment of our moral energies? What is the Nazareth of so termed "sacerdotalism" but the endeavour to treat as serious our Saviour's promises of authorization and support to those weak human agencies by which from age to age He asserts His power and His love among the sons of men? Yet is not this Nazareth too often banned, as if nothing higher than some unworthy and selfish effort to increase the wealth or power of a clerical order could be expected to come out of it? And do you suppose, my liberal brethren, that in surrendering your imaginations to such prejudices as these you lose nothing; that you debar yourselves from access to no wide fields of truth, which else were open to you; that you cut yourselves off from the enjoyment of no moral beauties, which you too most assuredly would know how to honour and to profit by, not less than we?

Certainly the temptation to hold that no good thing can come out of this or that department of human interest and work, be it social, political, philosophical, or religious, is not extinct. But in the name of whatever truth there may be, and some truth there must be, in each and all of them, the University, as a kindly mother, bids us "come and see." Here we have no excuse for intellectual or moral isolation: interests and states of mind, which elsewhere are unavoidably found apart, are brought into close juxtaposition in Oxford, as a necessary result of our work and circumstances. Here, if anywhere, it might be hoped that explanations might be made, and reconciliations effected, which elsewhere are improbable: between love of the past and aspirations for the future; between the energies of philosophical and scientific enterprise and the claims of faith; between the intellectual hardness of the critical spirit, and the tender enthusiasms of devotion to our Living Lord. But if this is to be, we must be sufficiently generous, let me rather say sufficiently truthful, to conquer prejudice. Some of us might wish that there were no such tasks as these before us; but we have no more the making of the speculative than of the material world. Our duty is to make the best of what God has given us.

Nor let me be misunderstood. This willingness to test and to unlearn a prejudice is a very distinct thing from the surrender of a fundamental conviction. A faith which is sufficiently strong and philosophical to lay surrounding thought and knowledge more or less under contributions, is a very different thing from a feeble eclecticism, which goes smiling about the world, paying unmerited compliments to incompatible theories, and ending by the discovery that it is itself able to rely upon no one truth as absolutely certain. It is neither charity to man nor loyalty to God to ignore differences of conviction which are really serious, perhaps vital; or to attempt to bury them beneath words or acts which imply their insignificance. We should pay dearly for our contact with the many sides of knowledge exhibited here, with the many gifted minds that are at work on it, with the varying opinions that are to be found respecting some of the gravest problems, if we should weaken or lose our hold on those priceless truths which cannot be forfeited with moral and spiritual impunity. To learn that goodness, even the Highest and the Best, could come from Nazareth, was, in Nathanael's case, not to forfeit a faith, but to invigorate and confirm it.

III.

"Come and see." From St. Philip's day until now, this invitation has been addressed to mankind by the Church of Christ. It is her first step in meeting our difficulties; it is a condition of the cure she would administer to moral as well as to mental pain. Christianity is not to be really understood, when looked at only in the intellectual landscape, as if it were but one out of the many elements which make up the thought and life of the human race. Kind distance may lend enchantment to a picturesque falsehood; it can be no gain to truth. If the Gospel had really issued from some mystic or scholastic Nazareth, and could, in the last analysis, be accounted for as a natural product of the mind and heart of man, St. Philip's invitation would be an imprudence in the mouth of its preachers. As it is, the Church of Christ pleads ever with humanity: " Give yourselves a chance. Come and see. Do not only talk about the Kingdom and the Power of the Son of God; understand that He is alive; acquaint yourselves with Him. Ask that you may see Him, not merely with the eye of the natural intelligence, but with the eye of the illuminated spirit. Do not waste life in framing theories of the beautiful, but come, as did Nathanael, into the presence of Christ. Mark the story of His earthly life in the Gospels, and reflect that what He was then He is now. Speak to Him in prayer as to an all-powerful Friend Who hears, and Who, as He sees best, will answer. Touch the garment of His Humanity in sacraments, that upon you too, as upon one of old, virtue may come out of Him. Open your conscience to the purifying and consoling influences of His Spirit; open your hearts to the constraining generosities of His Dying Love." . . . The real difficulty with thousands in the present day is not that Christianity has been found wanting, but that it has never been seriously tried. They have been interested in it, but have remained at a distance from it. They have passed their best years in supposing that Christ's religion is a problem to be ceaselessly argued about, when, lo! it is a life to be spent at the feet of a Living Master, and it justifies itself only and completely when it is lived.

At a time like this,[1] when every child understands the tragic interest of what is passing, when events of the first magnitude, and pregnant with incalculable consequences, are almost hourly expected or announced, it might seem that an invitation, which can lay no claim to novelty, and which repeats itself in the language of nineteen centuries, has but a slight chance of being listened to. And yet, what is the real lesson of the scene of devastation and slaughter which is absorbing our thoughts and sympathies? Is it not a comment which all can read, written as it is in characters of blood, upon those sunny theories of human progress and perfectibility, by which sometimes commerce, sometimes intellectual culture, sometimes even the polish and refinement of the surface of modern life, were supposed not long since to have effected, or almost to have effected, that which the Eternal Christ, as we were told, had failed to work—a real regeneration, a true, lasting elevation and change in the heart and thought of man? So we were told; so it already was, or was presently to be; when lo! the foremost nations of Europe—foremost as leaders of its thought, foremost as producers of all that embellishes its outward life—feel a glow of the old passionate savagery of barbarous man stirring within them in all its ancient force, and bend the whole power of their cultivated thought and their strenuous will, to achieve the largest possible measure of mutual destruction. And thus, already commerce has withered away, and intelligence, except so far as it is military or political, is silent, and some of the best treasures of art and literature [2] are either perishing or are menaced with impending destruction, and besides the thousands who have been slaughtered on the field of battle, entire populations are threatened with the extremities

---

[1] The reference is to the Franco-German war of 1870-71.

[2] The Library at Strasburg had been already destroyed, and the Cathedral seriously damaged. Paris was besieged.

of want. Ay, and an evil which is even worse than these is beginning to show itself; men are growing to be indifferent to human suffering, because, forsooth, suffering is on so great scale that the imagination cannot master it in detail, and because national feeling is degraded down to the point at which human life weighs for very little against schemes of military conquest. The true import of this may be disguised beneath high-sounding formulas, but it means the abasement of the leading nations of the world; it means the political and social depression of the vanquished; it means, too probably, the moral degradation of the conqueror.

And think you that we Englishmen shall be or are unscathed, that we are really uninfluenced, while we gaze from our safe island home on those sieges, those battlefields, those desperate efforts of vengeance, those fierce reprisals? No; it is impossible. It is not too much to say that the character of each one of us has been modified, however imperceptibly to ourselves, by the successive incidents of this terrible war. Events of such magnitude and character cannot but have affected our ways of thinking and feeling about the actions of our fellow-creatures and the Divine government of the world; so that if ever there was a moment when the souls of men needed to be brought back to their true bearings, to be disciplined, restrained, upheld, chastened, made strong yet humble, resolute yet tender, by the true sight of the one Perfect Man, of the one Hope and Model of Humanity, of the Everlasting Christ, that moment is now. Much may depend—far more than we think—within the next quarter of a century, on our seriously accepting the invitation to "come and see" Him, as perhaps we have never seen Him yet. History is made up of the action of nations, and nations in their action do but express the collective will of individuals. As learners in the school of Christ, we may do more than we think for others: we cannot fail to improve ourselves. Those of us who know Him least or not at all may forthwith know much of Him, if we will. Those who know something of Him will feel and confess that a nearer approach, a more penetrating sight of Him, is always possible; so that as the years pass, the soul may, by living experience, take possession more and more completely of that truth which it has hitherto held more or less in deference to authority; that it may learn to say with the Samaritans of old, "Now we believe, not because of thy saying; for we have heard Him ourselves, and know that this is indeed the Christ, the Saviour of the world."[1]

[1] St. John iv. 42.

SERMON II.

HUMILITY AND TRUTH.

1 Cor. iv. 7.

Who maketh thee to differ from another? And what hast thou that thou hast not received? Now if thou didst receive it, why dost thou glory, as if thou hadst not received it?

THIS earnest inquiry was occasioned by the serious divisions which seem to have shown themselves in the Church of Corinth soon after its foundation. Within this local Church there were at least four distinct sections, if not camps. Each had its practical aspirations, its characteristic currents of feeling, its rallying cries, its party names. The great name of St. Peter would have been claimed by the adherents of Jewish observances. St. Paul would have been appealed to by the advocates of an entire—it may be a somewhat antinomian—freedom from the ancient law. Apollos, in all probability, was the favourite teacher of a smaller section, interested in his personal acquirements, and in the attractive graces of Alexandrian culture. Even the holiest of names was not spared. "I am of Christ" was a party cry, apparently put forward by some, who, priding themselves on their superiority to all party distinctions, and on their indifference to the claim of any human names, were yet unconsciously narrow, exclusive, uncharitable, even beyond the measure of their brethren.

It is a mistake to suppose that St. Paul is here apostrophising a false teacher: he is appealing to each individual member of this divided and distracted Church. He is not dealing with the arguments, the characteristics, the particular spirit of any one of its sections, but with the fundamental evil, which was common, more or less, to all of them. In his eyes the cause of the differences was less corporate than individual, less intellectual than moral. The names of Paul, Apollos, Cephas, were used—we know in one case, we may be very sure in the others—without the permission of their bearers, and by people who differed, as we should say, upon questions of Church policy. The deeper divisions of later times, touching the Person of the Redeemer and the means of Grace, were unknown in that first age. Despite the vivid pictures which an imaginative criticism has drawn of essentially different Gospels radiating from the minds of the most prominent Apostles, it is certain that the faith of the earliest Church was essentially one. The questions which divided it were, at least chiefly, of such a character as not to touch the daily inward life of the servants of Christ.[1] St. Paul's language about the Judaizers in the Epistle to the Galatians, and the trenchant references to antinomian exaggerations of St. Paul's doctrine in the messages to the Asiatic Churches of the Apocalypse, alike bear upon individuals and societies which were already severed or were severing themselves from the great body of the faithful. The discussions which were possible without violating Church communion were personal and disciplinary, rather than doctrinal, although no doubt they had an increasing tendency, of varying strength in different Churches, to

[1] In 1 Cor. xv. the Apostle is not "treating with a denial of the Resurrection as a permissible form of Christian opinion." He is pointing out its real character, as fatal to all Christian faith (cf. ver. 17). There is no trace of any large number of persons being definitely committed to it, and yet remaining under Apostolic sanction in communion with the Church.

raise sooner or later purely doctrinal issues. The Corinthian party controversies were exactly of this transitional character; and accordingly St. Paul deals with them as involving moral rather than theological error. If the Corinthians were so divided that Christian society was resonant with their war-cries, this was because they were individually false to the Christian character rather than to the Christian Creed. If the Corinthian Christians could only learn to be individually humble, the Church of Corinth would soon again be one.

It is often as unprofitable to address corporate bodies as to address metaphysical abstractions; and St. Paul therefore, with his practical genius, deals with the Corinthian Church in the person of each Corinthian. The Corinthians, he says, are puffed up;[1] the new world of thought and feeling to which they had been introduced by the faith of Christ had only furnished them with materials for enhancing their individual self-importance. They approved of this Apostle; they disliked that Apostle; they forgot that an Apostle was only a minister by whom the faith was propagated; they made of him a sectional leader, in whose favour they gave their suffrages. It followed that they were the important people, not he; it was they who discriminated, who approved, who conferred moral authority; upon them the success or popularity of their chosen representative was inevitably reflected. Thus each member of the Church became, in his own thought, its centre; while its real pioneers, and workmen, and rulers —and, what was unspeakably more serious, One infinitely higher and holier than them all—were virtually banished to the circumference. Christianity was already ministering to a temper which it was its business and its triumph to destroy: religious language was the vehicle and the sanction of a profoundly irreligious deterioration.

[1] 1 Cor. iv. 6, εἷς ὑπὲρ τοῦ ἑνὸς φυσιοῦσθε κατὰ τοῦ ἑτέρου.

The Apostle does not deal tenderly with so serious an evil: he does not wish to give it any chance of resistance; he will tread it out at once. He heaps question upon question, without waiting for an answer; he would be guilty perhaps of what the logicians call the fallacy of many questions, if any of his questions could really have been answered.[1] He strips off, with no gentle hand, the disguise which hid the Corinthians from themselves, and which made their self-assertion tolerable. They assumed that they were what they were in virtue of some original and inherent right to be so; they supposed that they possessed what they had as owners of some indefeasible title to possession. The truth was that they were simply pensioners; pensioners upon a Bounty Which had given them their all. And it was necessary that they should be reminded of their dependence.

"Who maketh thee to differ from another, whether he be a heathen or a brother in the faith? And what hast thou of social or moral, or mental or spiritual wealth, that thou didst not receive? Now, if thou didst receive it, why dost thou glory as if thou hadst not received it?" As we think over St. Paul's question, we perceive that its range of application is wider than that which the Apostle's first readers would have assigned to it. It does not merely deal with an incidental and local form of moral mischief; it probes, and to the quick, a constant and world-wide tendency in human beings. It is addressed not merely to Corinthian, but to human nature; and as we stand before the Apostolic examiner, the Church of Corinth, with its chiefs, its parties, its heart-burnings, recedes from view and disappears; we hear this master of moral truth speaking to us of to-day—speaking to us all—speaking to each of us.

[1] 1 Cor. i. 13.

I.

There are probably two leading objections in a great many minds to cultivating humility; objections which lie generally against the whole of the self-repressing side of Christian ethics. In plain words, humility seems to involve a risk of tampering with sincerity, and a risk of losing moral force. Now, the first of these objections takes it for granted that humility is something dramatic and unreal; that it consists in word or manner which is put on for an occasion, without being dictated by sincere feeling or conviction. This is, however, no more humility, than an outward semblance of reverence in church, while the mind is wandering everywhere except in the direction of God's Throne, is devotion. Humility is essentially the recognition of truth; it is the taking in act and word and thought that low estimate of ourselves which is the true estimate. If we do not seriously think that such an estimate is the true one, it is only because we have never seen ourselves as we really are. We have yet to learn our real relationship to the Being to Whom we owe our existence, and the weakness which impairs our moral force, and the evil that clings to us within. In the meantime, no doubt, it is better not to pretend that we have done so; while it is certain that such pretence, if we should be guilty of it, would not be rightly termed humility. The same notion of humility, as something necessarily dramatic and fictitious, is at the bottom of the apprehension that it involves a loss of moral strength. Of course moral force is lost by every form of untruthfulness, even the least; but genuine humility is in its essence the planting our foot upon the hard rock of truth and fact, and often when it costs us a great deal to do so. To confess ignorance, to confess wrong, to admit incapacity, when it would be useful to be thought capable, to decline a reputation to which we have no right,—these things, and others of the same kind, are humility in action. They are often notoriously hard and painful; they are always of the greatest possible value in bracing the character; they are so far from forfeiting moral force that they enrich us with it just as all approximations to falsehood forfeit it. If we are weak, sinful, corrupt, it is better to learn and to feel the true state of the case, than to live in a fool's paradise. The great and unfortunate country which now lies wounded and bleeding on the soil of Europe, must surely feel that she would not at this moment be worse off if she had discovered and confessed to herself the real truth as to her resources seven months ago.[1] Every man is the stronger for knowing the worst he can know about himself, and for acting on this knowledge. And if religious men such as David and St. Paul use language[2] about themselves which seems to any of us exaggerated in the excess of its self-depreciation, this is because they saw much more of the Holiness of God, and of the real nature of moral evil, than we do: to them such language is only the sober representation of a plain fact. These great servants of God were not dazzled by any of the inherited or acquired decorations which hide from so many of us our real selves, and which the Apostle in the text is so determined to strip off from us.

II.

The founder of this Sermon[3] was probably of opinion that there were particular reasons for addressing it year by year to an academical audience. If we may form an estimate from the drift of the somewhat restricted number

---

[1] The allusion is to the later stage of the Franco-German war, 1870-71.
[2] Ps. li. 1-3. 1 Cor. xv. 9.
[3] The Humility Sermon, preached on Quinquagesima Sunday.

of passages from Holy Scripture which he has prescribed for the preacher's use on this occasion, he would seem to have thought that there were three features of University life which make humility more or less difficult of attainment. Although a change has taken place within the last quarter of a century, those who study here still belong for the most part to the wealthy classes. And the culture of the intellect, which is the proper work of the students at a University, has dangers which are too obvious to be disputed. Nay, more, the interest in religious questions, which is a product of all intellectual activity, may very easily combine loyalty to truths which men have sincerely at heart, with an estimate of self and an estimate of others which these truths condemn.

"Who maketh thee to differ from another? And what hast thou that thou hast not received?" How does this question apply to the case of a young man who comes to Oxford with good social connections, perhaps with a title, with a large allowance, and a prospect of a fortune in course of time? If we could dissect his thought about his position and means, what is the idea which underlies all the rest, and upon which he habitually dwells? It is the idea of *right*. He has a *right* to his position; to have what he has; to be what he is. And, legally and politically speaking, he is not mistaken. There is no flaw in the title-deeds of his estate; and the law will guarantee him and his heirs in its possession until the law itself shall have been fundamentally modified, or altogether repealed by some social revolution. Nay, he is morally justified in resting on this conviction of his right, at least in a certain measure. The idea of property, provided that there be an adequate sense of responsibility in the possessor, is a moral idea. Unless property have a moral basis, the eighth and the tenth commandments are unmeaning.

Property is a product of moral laws, and of circumstances which operate inevitably in human society. Thus it belongs to the Divine Government of the world; and an indistinct apprehension of this truth sanctions more powerfully than any legal technicality or document that idea of right which lies at the bottom of the young man's mind about his fortune and place among his fellows. So far there is no fault to be found with him: but then, what are his thoughts about the origin of this right which he has to his position and property? Upon the answer which he gives to that question in his daily thoughts will depend his bearing before God and men. If he pays no heed to this matter; if he says to himself, "Fact is fact, and right is right; I find myself in these circumstances; I am a fortunate man, and mean to make the best of my good luck;" then it is probable that he will presume upon what he has, and is, in his dealings with his fellow-creatures, and in his thoughts towards his God. He tacitly assumes that there is some indefeasible title, some necessity rooted in the nature of things, for his having and being what he has and is. He cannot, it seems, so far exercise his imagination as to picture the world and society to himself, with himself in a different position—say quite at the other end of society. Hence he naturally deals with his position and income as giving him a right to all the superiorities which he can assert over others, and especially as giving him a right to feel independent; independent of his fellowmen; independent of all but extraordinary circumstances; yes,—he would not say it, but such are his secret thoughts—independent of his God. The poor, he thinks, may well be anxious, and anxiety is the mother of prayer: but he, why should he be anxious, when all the luxuries of life are secured to him? and if he is not anxious, why,—except as a matter of pathetic sentiment or of early habit, —why should he pray? Prayer is the language of a consciously dependent being, and he cannot pretend to say that he feels himself dependent upon anybody. Prayer is the language of humility, and it would be affectation in him to act as if he were humble, or thought it desirable to be so.

Yet what is the truth? The truth is that his idea of right, upon which all else reposes, is a caricature of the real right which he has to his position. His real right is that not of an original landlord, but of a tenant at will. Speaking strictly, there is only One Landlord in this world: it is He Who made it. All else are but His tenantry; and although He ejects His tenants when it pleases Him, sometimes very summarily indeed, they have against Him, neither in right nor in fact, any plea or remedy. They have indeed the rights of tenants at will, but that is all. They are in every sense His pensioners, and to take any other view of their position is to incur the risk, or rather the certainty, of being one day rudely undeceived.

There are in the literature of the Church few treatises more abounding in noble and invigorating thoughts than that "On Consideration," which was addressed by St. Bernard to Pope Eugenius III. Eugenius had been a Cistercian monk; and in raising him to the Papal Throne after the violent death of Lucius II., the Roman Court may have been anxious to avail itself of the vast political influence which was wielded beyond the Alps by the Abbot of Clairvaux. The consciousness of this will in part explain the freedom of St. Bernard's words. But Eugenius was not a man to be any one's tool, and at that date the Roman Chair was surrounded with a halo of prestige and power to which the modern world affords no parallel. Yet St. Bernard does not merely write as an old friend, frankly discussing the details of a new position; he does not merely point out the vices, the extortions of the Roman Court, the corrupt traditions of the Papal administration at home and abroad. He addresses himself to Eugenius personally, and in terms which few men in such a station often listen to. Let Eugenius strip from his eyes all the veils and bandages which may disguise from him the true state of his case. He is still merely a man and a sinner, only charged with heavier responsibilities than his fellows. Grant that he is the heir of the Apostles, the first of the Christian Bishops; grant that Abel and Noah, and Abraham and Melchisedek, and Aaron and Moses, and Samuel and Peter, and One infinitely Higher than them all, are represented in him; what does this mean? Not pre-eminence in dignity, so much as pre-eminence in labour. Dignity of itself, exclaims St. Bernard, is not a certificate of virtue. Let Eugenius look to it, that he be in spirit the successor of Peter, not the successor of Constantine.[1] If he is chiefly thinking of his honours, he has his part, not with the Apostle, but with Nebuchadnezzar, with Alexander of Macedon, with Antiochus Epiphanes, with Herod. Let him forget the robes he wears, the gems which sparkle in his tiara, the plumes which wave around him, the precious metals which adorn his palace, his vast influence over the Western world. These, exclaims St. Bernard, are but as the mists of the morning. They are already passing; presently they will have passed for ever. "Dele fucum fugacis honoris hujus, et malè coloratæ nitorem gloriæ, ut nude nudum consideres quia nudus egressus ex de utero matris tuæ."[2] All that has been superadded will as certainly be removed, and beneath all there remains, on the Papal Throne as in the humblest of peasant dwellings, "man that is born of woman, having a short time to live, and being full of misery; man that cometh up, and is cut down as a flower, and fleeth as it were a shadow, and never continueth in one stage."

[1] *De Consid.* p. 76.
[2] *Ibid.* p. 40, ed. Berlin. Cf. Milman, *Latin Christianity*, vol. iii. p. 396.

It may be thought that the social foes of humility are less powerful now than in bygone years, that good taste on this side, and the strong and strengthening current of political democracy on that, have in this matter already done, or bid fair to do, the proper work of the Gospel. But this is to forget that the essence of all true moral excellence lies not in external conformity to a conventional standard, but in an inward disposition under the control of recognised principle. The formulas of good taste are merely an elegant translation of the common opinion of contemporary society. The humility of good taste is strictly an affair of appropriate phrases, gestures, reserves, withdrawals; it is the result of a socially enforced conformity to an outward law. The humility of democratic feeling is often a very vigorous form of pride, which is scarcely at pains to disguise its real character. The demand for an impossible social equality, which has done so much to discredit some of the noblest aspirations for liberty that the modern world has known, is due to the temper which creates a tyranny, only working under circumstances which, for the moment, forbid it. The impatience of an equal in the one case is the impatience of a superior in the other. The humility of a democracy is largely concerned with enforcing an outward conformity to this virtue on the part of other people; and both it and the humility of good taste may remind us of those cannibals who have walked in our parks clothed in the dress and affecting the manners of European civilization, and yet have found it difficult to restrain themselves from indulging old habits when there has been much to tempt them. Humility, to be genuine, must be based on principle; and that principle is suggested by the Apostle's question, which warns every human being that, be his wealth, his titles, his position, his name among men, what they may, they afford no real ground for self-exaltation, because they are external to his real self, and are in fact bestowed on him from above.

"Who maketh thee to differ from another? And what hast thou that thou hast not received?" This is a question too for those who have good abilities, and who have made the best of them. The day has probably gone by when clever idleness was of more account in this place than hardworking mediocrity. We have ceased to think that there is anything intrinsically respectable in the possession of abilities which men do not use. But then this higher and more moral estimate of mental accomplishments, which has more reverence for the hardly won results of patient work than for the flashes of genius, which cost men nothing, is not unlikely to obscure the truth before us. To those who believe in a Creator at all, Who made us all and each exactly what we are, there can be no question as to the true source of natural ability. But work is the activity of a human agent, and the results of work are the products of that activity, and these results are not, like inherited income or titles, external to the real man; they become the furniture of one very important part of his being: his memory and his understanding are permanently enriched by them. Is it possible to say in the case of the hard-working student, who has disciplined and stored his mind, that he too has nothing which he has not received? Has he not won a great deal that he possesses? is not his knowledge, as well as his capacity, a result of his persevering energy? And is he not on this account entitled in reason to a regulated self-confidence, which proclaims that he is the creation of his own efforts; which asserts his superiority, in this very respect, to men who are only what God and circumstances have made them?

Undoubtedly we here meet with a feature which is wanting in the case already considered; here is the active co-operation of a self-determining will. But if we except the will, all besides is independent of the worker. For instance, to intellectual success in this place, three conditions, speaking generally, are essential; preparatory training, abilities of a certain order, and fairly good health. Certainly, in some cases one or more of these conditions have been dispensed with. Some men have succeeded by dint of sheer perseverance, although their education may almost be said to have begun here. Others have done well whose abilities have appeared at the time and afterwards—to their great credit—altogether below the level of their honours. Others again have distinguished themselves whose work has cost them hours of weary pain, and who have triumphed at last only to sink into an early grave. Such cases will occur to the memories of those of us who have resided in Oxford for any number of years. But these cases are exceptions to the general rule; and in each one of these cases there is generally some physical or mental endowment which enables the student to conquer his disadvantages, and which is itself God's gracious gift. But the will: is that His gift too? Surely it is; only here His generosity is of that delicate kind which conceals His Hand, and allows His pensioner to imagine for a moment that he has something which he can really look upon as originally his own. The kindly stranger who would not wound the sensitiveness of an impoverished gentleman, hid the purse of gold at a spot in the garden where it could not but presently be found, and then retired to a thicket from which, without risk of being observed, he might enjoy the sight of the discovery. And thus God allows man for the moment to imagine that the will is a power for which he is indebted to no other being, since it is the movement and energy of the man's own self, of his inmost being. So it is: but then, is man his own creator? Does he indeed owe his central, his deepest life to no other? Is his personal self-determining spirit self-originating? Is there, in short, anything in man which makes him differ so vitally from or the creatures that he has in it that which he has not received?

It is often said, and more frequently thought, that such rank weeds as pride of intellect grow more readily and more thickly in the soil of University life than elsewhere. Nor do I deny that there are reasons for such an apprehension, especially when life is passed in cultivation of the intellect for its own sake, without any corresponding discipline of the heart and character, and without any sufficient recognition of the fact that no man has any right to cultivate his intellect without reference to his duties to his fellowmen. But is this necessarily or generally the case? Surely not. University life offers some advantages for learning humility which are scarcely attainable elsewhere. It is a misfortune for a man to be placed early in life in a position where he has few or no equals, while a number of inferior minds constantly depend on and defer to him. In such a position, even good men have imperceptibly acquired an estimate of themselves, of their judgment, their abilities, their services to God and to their fellows, which is inconsistent with fact, and fatal to humility. To those who spend life here this danger can hardly present itself. Probably no body of men is less controlled by conventional and fictitious standards of importance than are the resident members of the University. Here a man's intrinsic worth, or what is believed to be such, is the measure of the consideration extended to him. Every resident must feel that he lives in the presence of men who are in some ways his superiors. Even the most accomplished must recognise those who excel himself, if not in investigating this department of truth, yet in mastering that; if not in the cultivation of this faculty, yet in disciplining another; if not in mental, at least in moral attainments; if not in this form of moral beauty, then in that. How great this blessing is, any man can say, who, while living here, has been taking pains with his character, and using the opportunities for training it which

God has thus put in his way. And indeed, if this aid to humility were wanting in Oxford, there is another, which must occasionally obtrude itself with painful importunity upon the thoughts of all of us. Living, as we do here, with more or less power of controlling our time, with learning in so many ways made easy to us, with libraries, teachers, traditions around that invite us so gracefully, so persuasively, to make some little portion of truth our own; can we forget —we cannot forget—the thousands, the tens of thousands, of working men who toil in our great centres of industry; men with hearts not less warm, with an interest in life and a sense of its capabilities not less keen, with intellects, be sure, at the very least, not less strong or less acute than our own, yet denied by their circumstances the very least of our advantages, and knowing full well what this exclusion implies, and wondering that we who live in what seems to them a very paradise, do not make more of it. What would they not achieve, if they too, instead of working with their hands for bread throughout each long day, could take our places? What might not we do, if we would but steadily reflect on the simple fact that there is absolutely no reason whatever, save the free and unmerited bounty of God's Providence towards us, for our taking theirs? Well; what we or they would do under other than our actual circumstances is an intricate question, which it may be useless to discuss; but one result should surely follow from the most passing and superficial consideration of such a subject; if it did nothing else, it should make us humble.

"Who maketh thee to differ from another? And what hast thou that thou hast not received?" The question especially concerns those who possess, or believe that they possess, religious truth and religious advantages. It was to such persons that the Apostle himself addressed it. The Corinthian of whom the Apostle is thinking believed himself to differ from his fellow-Christians, not in social standing or intellectual culture, but specifically in the possession of a truer religious faith. If the Apostle had shared some modern opinions as to the importance of Christian doctrine, he would have epigrammatically dismissed the several points that were discussed at Corinth as having no real claim to serious consideration. But although St. Paul knew how to insist upon the non-essential character of certain open questions, which weak or narrow brethren, to the detriment of the Church's true comprehensiveness, would fain have closed,[1] he was far too keenly alive to the conditions under which alone intellectual loyalty to a Revelation claiming to be from God is possible, to affect or encourage indifference about matters that might even remotely touch its substance.[2] The personalities that were exchanged at Corinth did conceal tendencies towards really divergent convictions; and all these tendencies could not be equally directed towards truth, since some of them were mutually exclusive of each other. St. Paul, then, does not tell the Corinthian that the idea of his differing from another is of itself a presumptuous absurdity; he assumes the difference to exist, and even to be legitimate; he concentrates the point and strength of his question upon the source of the difference. "Who *maketh* thee to differ?" The Corinthian of whom he is thinking had taken it for granted that his religious orthodoxy, supposing it to be such, was, like a conquest of the natural intellect, simply a result of his own industry or sharpsightedness. Even if this had been the case, the natural faculty and the strength which employed it would still have been God's gifts. Yet, when religious truth is learnt to any purpose, it is learnt not merely as a problem which is grasped by the understanding, but as a rule of thought and life which is freely

---

[1] Rom. xiv. 3.   1 Cor. viii. 9.   [2] Gal. i. 8, 9; v. 2-4.   Tim. i. 19, 20.

accepted by the will, and especially as a tender devotion towards an unseen Person that can possess and govern and absorb the heart. These things are separable in treatises on religious psychology; they are inseparable in the practical experience of the living Christian to whom his creed is a serious reality. They carry us, if we are to account for them in their entirety, far beyond the range of any human energy or forethought. We are here on the traces of the work of the inward Teacher, Whose task was already heralded by prophecy; Who was to write the Will of God upon the hearts of men; Who was to supplement, and at times to supersede, natural methods of inquiry by an inward illumination. We are here close to a phenomenon, higher, more complex, more beautiful in every way more worthy of attention, than any which we find within the frontiers of the natural universe. We are already thinking of Divine Grace. Apart from Grace the religious life of Christendom is a thick tangle of unintelligible mysticism: in view of it, antecedents and effects are scarcely less clearly traceable than in the heavens above us, or in the beautiful clothing of the earth beneath our feet, or in the machinery and functions of our bodies. Or, to be more exact, Grace may remind us of the action of such mysterious forces in nature as is electricity, which, although ever under the governance of law, is at one while so independent of us as to threaten us from the clouds with ruin and death, and at another so wholly within our power that, like a public messenger or a household servant, it does our bidding with docile precision.

But if there be one thing more than another characteristic of Grace, it is that we have nothing to do with winning it. We may co-operate with it; we may forfeit it if we neglect it; we may or may not have predispositions for receiving it. But in itself it is, as its name implies, a free gift; i is given by Him Who might withhold it. We cannot either claim it as a right; or possess ourselves of it surreptitiously; or galvanize our natural faculties into doing its work, so as to diminish our sense of obligation towards the Giver. In its wider and its narrower sense, Grace is His Gift. The whole economy of Redemption, the Incarnation of the Divine Son, His perfect Teaching, His sinless Example, His Expiatory Death, His Rising from the Grave, His Ascension on High, His perpetual pleading in that world beyond the stars; whence is all this but from the free, undeserved bounty of the Infinite Mercy thus lavished upon us, the children of the Fall? And Grace, in the specific sense of the action of the Holy Spirit, by Whom the whole Church is governed and sanctified; by Whom the individual heart is filled with light and love; and Whose work especially it is, sometimes freely, sometimes through channels accurately defined and known, such as are the Sacraments, to knit our frail and perishing nature to the Divine Humanity of the Saviour; what is Grace, in this narrower and more accustomed sense but a free gift from first to last? Assuredly, if there be aught good in us, Grace has made us what we are, and without it our life is as nothing, or worse than nothing before the Sanctity and the Justice of God.

"What hast thou that thou hast not received?" So far as the spiritual life is concerned, there is but one answer to that question. And when that answer is sincerely meant, it makes the assumption of personal superiority, on the ground of possessing a higher truth or fuller religious privileges than others, utterly impossible. For there is indeed one possession which we have not received, and which is wanting to none of us. We can reasonably call it our own, since He Who gave us all else would most assuredly never have given us this. It is the fatal product of our misused liberty: it is the wrong-doing which we individually have contributed to increase the stock of moral evil which God for wise purposes permits, but which nevertheless is an affront and a dishonour to Him. Sin is the one thing which we have, and which we have not received. Think well on this, and you will learn the spirit of the fifty-first Psalm, which is the essential spirit of humility. Make this truth your own, and you will understand the lines which Copernicus traced for his tombstone—

> "Non parem Pauli gratiam requiro,
> Veniam Petri neque posco, sed quam
> In Crucis ligno dederas latroni
> Sedulus oro."

Forget this; and sooner or later you will be a Pharisee.

The fundamental thing in Pharisaism was not the sustained acting of a part with a view to keeping up appearances before the eyes of men; it was rather the fond claim and boast, cherished in secret thought, and proclaimed in the ears of men, that the religious position and privileges of Israel were of themselves a ground of merit and honour.[1] Such a boast would have been silenced if the Pharisee had had any true sight of an All-Holy God, or any accurate estimate of the strength and variety of the forms of moral evil within himself. And when the spirit of Pharisaism, which lives on in the human heart with energetic vitality, has reared itself beneath that Cross which rebukes all human self-sufficiency, it has been sustained by this same insensibility to the Sanctity above, and to the evil within us. Christian Pharisaism is possible only when men have forgotten that they have received all that God can accept hereafter, and that all that will embarrass and confound them before Him is indisputably their own.

"What hast thou that thou hast not received?" It is a searching question; but the true answer to it ought to leave us other men than perchance we are; more considerate and generous towards our fellows, more tender

[1] Rom. ii. 17-20.

and sympathetic, more capable of making allowance for difficulties which we have ourselves experienced, or for difficulties which we can at least imagine, more slow to condemn what looks like evil, more eager to acknowledge merit and to proclaim superiority, more considerate and respectful when dealing with inferiors, more resolute in the endeavour to crush and cast out the scorn and bitterness that wells up too readily from an unhumble heart. It is not easy all this, but it is humility in practice; and persevering endeavours after a true self-knowledge, together with constant recourse to a Higher Power, will, in God's good time, help us on our way. For as the years pass, and first one friend and then another is withdrawn, and the home circle is so gradually narrowed up as to leave a man almost alone in his generation, and the ideals which sustained energy in earlier life have one by one been broken, and the interests which were absorbing have lost their charm or have faded quite away, and disease has already laid its heavy hand on this frame which the spirit still tenants; there is one virtue among many—pre-eminently one—that he needs and will need increasingly,—Resignation. Resignation,—not to a whirlwind of inexorable forces, not to a brutal fate or destiny, not to powers who cannot see or hear or feel, but to One Who lives for ever and Who loves us well, and Who has given us all that we have, ay, life itself, that we may at His bidding freely give it back to Him. "Into Thy Hands I commend my Spirit!" They are the last words of Christian Resignation, most majestic in its self-content, most lowly in its recognition of the fact that we are recipients from first to last; they are the last words of a Resignation which He practised most perfectly Who is the Model and Prince of the humble; Who, being the Infinite and the Eternal, "made Himself of no reputation, and took on Him the form of a servant."[1]

[1] Phil. ii. 7.

SERMON III.

IMPORT OF FAITH IN A CREATOR.

(SEPTUAGESIMA SUNDAY.)

Gen. i. 1.

In the beginning God created the heaven and the earth.

IT is natural to inquire why we should begin to read the first chapter of Genesis on Septuagesima Sunday, when the Christian year is already some nine or ten weeks old. And the answer to that question is not to be found in any personal tastes or predilections on the part of the compilers of the Prayer Book. In this, as in much else, they simply handed on what they had received. The first chapter of Genesis had been for centuries read on this Sunday at Matins in the Breviary of the Western Church, before it occupied a corresponding place in the English Prayer Book. It is not altogether easy to say how the truths of the Christian Creed came to be laid out liturgically in the order which has come down to us, and which extends over rather more than half of the solar year. Work which in later ages has been formally undertaken by a Commission of Divines or by a Congregation of Rites was in earlier days produced by some prominent Church or by some leading Bishop, whose reputation for sanctity or for wisdom ensured the assent of his contemporaries. In a yet more primitive time liturgical arrangements, when they were not suggested by the Older Dispensation, would seem to have been arrived at instinctively by the Church's common spiritual sense of what was due to the truth she guarded. Here we see what it is that imparts so high an interest to the study of early liturgical documents. They spring from the fresh soul of early Christendom; they reveal the deep currents and impulses which swayed its collective life; they proclaim not merely the truths which were held by the Christian Church, but also the moods and character of the passion with which she pressed them to her heart.

The sudden change, then, from Isaiah to Genesis, is probably to be explained by the consideration that on Septuagesima Sunday we pass a great dividing line in the Church's year; and, as the name of the day implies, everything henceforth is relative to and preparatory for the great Easter Festival. Before again considering those stupendous facts which constitute the very heart and centre of the Christian Creed—the Passion and Resurrection of the Incarnate Son of God—we are led to take the measure of our own place in this universe, and of our relation to the Being Who made it. We fall back on these elemental truths that we may do justice to one important aspect of the Christian Creed, as filling up an outline, and affording relief from difficulties, which natural religion or elementary primitive traditions cannot fail to suggest. A serious Theism, like a reverent study whether of thought or of nature, is a true preparation for the Gospel. To know what God is, and what we are, is to know truths which will lead us on to other truths beyond; it is to have found a schoolmaster who, unless we are unhappily ingenious in misreading his directions, will, like the Jewish law of old, sooner or later bring us unto Christ.

When man looks out from himself upon the wonderful home in which he is placed, upon the various orders of living things around him, upon the solid earth which he treads, upon the heavens into which he gazes, with such ever-varying impressions, by day and by night; when he surveys the mechanism of his own bodily frame, fashioned in this precise shape and endowed with these faculties, with these limbs, and no other; when he turns his thought, as he can turn it, in upon itself, and takes to pieces by subtle analysis the beautiful instrument which places him in conscious relation to the universe around him,—his first and last anxiety is to account for the existence of all that thus interests him; he must answer the question, How and why did it come to be? Nor is this anxiety diminished, much less is it destroyed, when man has become familiar with the wonders around him; when he has multiplied his opportunities for observing them, and has catalogued his observations; when he has apparently reached general truths, and has tested them by experience, and feels himself to be making some acquaintance with his dwelling-house under the leadership of Science.

Certainly Theology, if she understands her own interests, can have no wish to disparage or discountenance this kind of knowledge. She will indeed decline to revise the Creed or the Bible in deference to some tentative hypothesis which the imagination rather than the positive knowledge of this or that eminent writer may suggest. But the mental habits which in its higher moods physical science encourages are all her own. Love of positive truth; perseverance under difficulties; intrepid accuracy—are virtues which Theology also cultivates. And she knows that there is a momentous problem near to her heart, and on which she has much to say, but which natural science also cannot but keep constantly before the mind of its votaries. It is the problem of the origin of the Universe. For whatever be the conquests of physical science in detail; whatever amount of light it may pour upon the working and structure of the material world,—all this does not dispose of the serious question, "How and why did this vast system of being come to be?" Science may unveil in nature regular modes of working, and name them laws; she may show that effects supposed to be due to some immediate interference from above are traceable to ascertained agencies below; she may substitute, and to a degree beyond present anticipations, some doctrine of gradually developed forms of life for the older belief in permanent distinctions between living species. But the great question still awaits her. Who furnished the original material for the presumed development? Who gave it the first impact, who has conducted it through the successive stages of its history? Why, in short, do we witness it at all?

Now, this question is answered by the first verse of the Bible, "In the beginning God created the heaven and the earth." And that answer is accepted by every believer in the Christian Creed: "I believe in One God, the Father Almighty, Maker of Heaven and Earth, and of all things visible and invisible."

I.

What is meant by Creation? Nothing less than the giving being to that which before was not. The Hebrew[1] word which is used to describe the Divine act of giving existence to the heavens and the earth does not of itself exclude the idea of some pre-existing material ready to the Hand of the Creator. But the text does not allow us to think of any such material; it carries us back to that

---

[1] ברא, which in the Piel means to cut, hew, in Kal means always to create. When used, *e.g.*, of the creation of man (Gen. i. 27), or of the new heart of the penitent (Ps. li. 10), the word doubtless describes a process of making out of something, but this idea of pre-existent material lies not in the word but in the context.

primal act whereby something that was not God first began to be. The expression "the heavens and the earth" is the most exhaustive phrase that the Hebrews could employ to name the universe; the universe is regarded as a twofold whole, consisting of very unequal parts. Writing for men, Moses writes as a man; an angel might have described the work of God very differently. But the moral importance of the earth, considered as the scene of man's probation, is a sufficient reason for the form which the phrase assumes. The word "heavens" includes not merely the material bodies which astronomy has in view, but those immaterial essences whose existence and activity were revealed gradually to Israel, and who are, as we know, much more ancient than man. The work of the fourth "day," or period, presupposes a creation of the "heavens," since the Hebrew word[1] translated "lights" might be rendered "lightbearers," and might thus suggest that the work of that period consisted in placing the already existing heavenly bodies in such a complete relation to the planet which was to be the abode of man as to influence its development.

How the Jews have understood the first verse of Genesis is sufficiently notorious. "Those," says Maimonides, "who believe in the laws of our master Moses, hold that the whole world, which comprehends everything except the Creator, after being in a state of non-existence, received its existence from God, being called into existence out of nothing. .... It is a fundamental principle of our law that God created the world from nothing." The mother of the Maccabean martyrs, when endeavouring to

---

[1] מָאוֹר is a luminous or light-bearing body. In Numb. iv. 9 it is used of a candelabrum. The sun and moon already existed; the work of the fourth "day" may have consisted in removing some intercepting atmosphere or other cause which hitherto had prevented them from giving light to the earth.

strengthen her youngest son for his last agony, bids him look upon the heaven and the earth, and all that is therein, and consider that God made them out of things that were not.[1] If the Alexandrian author of the Book of Wisdom speaks of God's making the Cosmos out of shapeless matter,[2] it does not follow that, like Philo afterwards, he had so yielded to Platonic ideas as to suppose that matter was eternal; he is speaking of God's later creative action, which gave form to matter that had been made before. Justin Martyr uses the phrase in the same sense; and St. Clement of Alexandria speaks of matter having no relation to time,[3] not meaning that matter is eternal, but that it had been created at a period when there were no "times or seasons or days or years." Tertullian holds that the Carthaginian artist Hermogenes, who probably had never unlearnt his heathen creed, really teaches the existence of a second God when he asserts the eternity of matter: "Duos Deos infert," says Tertullian, "materiam parem Deo infert."[4] And the common sense of Christian antiquity is expressed in the devout reasoning of St. Augustine: "Thou, O Lord, hast made heaven and earth; yet not out of Thine own Substance, for then heaven and earth would be equal to Thine Only Begotten, and, besides Thyself, there was nought else out of which Thou couldst make it: therefore hast Thou made heaven and earth out of nothing."[5]

In the Mosaic account of the Creation the sentence which rises high above all else, and compared with which all else is subordinate detail, is this: "In the beginning God created the heaven and the earth." Here is a truth which governs the theology of the Old and New Testament. It is vividly opposed to current doctrines in heathendom,

---

[1] ἐξ οὐκ ὄντων, 2 Macc. vii. 28.   [2] Wisd. xi. 17, ἐξ ἀμόρφου ὕλης.
[3] Photius attributes to him the expression ὕλη ἄχρονος.
[4] Tert. *adv. Hermog.* c. 4.   [5] Conf. xii. 7.

which regarded the world as emanating from a divine substance, or which ascribed all life and living beings to some unaccountable modification of primeval self-existing matter, or which took refuge from sterner thought in some graceful or grotesque legend, and traced both gods and men to a world egg, or a chaos. It may have influenced the formation of some heathen cosmogonies, as not improbably that of the Etruscan, which is ascribed by Suidas to a foreign source, and still more that of the Zendavesta, inspiring or shaping them through channels of intercourse of which there would have been no lack when men could travel or think at all. At the present day the truth of the creation is confronted sometimes indeed with avowed Atheism, sometimes with systematized Pantheism, but much more generally and frequently, at least in England, with a habit of mind which declines the question altogether, as lying beyond the range of experience, and belonging entirely to abstract speculation. Who has not fallen in with books which to an earnest Theist or Christian again and again suggest this grave subject, as the necessary issue of many a fruitful vein of thought, but in which, again and again, the Creator is significantly passed by, until at last He can be avoided no longer? And then we find ourselves suddenly enveloped in phrases of studied, nay, of profound reverence; phrases in which the writer bends before a something which is never named, we know not—perhaps he knows not—what. It may be that his purpose is to make all secure in case Theistic truth should turn out to be true after all; it may be that he desires, on grounds of early association, to stand well with the millions who still believe in a Creator; it may be that he is endeavouring to veil an embarrassment which inwardly shrinks from the whole subject, but which reflects that it can lose nothing by being graceful.

As for us Christians, " through faith, we understand that

the universe was framed by the word of God, so that it was not out of things that are apparent to the senses that the visible world came into existence." [1] Creation is a mystery, eminently satisfactory to reason, but strictly beyond it. Nothing within the range of our experience enables us to understand the process of calling beings into existence out of nothing. We men can do much in the way of modifying and controlling existing matter. But we cannot create the minutest particle of it. That God summoned it into being is a truth which we believe on God's authority, but which we never can verify. If, as is probable, the Mosaic cosmogony is much older than Moses, and was embodied in the Thorah as being a primeval revelation, still it must have been, to whomever given, strictly a revelation. No created being can have witnessed the act by which the Creator ended the solitariness of His Eternity, and surrounded Himself with forms of dependent life. And that which it is now important to insist on, is the practical value of this belief in Creation; its value in thought and its value in practice.

II.

Belief in the creation of the universe out of nothing is the only account of its origin which is compatible with belief in a personal and moral God.

Mankind may conceive, has conceived, of the relation between the universe or world and a higher Power in four

---

[1] In Heb. xi. 3 ἐκ μὴ φαινομένων is understood by St. Chrysostom and Theodoret to mean "out of nothing." If by "nothing" is meant "nothing material," the sense thus yielded is indisputable, though not that which the word suggests. The μὴ φαινόμενα are the Divine ideas from which the visible universe sprang into being, and which were drawn from their seclusion in the Divine Mind by the act of creation. A fundamental doctrine of the Epistle to the Hebrews is that there is an archetypal heavenly world, containing the types and ideas of this (Heb. viii. 5). Compare Delitzsch, *Hebräerbr. in loc.*

different ways.[1] Either God is a creation of the world—that is to say, of the thinking part of it—or God and the world are really identical; or God and the world, although distinct, are co-existent; or God has created the world out of nothing.

Now if God is a product of the human and thinking world; if He is produced by and only exists in the thought or the imagination of a certain section of the inhabitants of this planet, He is on a par with any other pure hypothesis. You may pay compliments to a creation of the human mind, or you may dislike and denounce it as mischievous and superstitious; but in either case you do not mistake it for something which it is not. Whatever may be the popular power of what you know to be only a form of current opinion, you do not reckon with it as if it were a substantial or living thing when you think or act. Your loyalty to truth naturally leads you to dismiss somewhat impatiently a phantom which might well have daunted the childhood of our race, but which has no business to flit about the brain of its manhood. If instead of believing in God, the Father Almighty, Maker of heaven and earth, you believe in the human mind as the maker of God, the conclusion is obvious. If God is not a real objective Being, apprehended by man's thought, but Himself utterly independent of such apprehension, then it follows that the universe is self-existent, and that it alone exists. A purely subjective deity is in truth no deity at all.

If, again, God and the world are two names for the same thing; if the universe is only the self-development of the Infinite, and man only that point in its self-evolution at which the Infinite attains self-consciousness; then surely we are playing with words in giving to this "Infinite" the solemn name of God. This Infinite is not God in the sense of the Bible; it is not God in the sense of the human

---

[1] I owe this method of stating the problem to Dr. Pusey.

heart. The name is retained; the reality has vanished just as truly as in the blankest Atheism. For such a deity is neither personal nor moral. He is not personal, since he lacks the first elements of personality: he is not an individual free-will or a self-consciousness; he is only a force which, for some unexplained reason, ultimately becomes self-conscious in a number of thinking subjects. The philosophy which cradles him is intolerant of the very idea of personality. And, apart from the difficulties of supposing morality in an impersonal subject, this deity is not moral, because he is, by the hypothesis, identified with all that is done by all the agents in the universe. The revealed belief in the Divine Omnipresence, which sees God everywhere, and therefore recognises His upholding Hand in the evil beings which war against Himself, is yet ever careful to distinguish between the perverted will, in whose activity alone evil is resident, and the action of the All-holy Creator. This last distinction is annihilated by the philosophy which identifies its god with the universe; and the necessary consequence is the annihilation of morality. Murder and adultery become manifestations of the life of the Infinite One as truly and in the same sense as benevolence or veracity.

But if, to avoid this revolting blasphemy, we suppose God and the world to be distinct, yet eternally co-existent, do we thereby secure in human thought a place for a moral and personal God? Surely not. For this last hypothesis involves a sacrifice of that which lies at the base of any real idea of God in our minds at all, namely, His solitary self-existence. If the universe had, from eternity, co-existed along with Him, though it were only as force and matter, so that the gradual elaboration of form and life was still reserved to Him, as being within these limits the all-controlling Agent, He would have been a different being from God. A second self-existence is a supposition which annihilates God. God has ceased to be if we are right in imagining that there never was a time when something else did not exist independently of Him. In the theogony of Hesiod it was possible to conceive of the gods as coming into existence at the same time as the world; but then God, in the Christian and Theistic sense, was not even conceived of, and the Greek mythologists do not attempt to account seriously for the origin of the universe. The supposition before us belongs in fact to a transitional stage of thought, when men are provisionally attempting intellectual compromises which cannot be permanently maintained. It necessarily throws us back upon a universe without a God, Who transcends while He sustains it in being, or upon a universe which is itself God; it leads inevitably to Atheism or Pantheism; it renders any serious belief in God impossible.

It is necessary, then, to believe in the creation of the universe out of nothing if we are to believe also in God's self-existent, personal, moral Life. But this faith in God's original act of creation does not exclude belief in some subsequent modification of His works through a progressive development, guided by more or less ascertainable law. The assertion of a recent writer, that the Jews failed to understand the full significance of creation because in Judaism the world is regarded as *creatura*, not as *natura*, as κτίσις, not as φύσις, can only be understood of later Jewish tradition. It is inapplicable to the language of the Bible. Certainly the Biblical account of the creation of light and of the animals stands in sharp contrast to the Greek conceptions of life and freedom fighting out their way by their own inherent powers from among the blind forces of nature; but the narrative of Moses includes a cosmogony as well as a creation: it describes modifications of existing matter as well as the creative act which summoned it into being. The recognition of God's continuous working in nature, in the form and according to the methods of law, is not a concession which has been wrung from theology by the advance of science. In a remarkable passage, where he is describing the opinions which may be held respecting the creative activity of God, Peter Lombard[1] employs terms which almost read like a tentative anticipation of Dr. Darwin's doctrine of the origin of species; although of course the Master of the Sentences, with his eye on the text of Genesis, would have often hesitated or demurred where the modern physicist is confident or aggressive.

But, even if we could reasonably and religiously carry evolutionist theories so far as to trace back all living beings to some germ or monad, the real question—the question of questions—would still confront us. How did the monad, whose development we can, as we may think, trace through successive stages of self-expansion, ever originally come to be? And upon the answer to this question depends nothing less than a man's belief in the Being Who, if He exists at all, must have infinitely more important claims on our attention than any one of the creatures which He has made, or than all of them together.

Again, belief in the creation of the universe by God out of nothing naturally leads on to belief in God's continuous Providence, and Providence in turn, considering the depth of man's moral misery, suggests Redemption. No such anticipation would be reasonable, if we could suppose that the world emanated from a passive God, or that, *per impossibile*, it had existed side by side with Him from everlasting. But if He created it in His freedom, the

[1] *Sentent.* lib. ii. distinct. xv. : "Quædam vero non formaliter sed materialiter tunc facta fuisse, quæ post per temporis accessum formaliter distincta sunt ; ut herbæ, arbores, et forte animalia. Omnia ergo, in ipso temporis initio facta esse dicunt ; sed quædam formaliter et secundum species quas habere cernimus, ut majores mundi partes ; quædam vero materialiter tantum."

question will inevitably be asked, why did He create it? Could it add anything to His Infinite Blessedness and Glory? could it make Him more powerful, more happy, more wise? Revelation answers the question, by ascribing creation to that attribute of God which leads Him to communicate His life; that generous attribute which is goodness in its relation to the irrational and inanimate universe, and love in its relation to personal beings. "I have loved thee with an everlasting love, therefore with loving-kindness have I drawn thee."[1] But if love or goodness was the true motive for creation, it implies God's continuous interest in created life. If love urged God to reveal Himself by His work under finite conditions—and both David and St. Paul insist upon the high significance of creation as an unveiling of the hidden life of God—surely love might urge Him to reveal Himself yet more distinctly under finite conditions, as "manifest in the flesh."[2] The formula that "time has no meaning for God," is sometimes used even by writers of consideration, in senses which are incompatible with the idea of creation. If it is not beneath God's dignity to create a finite world at all, it is not beneath His dignity to accept the consequences of His work; to take part in the development of His creatures; to subject Himself, in some sense, to the conditions imposed by His original act. If in His knowledge He necessarily anticipates the development of His work, so that to Him a "thousand years are as one day;"[3] by His love, on the other hand, which led Him to move out of Himself in creation at the first, He travails with the slow onward movement of the world and of humanity; and His Incarnation in time, when demanded by the supreme needs of the creatures of His hand, is in a line with that first of mysteries, His deigning to create at all. For thus, God having created the rational and human world, so loved it, that He gave His only

---

[1] Jer. xxxi. 3. [2] 1 Tim. iii. 16. [3] 2 Peter iii. 8.

begotten Son, that whosoever believeth on Him should not perish, but have everlasting life.¹

Of this property of the Life of God there is on earth one most beautiful and instructive shadow—the love of a parent for his child. That love is the most disinterested, the purest, if not the strongest of human passions. The parent hopes for nothing from his child; yet he will work for it, suffer for it, die for it. If you ask the reason, it is because he has been the means of bringing it into existence. Certainly, if it lives, it may support and comfort him in his old age; but that is not the motive of his anxious care. He feels the glory and the responsibility of fatherhood; and this leads him to do what he can for the helpless infant which depends on him. Our Lord appeals to this parental instinct when He teaches us the efficacy of prayer. If men, evil as they are, give good gifts unto their children, how much more shall not a moral God—your heavenly Father—give the best of gifts, His Holy Spirit, to them that ask Him.² But in truth the principle is of wider application; and it explains how it was that "the philanthropy and love of God our Saviour toward man appeared, when, not by works of righteousness which we had done, but according to His mercy, He saved us."³

Belief in creation indeed must govern the whole religious thought of a consistent believer. It answers many *a priori* difficulties as to the existence of miracle, since the one supreme, inexplicable miracle, compared with which all others are insignificant, is already admitted. It precludes difficulties on the score of the condescension of God in the Incarnation, in the Crucifixion, in the Sacraments; for the greatest condescension of all was the act which at the first summoned creatures into being. If the doctrine of final causes be discredited for a while in this or that region of human thought, it will reassert its claims

---

¹ St. John iii. 16.   ² St. Matt. vii. 11.   St. Luke xi. 13.   ³ Tit. iii. 4, 5.

in a higher atmosphere. The creation of the world by a free, personal, living God, cannot be contemplated apart from such a doctrine; and reason is already prepared for the statements of Scripture, that God's own Glory, His own Being or Self, was, as it could not but be in the case of the Supreme, His own end in creating.[1] And thus creation prepares us to see a purpose, whether fully or partially discernible, running through the whole course of human history, and we find it easy to understand that every single human soul—as its life lies out in all the complexity of movement and will and passion, before the All-Seeing One—is to Him a matter of the tenderest concern, so that each one of the sons of men might exclaim with the Apostle, "He loved me, and gave Himself for me."[2]

Once more, belief in Creation is of high moral value. Such a belief keeps a man in his right place; it is not less powerful in controlling his secret thought than his outward action. The disinclination to be under an obligation is always more or less natural to us, and it is particularly natural to those who are in rude health and high spirits, who have never yet known anything of real sorrow or of acute disease. It grows with that jealous sentiment of personal independence which belongs to an advanced civilization; and if it is distantly allied to one or two of the better elements of human character, it is more closely connected with others that are base and unworthy. The Eastern emperor executed the courtier who, by saving his life, had done him a service which could never be forgotten, perhaps never repaid; but this is only an extreme illustration of what may be found in the feelings of everyday life. A darker example of the same tendency is seen in the case of men who have wished a father in his grave, not on account of any misunderstanding, not from a coarse desire of succeeding to the family property, but because in the father the son saw a person to whom he owed not education

[1] Prov. xvi. 4. [2] Gal. ii. 20.

merely, but his birth into the world, and felt that so vast a debt made him morally insolvent so long as his creditor lived.

If men are capable of such feeling towards each other, we can understand much that characterizes their thought about and action towards God. By His very Existence He seems to inflict upon them a perpetual humiliation. To feel day by day, hour by hour, that there is at any rate One Being before Whom they are as nothing; to Whom they owe originally, and moment by moment, all that they are and have; Who so holds them in His Hand that no human parallel can convey a sense of the completeness of their dependence upon His good pleasure; and against Whose decisions they have neither plea nor remedy:—this they cannot bear. Yet if God exists, this, and nothing less than this, is strictly true. The truth is not diminished by any of the intellectual projects whereby men instinctively endeavour to lessen the sense of an overwhelming obligation. Evolution implies an original impulse; physical law implies a Lawgiver; God is recalled to human thought by the expedients which man invents that he may hide out of sight the mighty, all-including, all-conferring activity of the Creator. After all, brethren, "it is He that hath made us, and not we ourselves."[1] Not we ourselves. Of course we never should say in so many words that we were our own creators; but we may morally assume it. We may ignore the One Being Who made us and all besides, and Who will judge us: we may forget Him so entirely as to live as if He did not exist at all. Thousands do so forget Him: it is written on their lives that they have no notion that they have a Maker to think about and to live for. Yet, even if such forgetfulness had no lasting consequences, it were surely better to be true—true to the real law of this universe, true to a truth which alone can keep us in our proper place, of humble, submissive, resigned, obedient,

[1] Ps. c. 2.

yet withal hopeful and thankful, and diligent service. The service of the Great Creator may well be hopeful and thankful, for a moral God will not despise the work of His own hands, and Creation leads up to Redemption.

A traveller in Cornwall, when gazing at the masses of granite rock which defy, and look as if they might defy for ever, the continuous onset of the Atlantic, has expressed a thought which comes to most men at some time in their lives. The magnificence and the awe of nature fills him with an oppressive sense of the relative insignificance of man. A few years hence and he will be beneath the sod; but those cliffs will stand, as now, facing the Ocean, incessantly lashed by its waves, yet unshaken, immoveable; and other eyes will gaze on them for their brief day of life, and then they too will close. Yes, at first sight man is insignificant when thus confronted with external nature. The purely material world seems to have more in common than we with the unchanging and everlasting years of the Great Creator. Yet we know that it is not so. In reality the rocks are less enduring than man. Each man's personal self will still survive for weal or woe, when another catastrophe shall have utterly changed the surface of this planet, and the elements shall have melted with fervent heat, and the earth also and all things that are therein shall have been burnt up.[1] Let us think of that day, warranted by His Word, Who has made all that we see. It may be deferred for ages, but it will surely come at last; it will not tarry.[2] Practically speaking, there are for each one of us two supreme realities—God and the soul. The heavens and the earth will pass away. But the soul will still remain, face to face with God; and the Word of the Creator, His Word of Mercy, as well as His Word of Justice, will not pass away.[3]

[1] 2 St. Peter iii. 12, 13. [2] Hab. ii. 3. [3] 1 St. Peter i. 24, 25.

SERMON IV.

WORTH OF FAITH IN A LIFE TO COME.

REV. vii. 9, 10.

I beheld, and lo, a great multitude, which no man could number, of all nations, and kindreds, and people, and tongues, stood before the throne, and before the Lamb, clothed with white robes, and palms in their hands; and cried with a loud voice, saying, Salvation to our God Which sitteth upon the throne, and unto the Lamb.

AS a man passes into middle life, or beyond it, autumn, it has been said, whispers more to his soul than any other season of the natural year. It is not difficult to see why this should be, if it be, the case. The few hours of sunlight, the generally beclouded sky, as

"Chill and dun,
Falls on the moor the brief November day,"[1]

the cold damp atmosphere, the sense of advancing collapse and dissolution which the withered and decaying leaf everywhere suggests, and the knowledge that, as the days succeed each other, the season will pass into a yet deeper gloom—these features of November dispose us to think of the close of human life, and of the world which follows it. And the Church, with her fine practical instinct, seems to have made the most of such characteristics of the month as these, by placing at its commencement the festival which guides our thoughts upwards to the

[1] *Christian Year*, Twenty-third Sunday after Trinity.

home of all the Saints in glory, and by closing it with Advent Sunday,—that yearly anticipation of the great day of doom, when all that belongs to the present order of things here below will finally pass away.

Let us then endeavour to bring our thoughts into some sort of harmony with the time of year by considering a commonplace but always important subject, namely, the value of a serious belief in a life to come. Time was, and that not long past, when it might have been deemed needless, and even inexpedient, to insist upon such a topic as this. But none who know what is being said and written in our midst will be of this opinion now. The reality of a life after death is nowadays discussed, and indeed disputed, in popular reviews and in general society; and one consequence of such indiscriminate discussion, upon a not inconsiderable number of minds, is too patent and too serious to be overlooked. Men are endeavouring to persuade themselves that, whether true or false, the doctrine of a life to come may be treated as a purely speculative question, which has no necessary or indispensable relation to our present life and its duties. Whether we exist after death or not, this life at any rate, they argue, may be viewed as a thing complete in itself: we may live it, and make the most of it, without committing ourselves too definitely to any hypothesis as to what will or will not follow it. This life, they think, needs no motives drawn from the imagery of a distant world or of a supersensuous future; it can dispense with all stimulants to action or to self-control which it does not of itself suggest. A physical basis has been provided for morals which renders them independent of any theological sanction; or, at least, a ground has been cleared for so much morality as is really wanted upon a common-sense estimate of human existence. And for the rest, human society is no longer young; it has now had time for a great deal of varied experience; and it may be trusted to take care of itself, and to guard the lives and property of its members by the resources which are at the command of law. This being so, it is contended, the question of a future life may be postponed; it cannot be considered urgent; although, no doubt, it will always be interesting to speculative minds of a certain type, and will at least take rank with the inquiry whether the planets are inhabited, and by what kind of creatures.

Here then we have to consider the question what it is that faith in a life to come does, or in reason ought to do, for the man who seriously entertains it. And in order to limit the subject, I will not enter upon the connected topics of a judgment which awaits us, or of the sterner side of that doctrine of the future life which natural reason suggests and which the Christian Faith so distinctly proclaims. Let us think to-day of the prospect of sharing in a sublime and blessed existence such as is portrayed in the text of the Apocalypse before us, and let us ask ourselves whether it should or should not make any difference in our present state of being.

I.

First, then, reflect upon the importance to every thinking agent of forming an accurate estimate of his powers, of taking a true measure of himself. It is fatal enough, we all of us know, and it is not uncommon, to think that we are of more importance, cleverer, wiser, better, than we are. This is a mistake as to the nature of which the Gospel and the social common sense of man are entirely agreed. But it is only less fatal not to recognise the powers and opportunities which God has really given us, and to bury in a napkin some talent which is part of the endowment of our being. In this, as in all other matters, simple truthfulness is of the first importance. And life is worthily lived when a man has ascertained what his stock of capacities really are, and has resolved, God helping him, to make the best of them.

Thus, then, it is plain that the question whether we exist or not after death challenges attention on utilitarian grounds. It enters directly into any serious estimate of what is meant by human life, and to form such an estimate cannot be other than a matter of the first practical importance to all of us. For man as a moral being is a workman, working at himself; and a workman must know what he has to handle if he is to do his work well. What is this creature for the improvement of which we are each of us responsible? You and I find ourselves at this moment endowed with the blessed but awful prerogative of life. There was no necessity for our existing, and yet here we are. We may indeed pass days, weeks, months, years, without reflecting on what it is to live. But there are times, I believe, in almost every life, when thought is turned back upon itself, by some shock or sorrow, and when a man stands consciously face to face with the dread mystery of his own existence. What is it that we mean by that which each of us terms so lightly "I;" that inner being which thinks and feels and acts; which knows that it thinks and feels and acts; which determines its thought and its feeling and its action? What is this essence, the seat of reflection and memory and will, which, although far removed from the touch of sense, is yet everywhere present behind the senses; which looks out from itself upon the beings and things around it, and knows itself to be utterly distinct from each and all of them? This inner essence is a fact; it is at least as recognisable a fact as some lump of matter which lies passive and helpless as you handle it. It is not less a fact, because it is endowed with the prerogative of being conscious that it is what it is; and we ask, what is it worth, both in itself and as compared with things and beings around it? how long will it last? why is it here? whither is it going? what is its origin? what its destiny?

We are told that the difference between belief and disbelief in a life after death is only a difference between two theories about the relation of human nature to a remote future, and to an abstract conception of existence. Two theories! My brethren, there are theories and theories. There are theories, no doubt, high up in the air of speculation which do not touch, ever so lightly, the practical interests of human beings. But there are also theories which are not thus remote and ornamental; theories the subjects of which penetrate the very bone and marrow, the inmost recesses of our life, so that, if we would, we cannot detach and thrust them from us, and affect towards them the polite indifference which may be awarded to purely abstract speculations. In fact, we do not think or speak of them as theories; we call them by the graver name of doctrines. As doctrines they are for us either true or false; if false, then in varying degrees mischievous falsehoods; if true, then very solemn and momentous truths. And surely this question, whether we become extinct at death or exist continuously after it, in a higher and freer form of life, comes too directly home to every human being to be discussed, as our neighbours would say, academically; as if forsooth it were only to be thought of as furnishing opportunity for skilful fencing between one set of intellectual combatants and another.

If, when a man tries to take stock of his existence, he says to himself, "I am a higher sort of animal, who will certainly have ceased to exist altogether in the course of some twenty or thirty years," then he will probably do the best that can be done with life from a purely animal point of view. The outlook is closely bounded by a lofty fence, on which is traced the word "Annihilation;" and there is much in nature which whispers the old advice—

> "Dona præsentis rape lætus horæ,
> Linque severa"—

or which bids him, in more modern phrase, enjoy to the full the successive sensations, one by one, of his fleeting period of animation.

But suppose, on the other hand, that a man's thoughts run thus: "I am here, clothed in a frame of flesh and blood which must soon be subjected to decay and dissolution. But this stage of my existence is only a brief preface to another which will follow it, and of which there will be no end." To think thus, most assuredly, is to form another estimate of the best use to make of the remaining years of life. That vast illimitable existence beyond the grave already casts across a man's path some shadows, at the least, of its own magnificence; and it is felt that there is solemn work to be done, within and without him, while the day of preparation lasts. To say that the question at issue is theoretical or abstract is to disguise very serious issues beneath the pedantries of phrase. It is not a matter of merely abstract interest whether Newton ceased altogether to exist on March 20, 1727, or whether he is living somewhere at this moment, and, it may be, in the splendour of of a higher intellectual and moral life. The real question in dispute is whether man is a creature of one kind, or a creature of another and an utterly different kind; whether he is to think of his life and its duties as may befit a perishing and on the whole a very unfortunate animal,— unfortunate, because too highly endowed for purely animal wellbeing,—or whether he is to measure his opportunities as a spirit should measure them which knows itself to be confronted by high hopes and by terrific possibilities; which knows that it already belongs by the tie of an imperishable existence to an eternal world.

II.

Secondly, human beings, as such, require a prospect of something beyond the immediate present, and are powerfully acted upon by possessing it. No one who has ever observed human nature, either in himself or in others, can doubt the importance to every man of his having something before him of which he is not yet in actual enjoyment. The present, at its very best, does not satisfy: it only appears to satisfy when it is reinforced by the assurance that it is to be succeeded. It is haunted by the sense of imperfection, by the thirst for that which it imperfectly suggests; its outlook is bounded somewhat abruptly by the material and the perishing; and there is that in the depths of the human soul which is capable of and was made for something greater. "I sought in mine heart to give myself unto wine, yet acquainting mine heart with wisdom; and to lay hold on folly, till I might see what was that good for the sons of men, which they should do under the heaven all the days of their life. I made me great works: I builded me houses: I planted me vineyards: I made me gardens and orchards, and I planted trees in them of all kinds of fruits: I made me pools of water, to water therewith the wood that bringeth forth trees: I got me servants and maidens, and had servants born in my house: also I had great possessions of great and small cattle above all that were in Jerusalem before me: I gathered me also silver and gold, and the peculiar treasure of kings and of the provinces: I gat me men singers and women singers, and the delights of the sons of men, as musical instruments, and that of all sorts. So I was great, and increased more than all that were before me in Jerusalem: also my wisdom remained with me. And whatsoever mine eyes desired I kept not from them: I withheld not my heart from any joy; for my heart rejoiced in all my labour: and this was my portion of all my labour——"

And what was the conclusion of this writer,—the wisest probably of the sons of men?

"Then I looked on all the works that my hands had wrought, and on the labour that I had laboured to do: and behold, all was vanity and vexation of spirit, and there was no profit under the sun."[1]

Such is the law of our existence: we do not find real satisfaction in the temporary and the evanescent, and, as a consequence, we look forward. We look forward, as is natural, first of all, to reaching the nearest horizon that bounds our view. As little children, we look forward to the strength and capacity of boyhood; as boys, we anticipate the freedom and completeness—for such in the distance it seems—of being men. As men, we are still expectant; when we have gained the range of hills which from a distance seemed erewhile so blue and picturesque, we are at least partly disappointed; and, moreover, we have caught sight of another range beyond it. Thus we pass through life; anticipating first this and then that stage of our career, until at last the warning—if it be deferred so long—comes to us, that there is not much more, at least here, to be anticipated. We may perhaps attempt to continue the life of expectation by embarking it in the fortunes of those who will succeed us on earth; but this precaution does not satisfy a being who cannot but be conscious of himself possessing an existence which is utterly and necessarily distinct from all around it. Lucretius does not disguise his vexation at the reluctance of human nature to acquiesce in the fiat of extinction at death which is pronounced by the materialist philosophy:—

"Quid tibi tantopere est, mortalis, quod nimis ægris
Luctibus indulges? quid mortem congemis, ac fles?

---

[1] Eccles. ii. 3-11.

> Cur non, ut plenus vitæ conviva, recedis,
> Æquo animoque capis securam, stulte, quietem?"

No! this refusal to be satisfied with the banquet of our earthly life is an honourable discontent; it is the instinct of a being who cannot suppress the promptings of a higher destiny; who even on the threshold of death must look forward still and demand a future.

How this requirement of our nature is provided for in the Christian Revelation is familiar to all of you. The well-known sarcasm of Gibbon, when he is discussing the second of his five causes of the growth of Christianity,[1] is, in fact, the statement of a simple truth. That which philosophy could not do, notwithstanding some noble efforts, towards giving man assurance of his true destiny, was achieved by the Gospel. In words which haunt the memories even of those who have ceased to believe that they are words of God, the Bible warrants, by an ascending series of proclamations, the bright and cherished prospect of the life after death. It is already hovering before the vision of Hebrew psalmists: "As for me, I will behold Thy face in righteousness: I shall be satisfied, when I awake, with Thy likeness."[2] "With Thee is the fountain of life: and in Thy light shall we see light."[3] "Thou wilt show me the path of life: in Thy Presence is the fulness of joy, and at Thy right hand there are pleasures for evermore."[4] It underlies the language of prophets, even when they are thinking of some nearer blessings: "The redeemed of the Lord shall return, and come with singing unto Zion; and everlasting joy shall be upon their head: they shall obtain gladness and joy, and sorrow and mourning shall flee away."[5] "Thy sun shall no more go down, neither shall thy moon withdraw itself:

---

[1] *Decl. and Fall*, c. xv. vol. ii. p. 170, ed. 1862.
[2] Ps. xvii. 15. [3] Ps. xxxvi. 9.
[4] Ps. xvi. 11. [5] Isa. li. 11.

for the Lord shall be thine everlasting light, and the days of thy mourning shall be ended."[1] It is rendered certain by the words of our Lord Jesus Christ: "In My Father's house are many mansions: if it were not so, I would have told you: I go to prepare a place for you."[2] He it is Who foretells a time when "the righteous shall shine forth as the sun in the kingdom of their Father."[3] It is He Who draws the picture of a future in which His first disciples are to "sit on thrones, judging the twelve tribes of Israel."[4] He Whose presence is itself heaven, yet exclaims in prayer, "Father, I will that they whom Thou hast given Me be with Me where I am, that they may behold My glory."[5] His is the precept, "Lay up for yourselves treasures in heaven, where neither moth nor rust doth corrupt."[6] His the assurance, "The righteous shall go away into life eternal."[7] His the forecast of a state of existence where "they neither marry nor are given in marriage, but are as the angels of God in heaven."[8] His the promise, "He that loseth his life for My sake shall find it."[9]

And thus His first servants live in view of the prospect which He has opened to them. "It doth not yet appear," they say, "what we shall be; but we know that, when He shall appear, we shall be like Him, for we shall see Him as He is."[10] "We are joint-heirs," they reflect, "with Christ; if so be that we suffer with Him, that we may be also glorified together."[11] "The sufferings of this present time are," they argue, "not worthy to be compared with the glory that shall be revealed in" Christians.[12] "The exceeding and eternal weight of glory" is triumphantly contrasted by them with the "light affliction which is but for a moment."[13] "An

[1] Isa. lx. 20.
[2] St. John xiv. 2.
[3] St. Matt. xiii. 43.
[4] St. Luke xxii. 30.
[5] St. John xvii. 24.
[6] St. Matt. vi. 20.
[7] St. Matt. xxv. 46.
[8] St. Matt. xxii. 30.
[9] St. Matt. x. 39.
[10] 1 St. John iii. 2.
[11] Rom. viii. 17.
[12] Rom. viii. 18.
[13] 2 Cor. iv. 17.

inheritance incorruptible, and undefiled, and that fadeth not away," is reserved in heaven, so they proclaim, for those who through grace persevere unto the end.[1] Nay, heaven is open to them in ecstasy, and they tell us what they see and what they hear. "There shall be no night there; and they need no candle, neither light of the sun; for the Lord God giveth them light: and they shall reign for ever and ever."[2] The martyred and blessed dead are "before the throne of God, and serve Him day and night in His temple: and He that sitteth on the throne shall dwell among them. They shall hunger no more, neither thirst any more: neither shall the sun light on them, nor any heat."[3] "God shall wipe away all tears from their eyes; there shall be no more death, neither sorrow, nor crying, neither shall there be any more pain."[4] And, in the vision of the text, "a great multitude, which no man could number, of all nations, and kindreds, and people, and tongues, stood before the throne, and before the Lamb, clothed with white robes, and palms in their hands; and cried with a loud voice, saying, Salvation to our God Which sitteth upon the throne, and unto the Lamb."

Yes, this is the great anticipation of the human soul: this is the great announcement of the Gospel. It gathers up into itself all that is best in the enthusiasm and poetry of our race; it consecrates each glimpse of true beauty that ever has visited the spirit of man. All that has seemed in past years to flit before us, as though a gleam of light from a brighter world; all that has lifted us for the moment, we knew not how, above our natural selves, into a region of thought and feeling which was strange and exquisite; all the presentiments, the ideals, the outlines of higher existence, which did but tarry for an instant with us and forthwith vanish away, are to be recalled, realized, perpetuated, surpassed. That subtle and various pleasure which

[1] 1 St. Pet. i. 4. [2] Rev. xxii. 5. [3] Rev. vii. 15, 16. [4] Rev. xxi. 4.

underlies the buoyant spirits of youth, and the strength of manhood, and the ripe wisdom and well-earned reverence of age, will be extracted, condensed, eternalized. What if those who know not God's revelation of Himself in Christ have anticipated a heaven which should correspond with their debased conception of "the best on earth"? Surely this does not prevent Christians from acknowledging that, though heaven is no creation of man's imaginative faculty, though its existence is just as objective as our own, yet God's heaven is all that is really best on earth, and more besides. The highest aspects of each condition of life are to heaven what the types of the Old Covenant were to the Messiah; they foreshadow, now one, now another side of a perfectly comprehensive excellence, till they lose themselves in that which they so variously portray.

Now, to maintain that serious belief in such a future as this is not calculated to make a great difference in the life and character of the man who holds it is to contradict all that we know about our common nature. In different senses of the saying, men in all ages are saved through hope: in other words, the anticipation of a better future is the leverage of their being. Even when it is only a dim future resting not even upon human assurances, but on some precarious calculation of possibilities, it is, at times, sufficient to mould a life. What was it that roused the young Hannibal to become the intrepid leader whom we meet in history, but the prospect set before him when a boy that one day he might avenge the wrongs of his country? What was it that has led discoverers like Columbus to attempt a perilous voyage into unknown seas, but the reports of a land beyond which might possibly reward persevering enterprise? How have those other, and scarcely less noble, discoverers who have enriched our world with the gifts of science been nerved to their work, but by the sustained expectation that there were secrets waiting to be wrung from nature if only men would seek them? How could even a John Howard have spent his days in what at first might well have seemed a thankless task, the rescue of thousands of prisoners from an aggravated wretchedness, and of society from the thoughtless barbarism which sanctioned it, had it not seemed to him to be within reach of his untiring philanthropy? What else indeed has supported all the men who have done most and best for their kind, under the pressure of difficulties and against appearances, but this faith in a possibly improved condition of things, for which they must needs labour and for which they might well be content to wait? And, if this be a true account of the matter, who shall call in question the moral importance of faith in a future life, or the immense moral loss which must result if it be renounced? That faith rests, as Christians believe, on stronger bases than any of the probabilities which in this life move good and enterprising men to vigorous action; and Christianity does the highest service to human nature here and now, when it tells man, without faltering and incessantly, that he has to live for another world.

It may indeed be asked whether the true satisfactions of religion are not present satisfactions? whether virtue is not its own reward? whether God is not the present possession of the Christian soul? whether the things that eye hath not seen, nor ear heard, but which God has prepared for them that love Him, are not things to be enjoyed on earth by the spirit of man?[1] whether, in fine, expectation of something yet to come is not the note of preparatory and imperfect dispensations, and unworthy of the Gift which was made to man by the Divine Incarnation?

To this it must be replied that Christianity, as a matter of fact, does not profess in this life to satisfy all the aspirations of man. It does a great deal for him, yet it

[1] 1 Cor. ii. 9.

leaves something still to be done; it holds something in reserve; and that for man's own sake, and with a view to his best interests. Thus, the Christian is an adopted son of God;[1] yet, since the redemption of the body from the empire of death is still future, he is also "waiting for the adoption."[2] The Christian is justified;[3] yet it is St. Paul who tells him that we Christians, "through the Spirit," still "wait for the hope of righteousness by faith."[4] Christians are said now to "have been made to sit together in heavenly places in Christ Jesus,"[5] and yet, "when Christ, Who is our life, shall appear, then shall ye also appear with Him in glory."[6] A Christian *has* eternal life;[7] and yet, although to live is Christ, to die is still, in some sense, "gain."[8] The conversation of a Christian is in heaven;[9] he has come to mount Zion, to the city of the living God, and to an innumerable company of angels, and to the general assembly of the church of the firstborn, and to the spirits of the just made perfect; and to Jesus the Mediator of the New Covenant;[10] the supernatural world is about him, and he belongs to it. And yet "we that are in this tabernacle do groan, being burdened;" "earnestly desiring to be clothed upon with our house which is from heaven."[11]

Thus the satisfaction which Christianity affords to the human soul is at once present and future; present in part, but future in its completeness: we have eternal life, yet we expect it; we possess God, yet we look forward to seeing Him as He is; we are in heaven in one sense, while in another we have yet to win it. The Treasure of the Gospel is ours, but only in part; enough is left to look forward to, to feed the high grace of hope, to exert upon the nature which God the Creator has given us that strong attraction,

---

[1] Rom. viii. 15. Gal. iv. 5. Eph. i. 5.   [2] Rom. viii. 23.
[3] Rom. v. 1, 9.   1 Cor. vi. 11.   [4] Gal. v. 5.   [5] Eph. ii. 6.
[6] Col. iii. 4.   [7] 1 St. John v. 13.   [8] Phil. i. 21.
[9] Phil. iii. 20.   [10] Heb. xii. 22-24.   [11] 2 Cor. v. 4, 2.

that indispensable stimulus, which belongs to anticipation of the future.

III.

Once more, the doctrine of a life to come affords entire and permanent satisfaction to the social instincts of man.

By the terms of his nature man is a social being; his social instincts are originally due not to what he has made himself, but to his manhood. In its three forms,—the family, the country, the race,—society takes possession of us. We are born into a family; long before we can determine and shape our course, other human beings are acting upon us with decisive power, and our affections are drawn out towards and engaged by them beyond recall. Then, as our horizon extends, we associate ourselves with society in the larger form of our country; its frontier, its enthusiasms, its apprehensions, its dangers, its aspirations become, in a sense, our own; a whole world of passion and interest which had slept unsuspected in the depths of our being is roused into activity, and we find ourselves capable of much whereof we little dreamt. But the human soul knows no limits to its higher aspirations, and the social instinct, in all noble-minded men, endeavours to be as wide in its range of exercise as the human race. To be a man, as heathens have felt, is to have sympathy with everything that is truly human.

When, then, our Lord Jesus Christ came to do the best that Divine Wisdom could do for us, He made provision for the social instinct in man. He knew what was in us, and He ordered accordingly. The new life which He brought us is not only a personal bond between each of us and our Maker, it is also a social bond between each of us and our brethren who share it. Thus Christianity becomes concrete and actual, not merely in the believing Christian, but in the organized and universal Church. A Christian is not only a man who is of a particular moral type and temper, or who knows and can say how man can come to be as he should be before God: he is also a man who knows and remembers that he is a member of a divinely-constituted society of men. For, if any one thing is written plainly in the New Testament it is that our Lord came to found a society; that He called this society by no less a name than that of the Kingdom of Heaven, in order to remind men of its true object and character; and that in well-ordered membership of this society, no less than in sincere personal faith and love towards the Author and Restorer of our being, does the true Christian life essentially consist.

But do these provisions in nature and in grace afford satisfaction to the social instinct? Must we not confess that they are even very far from doing so? How constantly is the family the scene of disagreements which are bitter in proportion to the sacredness of the ties which are violated! How often is patriotism only a name for party; how often is it, as in France under the First Napoleon, associated with enterprises which a strong sense of right cannot possibly approve! How often do cosmopolitan theories shade off into an unhealthy sentimentalism, if indeed they do not take the form of some subtle variety of selfish aggrandizement!

Nor can it be maintained that the social instinct is adequately, or rather finally, provided for in the Christian Church militant. The Catholic Church is indeed, by the will of its Divine Founder, "one body and one spirit, even as its members are called in one hope of their calling."[1] But in practice, even while Apostles are living and ruling, "one" of its members "saith, I am of Paul, and another, I of Apollos, and I of Cephas, and I of Christ."[2] Its divisions are chronic; they are reinforced by the strongest passions that can move mankind; they crystallize into separations

[1] Eph. iv. 4. [2] 1 Cor. i. 12.

that last for centuries; they create barriers which are fatal to the ebb and flow of the charities of Christ. We may well wish it had been otherwise; we must indeed pray that it may be otherwise. We may say, in our less reverent moods, that if the world was to be won to the Gospel, it ought to have been otherwise. We do not really escape from the difficulty by taking refuge in the largest but not the least changeful fragment of a divided Christendom, and by burying our heads ostrichwise in the sands of *a priori* theories, if haply we may persuade ourselves that this fragment is the whole. In these matters we have to submit to the empire of facts; and facts do not adjust themselves to our impetuous assumptions. Although the Church of Christ militant is bound up with all the best hopes for truth and charity which our race can entertain, it does not correspond to the ideal aspirations of the social instinct. It is the home of Divine grace; but it is also the home of human nature. And even in the Church human nature asserts its fallen propensities towards separation; even on this sacred ground the practical result disappoints the higher longings of man for a perfect society on earth.

And therefore for the social instinct, as for the need of a future, provision is made finally and adequately in the world to come. In that world there will be a reunion around the throne of Christ of all who have been separated here by the misunderstandings which are more or less inevitable in the twilight. The saintly characters, the high and pure intelligences, whose names are perhaps familiar to us, the outlines of whose thought or life have reached us through dim tradition, or whom we know through their writings, and have longed—as did St. Chrysostom when he read St. Paul—to have seen and heard in the flesh; these will be in that company. And others whom we ourselves have known in life, and who have passed away, and have never since on one single day been unremembered in our prayers, and have left in our memories an impression which is as fresh now as when they parted from us, and which will be what it is until we too lie down to die,—these too will be present in that vast assemblage as our fellow-citizens for ever, as members of the same great family of immortal beings. Is it conceivable that such a prospect of introduction to all who have been really great and noble among the sons of men should not influence those who enjoy it?. is it possible that they are living and acting only in the same moral world as are those for whom all that follows death is a dreary blank?

No, it is impossible. For closely allied to our desire for a future life, and for a purer association with other beings than we can here enjoy, is our desire for personal perfection. In some degree this passion lives in every human soul; if it has been trodden out or suffered to die away, it once was there; if it is too vague to have any clear account to give of itself, it is not the less an original feature of our nature. It gives impulse to all that moves upward in human life; it inspires art, it reconstructs society, it endeavours to renew individual character. It is at once a pleasure and a torment, an enjoyment and a reproach; and it is never satisfied in this life,—never. Certainly, we are bidden even here to be perfect;[1] we are told, in a variety of ways, that in this life, God, the Perfect Being, may be possessed by the human soul. "If a man love Me he will keep My words, and My Father will love him, and We will come unto him, and make Our abode with him."[2] But, in fact, the present possession of God by a soul in grace is, although a most real and priceless blessing, yet accompanied by drawbacks arising from our clinging imperfections, which will no longer exist in a better state. "Now we see through a glass darkly, but then face to face."[3] There will then be nothing between us and

---

[1] St. Matt. v. 48.   [2] St. John xiv. 23.   [3] 1 Cor. xiii. 12.

Himself. Certainly, He is now what He will be then; the same, yesterday, to-day, and for ever.[1] But we shall have been changed.[2] "Beloved, now are we the sons of God, and it doth not yet appear what we shall be; but we know that when He shall appear, we shall be like Him, for we shall see Him as He is."[3]

IV.

Until, then, human nature ceases to be what it is, the question whether there is, or is not, a life after death cannot but have great practical importance for mankind. Doubtless there have been, and are, men who have been, according to their light, conscientious and upright without believing it; just as there have been, and are, men who have professed to believe it without being upright and conscientious. But the question is as to the mass of men, not as to the exceptions. No one can doubt that in the case of the great majority of human beings, the presence or absence of such a belief as this must make all the difference in the world. Not that it would be a sufficient reason for asserting the doctrine to say that it is a doctrine of the highest ethical value; my position is, that being true, it is also of the greatest value, and that, if it could be disproved, the loss to mankind would be incalculably great.

And yet, we must all know, there are generous hearts in which the sad whisper is uttered, "Would that it were certain, but is it after all more than a beautiful dream?"

My brethren, it is, probably useless, nowadays, for the purpose of producing or recovering this great conviction, to insist upon such abstract considerations as those which are put forward in the Phædo of Plato, and from which so much has been so well developed in modern spiritualist philosophies, as to the intrinsic nature, the immateriality,

---

[1] Heb. xiii. 8.   [2] 1 Cor. xv. 51.   [3] 1 St. John iii. 2.

the indivisibility, the indestructibility of the soul. Many hard things have been said, and are being said, about the worth of these arguments; and of these modern criticisms themselves it may be said also that men who come after us are not likely to take them all for granted. But the intellectual temper of our day is unquestionably ill-disposed towards *a priori* argument dealing with subjects where there is great room for the mistakes which are due to necessary ignorance. Let me, however, suggest two considerations by means of which a man who has lost it may hope to recover faith in an existence after death.

Of these the first is the steady contemplation of the idea of justice, an idea of which no man can utterly divest himself, if indeed he would. It is a part of his humanity; if it is not born with his mind, yet it is inevitably admitted, like a mathematical axiom, when once placed before him. A man can neither reject it in theory nor dispute its right to practical ascendency; and yet, when he reviews our everyday human life by the light of this imperious idea, what is his conclusion? The success of crime, the misfortunes of virtue, are the commonplaces of experience. They are too numerous and too serious to be explained away. If anything is clear, it is that there is no sufficient room for the idea of justice in our present sphere of being. Justice demands some more extended sphere; justice demands an immortality; and if there be a moral Being of Whose intrinsic nature justice is a ray, then the immortality of man is a necessary truth.

Think well, brethren, on this idea of justice; and then, secondly, go into the presence of death, the death of one, it may be, in whose life we have felt—it is not difficult to feel this just now in Oxford [1]—what a beautiful and majestic thing a human life may be. Up to the last there is everything to betoken the unimpaired activity of a living spirit,

---

[1] The reference is to the late Mrs. Acland, Nov. 1878.

whose moral fervour and high intelligence have conspired to prove how little the pains of the dissolution which is taking possession of the body can disturb the lofty calm of its immaterial tenant. But at last a moment comes when the voice has failed, and the eye is dim, and the features are rigid in death. Is it conceivable that all which a few moments since carried us beyond ourselves into a higher world is buried beneath the folds of inanimate matter which lie before us? No, it is inconceivable. Is it whispered that this is an intrusion of human feeling upon ground where science only has a right to teach? I answer, that feeling is only thus confident and daring, because feeling is here the drapery of man's higher reason; and that reason protests against an assumption for which no really scientific warrant can be shown, and which is contradicted by all that is best worthy of trust in the instinctive judgment of the human soul.

And then, when we have cross-questioned the idea of justice, and gazed upon the face of the saintly dead, let us go in thought to the empty Sepulchre outside Jerusalem, and ask ourselves the meaning of the event which actually took place there eighteen centuries ago,—an event warranted by testimony which in all ordinary matters of human concern would be deemed conclusive. That event it was which opened the kingdom of heaven to all believers. Over the door of that Sepulchre we Christians, not without reason, will ever read the words of the first Apostle: "Blessed be the God and Father of our Lord Jesus Christ, Which according to His abundant mercy hath begotten us again unto a lively hope by the Resurrection of Jesus Christ from the dead, to an inheritance incorruptible, and undefiled, and that fadeth not away."[1]

Suffer me to add in conclusion a few words which may be remembered in days to come.

[1] 1 St. Pet. i. 3, 4.

The expectation of a life after death enables us to see things in their true proportions. The future life furnishes us with a point of view from which to survey the questions, the occupations, the events of this. Until we keep it well before us, we are like those persons who have never travelled, and have no standard by which to estimate what they see at home. Next to positive error, a mistake as to the relative proportions of truths is the greatest misfortune. Yet who does not feel, every day of his existence, how easily this mistake is made? Some occurrence which touches us personally appears to be of world-wide importance. Some book which we have fallen in with, and have read with sympathy, or perhaps have helped to write, seems to mark an epoch in literature or in speculation. Some controversy, with its petty but absorbing ferocities, lying far off the main current of tempestuous thought which is sweeping across our distracted generation, appears, through its present relation to ourselves, to touch all interests in earth and heaven. Self magnifies and distorts everything; the true corrective is to be found in the magnificent and tranquillizing thought of another life. As men draw near to the threshold of eternity they see things more nearly as they are; they catch perspectives which are not perceived in the days of business and of health. When Bossuet lay a-dying, in great suffering and exhaustion, one who was present thanked him for all his kindness, and using the Court language of the day, begged him when in another world to think of the friends whom he was leaving, and who were so devoted to his person and his reputation. At this last word, Bossuet, who had almost lost the power of speech, raised himself from the bed, and gathered strength to say, not without an accent of indignation, "Don't talk like that. Ask God to forgive a sinner his sins."

And surely those occupations should claim our first

attention which prepare us for that which after all is the really important stage of our existence. All kinds of earthly duty may indeed be consecrated to this work by a worthy motive; but direct preparation for the future is made in worship. In the most solemn moments which we can spend on earth, we hear the words, "The Body of our Lord Jesus Christ, which was given for thee, preserve thy body and soul unto everlasting life." Nay, all Christian worship is in proportion to its sincerity an anticipation of the life of the world to come. Worship is the earthly act by which we most distinctly recognise our personal immortality: men who think that they will be extinct a few years hence do not pray. In worship we spread out our insignificant life, which yet is the work of the Creator's hands, and the purchase of the Redeemer's Blood, before the Eternal and All-Merciful, that we may learn the manners of a higher sphere, and fit ourselves for companionship with saints and angels, and for the everlasting sight of the Face of God. Worship is the common sense of faith in a life to come; and the hours we devote to it will assuredly be among those upon which we shall reflect with most thankful joy when all things here shall have fallen into a very distant background, and when through the Atoning Mercy our true home has been reached at last.

SERMON V.

INFLUENCES OF THE HOLY SPIRIT.

(WHITSUN-DAY.)

St. John iii. 8.

The wind bloweth where it listeth, and thou hearest the sound thereof, but canst not tell whence it cometh, and whither it goeth.

WHO has not felt the contrast, the almost tragic contrast, between the high station of the Jewish doctor, member of the Sanhedrin, master in Israel, and the ignorance of elementary religious truth, as we Christians must deem it, which he displayed in this interview with our Blessed Lord? At first sight it seems difficult to understand how our Lord could have used the simile in the text when conversing with an educated and thoughtful man, well versed in the history and literature of God's ancient people; and, indeed, a negative criticism has availed itself of this and of some other features in the narrative, in the interest of the theory that Nicodemus was only a fictitious type of the higher classes in Jewish society, as they were pictured to itself by the imagination of the fourth Evangelist. Such a supposition, opposed to external facts and to all internal probabilities, would hardly have been entertained, if the critical ingenuity of its author had been seconded by any spiritual experience. Nicodemus is very far from being a caricature; and our Lord's method here, as elsewhere, is to lead on from

familiar phrases and the well-remembered letter to the
spirit and realities of religion. The Jewish schools were
not unacquainted with the expression a "new creature;"
but it had long since become a mere shred of official
rhetoric. As applied to a Jewish proselyte, it scarcely
meant more than a change in the outward relations of
religious life. Our Lord told Nicodemus that every man
who would see the kingdom of God which He was found-
ing must undergo a second birth; and Nicodemus, who
had been accustomed to the phrase all his life, could not
understand it if it was to be supposed to mean anything
real. "How," he asks, "can a man be born when he is old?
can he enter a second time into his mother's womb, and
be born?" Our Lord does not extricate him from this
blundering literalism; He repeats His own original assertion, but in terms which more fully express His meaning:
"Verily, verily, I say unto thee, Except a man be born of
water and of the Spirit, he cannot enter into the kingdom
of God. That which is born of the flesh is flesh; and
that which is born of the Spirit is spirit. Marvel not that
I said unto thee, Ye must be born again." Our Lord's
reference to water would not have been unintelligible to
Nicodemus; every one in Judæa knew that the Baptist
had insisted on immersion in water as a symbol of the
purification of the soul of man. Certainly, in connect-
ing "water" with the Spirit and the new birth, our
Lord's language, glancing at that of the prophet,[1] went
very far beyond this. He could only be fully understood at a later time, when the Sacrament of Baptism had
been instituted, just as the true sense of His early allusions
to His death could not have been apprehended until after
the Crucifixion. But Nicodemus, it is plain, had not yet
advanced beyond his original difficulty; he could not
conceive how any second birth was possible, without alto-

[1] Ezek. xxxiv. 24, 25.

gether violating the course of nature. And our Lord penetrates His thoughts and answers them. He answers them by pointing to that Invisible Agent Who could achieve, in the sphere of spiritual and mental life, what the Jewish doctor deemed so impossible a feat as a second birth. Nature, indeed, contained no force that could compass such a result; but nature in this, as in other matters, was a shadow of something beyond itself.

It was late at night when our Lord had this interview with the Jewish teacher. At the pauses in conversation, we may conjecture, they heard the wind without as it moaned along the narrow streets of Jerusalem; and our Lord, as was His wont, took His creature into His service —the service of spiritual truth. The wind was a figure of the Spirit. Our Lord would have used the same word for both. The wind might teach Nicodemus something of the action of Him Who is the real Author of the New Birth of man. And it would do this in two ways more especially.

On a first survey of nature, the wind arrests man's attention, as an unseen agent which seems to be moving with entire freedom. "The wind bloweth where it listeth." It is fettered by none of those conditions which confine the swiftest bodies that traverse the surface of the earth; it sweeps on as if independent of law, rushing hither and thither, as though obeying its own wayward and momentary impulse. Thus it is an apt figure of a self-determining invisible force; and of a force which is at times of overmastering power. Sometimes, indeed, its breath is so gentle, that only a single leaf or blade of grass will at distant intervals seem to give the faintest token of its action; yet, even thus, it "bloweth where it listeth." Sometimes it bursts upon the earth with destructive violence; nothing can resist its onslaught; the most solid buildings give way; the stoutest trees bend before it; whatever is frail and delicate can only escape by the completeness of its submission. Thus, too, it "bloweth where it listeth." Beyond anything else that strikes upon the senses of man, it is suggestive of free supersensuous power; it is an appropriate symbol of an irruption of the Invisible into the world of sense, of the action, so tender or so imperious, of the Divine and Eternal Spirit upon the human soul.

But the wind is also an agent about whose proceedings we really know almost nothing. "Thou hearest the sound thereof;" such is our Lord's concession to man's claim to knowledge. "Thou canst not tell whence it cometh, and whither it goeth;" such is the reserve which He makes in respect of human ignorance. Certainly we do more than hear the sound of the wind; its presence is obvious to three of the senses. We feel the chill or the fury of the blast; and, as it sweeps across the ocean, or the forest, or the field of corn, we see how the blades rise and fall in graceful curves, and the trees bend, and the waters sink and swell into waves which are the measure of its strength. But our Lord says, "Thou hearest the sound thereof." He would have us test it by the most spiritual of the senses. It whispers, or it moans, or it roars as it passes us; it has a pathos all its own. Yet what do we really know about it? "Thou canst not tell whence it cometh, and whither it goeth." Does the wind then obey no rule; is it a mere symbol of unfettered caprice? Surely not. If, as the Psalmist sings, "God bringeth the winds out of His treasuries,"[1] He acts, we may be sure, here as always, whether in nature or in grace, by some law, which His own perfections impose upon His action. He may have given to us of these later times to see a very little deeper beneath the surface of the natural world than was the case with our fathers. Perchance we explain the immediate antecedents of the phenomenon; but can we explain our own explanation? The frontier of our ignorance is removed one stage

[1] Ps. cxxxv. 7.

farther back; but "the way of the wind" is as fitting an expression for the mysterious now as it was in the days of Solomon.[1] We know that there is no cave of Æolus. We know that the wind is the creature of that Great Master Who works everywhere and incessantly by rule. But, as the wind still sweeps by us who call ourselves the children of an age of knowledge, and we endeavour to give our fullest answer to the question, "whence it cometh, and whither it goeth?" we discover that, as the symbol of a spiritual force, of whose presence we are conscious, while we are unable to determine, with moderate confidence, either the secret principle or the range of its action, the wind is as full of meaning still as in the days of Nicodemus.

When our Lord has thus pointed to the freedom and the mysteriousness of the wind, He adds, "So is every one that is *born* of the Spirit." The simile itself would have led us to expect—"So is the Spirit of God." The man born of the Spirit would answer not to the wind itself, but to the sensible effect of the wind. There is a break of correspondence between the simile and its application. The simile directs attention to the Divine Author of the new birth in man. The words which follow direct attention to the human subject upon whom the Divine Agent works. Something similar is observable when our Lord compares the kingdom of heaven to a merchantman seeking goodly pearls; the kingdom really corresponds not to the merchantman, but to the pearl of great price which the merchantman buys.[2] In such cases, we may be sure, the natural correspondence between a simile and its application is not disturbed without a motive. And the reason for this disturbance is presumably that the simile is not adequate to the full purpose of the speaker, who is anxious to teach some larger truth than its obvious application would

[1] Eccles. xi. 5, where however the Authorized Version renders "spirit."
[2] St. Matt. xiii. 45, 46.

suggest. In the case before us, we may be allowed to suppose, that by His reference to the wind our Lord desired to convey something more than the real but mysterious agency of the Holy Spirit in the new birth of man. His language seems designed, not merely to correct the materialistic narrowness of the Jewish doctor, not merely to answer by anticipation the doubts of later days as to the spiritual efficacy of His own Sacrament of Regeneration, but to picture, in words which should be read to the end of time, the general work of that Divine Person Whose mission of mercy to our race was at once the consequence and the completion of His own.

It may be useful to trace the import of our Lord's simile in three fields of the action of the Holy and Eternal Spirit; His creation of a sacred literature, His guidance of a Divine society, and His work upon individual souls.

I.

As, then, we turn over the pages of the Bible, must we not say, "The wind of heaven bloweth where it listeth"? If we might reverently imagine ourselves scheming beforehand what kind of book the Book of God ought to be, how different would it be from the actual Bible! There would be as many Bibles as there are souls, and they would differ as widely. But in one thing, amid all their differences, they would probably agree: they would lack the variety, both in form and substance, of the Holy Book which the Church of God places in the hands of her children. The self-assertion, the scepticism, and the fastidiousness of our day would meet like the men of the second Roman triumvirate on that island in the Reno, and would draw up their lists of proscription. One would condemn the poetry of Scripture as too inexact; another its history as too largely secular; another its metaphysics as too transcendental, or as hostile to some fanciful ideal of "simplicity," or as likely to quench a purely moral enthusiasm. The archaic history of the Pentateuch, or the sterner side of the ethics of the Psalter, or the supernaturalism of the histories of Elijah or of Daniel, or the so-called pessimism of Ecclesiastes, or the alleged secularism of Esther, or the literal import of the Song of Solomon, would be in turn condemned. Nor could the Apostles hope to escape: St. John would be too mystical in this estimate; St. James too legal in that; St. Paul too dialectical, or too metaphysical, or too easily capable of an antinomian interpretation; St. Peter too undecided, as if balancing between St. Paul and St. James. Our new Bible would probably be uniform, narrow, symmetrical; it would be entirely made up of poetry, or of history, or of formal propositions, or of philosophical speculation, or of lists of moral maxims; it would be modelled after the type of some current writer on English history, or some popular poet or metaphysician, or some sentimentalist who abjures history and philosophy alike on principle, or some composer of well-intentioned religious tracts for general circulation. The inspirations of heaven would be taken in hand, and instead of a wind blowing where it listeth, we should have a wind, no doubt, of some kind, rustling earnestly enough along some very narrow crevices or channels, in obedience to the directions of some one form of human prejudice, or passion, or fear, or hope.

My brethren, the Bible is like nature in its immense, its exhaustless variety; like nature, it reflects all the higher moods of the human soul, because it does much more; because it brings us face to face with the infinity of the Divine Life. In the Bible the wind of heaven pays scant heed to our anticipations or our prejudices; it "bloweth where it listeth." It breathes not only in the Divine charities of the Gospels, not only in the lyrical sallies of the Epistles, not only in the great announcements scattered here and there in Holy Scripture of the magnificence, or the compassion, or the benevolence of God; but also in the stern language of the prophets, in the warnings and lessons of the historical books, in the revelations of Divine justice and of human responsibility which abound in either Testament. "Where it listeth." Not only where our sense of literary beauty is stimulated, as in St. Paul's picture of charity,[1] by lines which have taken captive the imagination of the world, not only where feeling and conscience echo the verdict of authority and the promptings of reverence, but also where this is not the case; where neither precept nor example stimulates us, and we are left face to face with historical or ethical material, which appears to us to inspire no spiritual enthusiasm, or which is highly suggestive of critical difficulty. Let us be patient; we shall understand, if we will only wait, how these features of the Bible too are integral parts of a living whole; here, as elsewhere, the Spirit breathes; in the genealogies of the Chronicles as in the Last Discourse in St. John, though with an admitted difference of manner and degree. He "bloweth where He listeth." The Apostle's words respecting the Old Testament are true of the New: "All Scripture is given by inspiration of God, and is profitable for doctrine, for reproof, for correction, for instruction in righteousness."[2] And, "Whatsoever things were written aforetime were written for our learning, that we through patience and comfort of the Scriptures might have hope."[3]

"But thou hearest the sound thereof, and canst not tell whence it cometh, and whither it goeth." The majesty of Scripture is recognised by man, wherever there is, I will not say a spiritual faculty, but a natural sense of beauty. The "sound" of the wind is perceived by the trained ear, by the literary taste, by the refinement, by the humanity of every generation of educated men. But what beyond? What of its spiritual source, its spiritual drift and purpose, its

[1] 1 Cor. xiii. [2] 2 Tim. iii. 16. [3] Rom. xv. 4.

half-concealed but profound unities, its subtle but imperious relations to conscience? Of these things, so precious to Christians, a purely literary appreciation of Scripture is generally ignorant; the sacred Book, like the prophet of the Chebar, is only "as a very lovely song of one that hath a pleasant voice, and can play well on an instrument."[1] Or again, the "sound thereof" is heard in the admitted empire of the Bible over millions of hearts and consciences; an empire the evidences of which strike upon the ear in countless ways, and which is far too wide and too secure to be affected by the criticisms that might occasionally seem to threaten it. What is the secret of this influence of Scripture? Not simply that it is the Book of Revelation; since it contains a great deal of matter which lay fairly within the reach of man's natural faculties. The Word or Eternal Reason of God is the Revealer; but Scripture, whether it is a record of Divine revelations or of naturally observed facts, is, in the belief of the Christian Church, throughout "inspired" by the Spirit. Inspiration is the word which describes the presence and action of the Holy Spirit everywhere in Scripture. But what does the Christian Church exactly mean by Inspiration? Many have been the attempts to answer that question precisely. It has been said of the late Dr. Arnold that during the later years of his life he spent more thought in the effort to construct a perfectly satisfactory theory of inspiration than on any other subject. In the Church of Rome there are at least three permitted opinions as to the nature of Biblical Inspiration. The more rigid, advocated by some Dominican theologians, regards the sacred writers as simply passive instruments of the Inspiring Spirit, so that every word and comma and point was dictated from heaven.[2] Other understand by inspira-

---

[1] Ezek. xxxiii. 32.
[2] Rabaudy, Ord. Præd. *Exerc. de Script. Sac.* ii. 3, sub fin., quoted by Perrone, *Prœl. Theol.* ii. 1082, ed. Migne.

tion a general *positive* assistance, prescribing what to write, what to omit, and guiding the general choice of language and of periods without dictating each separate expression.[1] The Jesuit divines of Louvain, Hamel and Lessius, confined inspiration to the purely negative function of protecting the inspired writer from error.[2] In the English Church the differences on the subject are, at least, as considerable as in the Church of Rome. The demand for an exact theory is natural enough, especially on the part of sincerely religious men, who have lost sight of the providential guidance of the Church, and who desire to enhance as far as possible the *definite* force of the authority of Scripture. Yet surely it is a matter for thankfulness that no part of the Catholic Church has formally committed itself to an authoritative doctrine of Biblical Inspiration, whatever may have been attempted by private writers of more or less consideration. Not merely because any possible definition would almost certainly add to difficulties which are suggested by negative criticism; but much more because, from the nature of the case, we are not really able to deal *ab intra* with such a subject. That Divine inspiration must postulate certain momentous results, positive as well as negative, may indeed be taken for granted; some positive informing guidance, as well as immunity from any moral or doctrinal error. But when we go beyond this, and endeavour to hold the balance between mechanical and dynamical theories, in other words, to determine how the Divine Spirit has acted upon the human, we are in a region where nothing is really possible beyond precarious conjecture. We know not how our own spirits, hour by hour, are acted on by the Eternal Spirit, though we do not question the fact; we content ourselves with recognising what we cannot explain. If we believe that Scripture is inspired,

[1] So Valentia, *Estius in* 2 *Tim.* iii. 16, quoted by Perrone, *Prœl. Theol.* ii. 1082, ed. Migne.   [2] Cf. Perrone, ubi sup. 1083, note (3).

we know that it is instinct with the Presence of Him Whose voice we might hear in its every utterance, but of Whom we cannot tell whence He cometh or whither He goeth.

II.

The history of the Church of Christ from the days of the Apostles has been a history of spiritual movements. Doubtless it has been a history of much else; the Church has been the scene of human passions, human speculations, human errors. But traversing these, He by Whom the whole body of the Church is governed and sanctified, has made His Presence felt, not only in the perpetual proclamation and elucidation of truth, not only in the silent, never-ceasing sanctification of souls, but also in great upheavals of spiritual life, by which the conscience of Christians has been quickened, or their hold upon the truths of Redemption and Grace made more intelligent and serious, or their lives and practice restored to something like the ideal of the Gospels. Even in the apostolic age it was necessary to warn Christians that it was high time to awake out of sleep; that the night of life was far spent, and the day of eternity was at hand.[1] And ever since, from generation to generation, there has been a succession of efforts within the Church to realize more worthily the truth of the Christian creed, or the ideal of the Christian life. These revivals have been inspired or led by devoted men who have represented the highest conscience of Christendom in their day. They may be traced along the line of Christian history; the Spirit living in the Church has by them attested His Presence and His Will; and has recalled lukewarm generations, paralyzed by indifference or degraded by indulgence, to the true spirit and level of Christian faith and life.

In such movements there is often what seems, at first sight, an element of caprice. They appear to contemporaries

[1] Rom. xiii. 11, 12.

to be onesided, exaggerated, narrow, fanatical. They are often denounced with a passionate fervour which is so out of proportion to the reality as to border on the grotesque. They are said to exact too much of us, or to concede too much. They are too contemplative in their tendency to be sufficiently practical, or too energetically practical to do justice to religious thought. They are too exclusively literary and academical, as being the work of men of books; or they are too popular and insensible to philosophical considerations, as being the work of men of the people. Or, again, they are so occupied with controversy as to forget the claims of devotion, or so engaged in leading souls to a devout life as to forget the unwelcome but real necessities of controversy. They are intent on particular moral improvements so exclusively as to forget what is due to reverence and order; or they are so bent upon rescuing the Church from chronic slovenliness and indecency in public worship as to do less than justice to the paramount interests of moral truth. Sometimes these movements are all feeling; sometimes they are all thought; sometimes they are, as it seems, all outward energy. In one age they produce a literature like that of the fourth and fifth centuries; in another they found orders of men devoted to preaching or to works of mercy, as in the twelfth; in another they enter the lists, as in the thirteenth century, with a hostile philosophy; in another they attempt a much-needed Reformation of the Church; in another they pour upon the heathen world a flood of light and warmth from the heart of Christendom. It is easy, as we survey them, to say that something else was needed; or that what was done could have been done better or more completely; or that, had we been there, we should not have been guilty of this onesidedness, or of that exaggeration. We forget, perhaps, Who really *was* there, and Whose work it is, though often overlaid and thwarted by human weakness and human passion, that we are really criticising. If it was seemingly onesided, excessive or defective, impulsive or sluggish, speculative or practical, æsthetic or experimental, may not this have been so because in His judgment, Who breatheth where He listeth, this particular characteristic was needed for the Church of that day? All that contemporaries know of such movements is "the sound thereof;" the names with which they are associated, the controversies which they precipitate, the hostilities which they rouse or allay, as the case may be. Such knowledge is superficial enough; of the profound spiritual causes which really engender them, of the direction in which they are really moving, of the influence which they are destined permanently to exert upon souls, men know little or nothing. The accidental symptom is mistaken for the essential characteristic; the momentary expression of feeling for the inalienable conviction of certain truth. The day may come, perhaps, when more will be known; when practice and motive, accident and substance, the lasting and the transient, will be seen in their true relative proportions; but for the time this can hardly be. He is passing by "Whose way is in the sea, and His paths in the deep waters, and His footsteps unknown."[1] The Eternal Spirit is passing; and men can only say, "He bloweth where He listeth."

Those who take God at His word will not doubt where His Holy Spirit is given. In sacraments which He has ordained; in a message which He has authorized; in prayer, public and private, to which He has pledged His presence,[2] this great gift is certainly to be found. The Spirit is the soul of the Church, and whatever be the weaknesses or diseases of parts of the body which He deigns to inhabit, the soul asserts itself as life in its furthest extremities.

But is His mission wholly confined to the Body of

[1] Ps. lxxvii. 19.   [2] St. Matt. xviii. 20.

Christ? has He no relations to separated groups of Christians, to seekers after truth in heathen lands, to lower forms of truth as well as higher, to philosophy, to science, to art, to all departments of human energy? Surely in recognising this larger sphere of His energy we do not blur the lines of His covenanted action; to believe in the mighty gift of Pentecost is not to deny that "the Spirit of the Lord filleth the world."[1] Doubtless in His activity there are many methods, many degrees of intensity, many ends in view. His influence is vouchsafed to those who hold only portions of truth, that they may be led on to that which as yet they do not hold; He prevents men with His most gracious favour before He furthers their efforts by His continual help. This may be understood most easily by those who most firmly believe in the revealed constitution and claims of the Church of Christ; and it suggests happier prospects than are otherwise possible amid the existing confusions of the world and of Christendom. Last year two American preachers[2] visited this country, to whom God had given, together with earnest belief in some portions of the Gospel, a corresponding spirit of fearless enterprise. Certainly they had no such credentials of an apostolic ministry as a well-instructed and believing Churchman would require. They knew little or nothing of God's revealed Will respecting those sacramental channels whereby the life of grace is planted and maintained in the soul; and their test of ministerial success appeared sometimes to mistake physical excitement or inclination for a purely spiritual or moral change. And yet, must not we, who through no merit of our own, have enjoyed greater spiritual advantages than theirs, feel and express for these men a sincere respect, when, acting according to the light which God had given them, they

---

[1] Wisd. i. 7.
[2] The allusion is to the visit of Messrs. Moody and Sankey, in 1875.

threw themselves on our great cities with the ardour of Apostles; spoke of a higher world to thousands who pass the greater part of life in dreaming only of this; and made many of us feel that we owe them at least the debt of an example, which He Who breatheth where He listeth must surely have inspired them to give us?

III.

Our Lord's words apply especially to Christian character. There are some effects of the living power of the Holy Spirit which are invariable. When He dwells with a Christian soul, He continually speaks in the voice of conscience; He speaks in the voice of prayer. He produces with the ease of a natural process, without effort, without the taint of self-consciousness, "love, joy, peace, long-suffering, gentleness, goodness, faith, meekness, temperance."[1] Some of these graces must be found where He makes His home. There is no mistaking the atmosphere of His presence: in its main features it is the same now as in the days of the Apostles. Just as in natural morality the main elements of "goodness" do not change; so in religious life, spirituality is, amid great varieties of detail, yet in its leading constituent features, the same thing from one generation to another. But in the life of the individual Christian, or in that of the Church, there is legitimate room for irregular and exceptional forms of activity or excellence. Natural society is not strengthened by the stern repression of all that is peculiar in individual thought or practice;[2] and this is not less true of spiritual or religious society. From the first, high forms of Christian excellence have often been associated with unconscious eccentricity. The eccentricity must be unconscious, because consciousness of eccentricity at once

---

[1] Gal. v. 22.   [2] Mill's Essay of Liberty, chap. iii.

reduces it to a form of vanity which is entirely inconsistent with Christian excellence. How many excellent Christians have been eccentric, deviating more or less from the conventional type of goodness which has been recognised by contemporary religious opinion! They pass away, and when they are gone men do justice to their characters; but while they are still with us how hard do many of us find it to remember that there may be a higher reason for their peculiarities than we think. We know not the full purpose of each saintly life in the designs of Providence; we know not much of the depths and heights whence it draws its inspirations; we cannot tell whence it cometh or whither it goeth. Only we know that He Whose workmanship it is bloweth where He listeth; and this naturally leads us to remark the practical interpretation which the Holy Spirit often puts upon our Lord's words by selecting as His chosen workmen those who seem to be least fitted by nature for such high service. The Apostle has told us how in the first age He set Himself to defeat human anticipations. "Not many wise men after the flesh, not many mighty, not many noble, are called;"[1] learned academies, powerful connections, gentle blood did little enough for the Gospel in the days when it won its first and greatest victories. The Holy Spirit, as Nicodemus knew, passed by the varied learning and high station of the Sanhedrin, and breathed where He listed on the peasants of Galilee; He breathed on them a power which would shake the world. And thus has it been again and again in the generations which have followed. When the great Aquinas was a student of philosophy under Albertus Magnus at Cologne, he was known among his contemporaries as "the dumb Ox;" so little did they divine what was to be his place in the theology of Western Christendom. And to those of us who can look back upon

[1] 1 Cor. i. 26.

the memories of this University for a quarter of a century or more, few things appear more remarkable than the surprises which the later life of men constantly afford; sometimes it is a failure of early natural promise, but more often a rich development of intellectual and practical capacity where there had seemed to be no promise at all. We can remember, perhaps, some dull quiet man who seemed to be without a ray of genius, or, stranger still, without anything interesting or marked in character, but who now exerts, and most legitimately, the widest influence for good, and whose name is repeated by thousands with grateful respect. Or we can call to mind another whose whole mind was given to what was frivolous, or even degrading, and who now is a leader in everything that elevates and improves his fellows. The secret of these transfigurations is ever the same. In those days these men did not yet see their way; they were like travellers through the woods at night, when the sky is hidden and all things seem to be other than they are—

> "Quale per incertam lunam sub luce malignâ
> Est iter in silvis, ubi cœlum condidit umbrâ
> Jupiter, et rebus nox abstulit atra colorem."

Since then the sun has risen and all has changed. The creed of the Church of Christ, in its beauty and its power, has been flashed by the Divine Spirit upon their hearts and understandings; and they are other men. They have seen that there is something worth living for in earnest; that God, the soul, the future, are immense realities, compared with which all else is tame and insignificant. They have learned something of that personal love of our crucified Lord, which is itself a moral and religious force of the highest order, and which has carried them forwards without their knowing it. And what has been will assuredly repeat itself. Some of you who listen, if you are living thirty years hence, will verify their experiences by your own.

In conclusion, our Lord's words suggest many lessons, but one of especial and incontrovertible importance; reverence for the presence and work of that Holy Visitor Whose festival this is. Reverence for Him, in the Bible which He inspires; in the Church which He governs and sanctifies; in the souls, whether our own or others, in which He deigns to dwell. It is easy to become familiar with the outward tokens of His presence; to use language which has no meaning apart from Him; to forget that He is the Lord and Giver of Life, without Whom Holy Scripture, the Church, the New Birth, the New Life, would be empty phrases. If nature is full of interest and wonder; if the bodily frame which we inhabit, like the sea or the sky, are ever presenting to us new material for thought; much more is this the case with the mysterious depths of the human soul. And few things, perhaps, weigh more heavily on those of us who know that life is already on the wane, and that the greater number of the years for which we shall answer hereafter must have already passed, than the recollection which at times steals over us, of that almost unnoticed multitude of thoughts, feelings, aspirations, pointing upwards and onwards, which have presented themselves in the presence-chamber of the soul, and then have vanished away, and left no trace behind. Whence came they? Those glimpses of nobler truth, those sudden cravings after a higher existence, those fretful uneasy yearnings, full of wholesome dissatisfaction with self, those whisperings, those voices, which would not for a while allow us to rest, but which, as the years have passed—is it not often thus?—have died away into silence. Whence came they; and whither should they have led us on? Ah! we have said to ourselves, or the world has said to us, that the foolish enthusiasm of youth has passed, and that with middle age we have succeeded to common sense and to ripe discretion. It may be so; but there is, at least in some cases, another way of reading the result. It is too possible that something more than fervid indiscretion has been lost with youth; that the bloom of the soul, the freshness and tenderness of the conscience, has been succeeded by a condition of thought and feeling, the true character of which we conceal from ourselves and from others when we label it "discretion" and "common sense." Depend upon it, my younger brethren, the bright, self-sacrificing enthusiasms of early manhood are among the most precious things in the whole course of human life. They may have their illusions, but they have their safeguards also; and when they emancipate us from all that would force us down, when they clear the spirit's eye and nerve the bodily arm, when they enable us to tread under our feet some clinging mischief which has made us wretched for years, and open out horizons of disinterested effort from which we already draw the inspiration of a higher life, surely we do well to cherish them. Amidst much which is depressing in the religious circumstances and prospects of this place, Christians have signal reason humbly to thank God the Holy Ghost for the impulse which He has given of late to missionary enterprise; for the noble men, known to not a few of us as teachers or as friends, whom He has sent out from our midst within the last two years to rule His flock in heathen lands;[1] and for the young, warm, and generous hearts whom human affection, deepened and sanctified by the supernatural love of God, has gathered around them as a band of devoted sons and workers. This assuredly is the "sound" of the wind from heaven, of that Eternal Spirit Who marks in every generation predestined souls for His higher

[1] Dr. Coplestone, Bishop of Colombo, and Dr. Mylne, Bishop of Bombay.

service; of Whom none can exactly say whence He comes to them or whither He is leading them; Who breatheth where He listeth, not in caprice or by accident, but because He knows exactly whereof each of His creatures is made, and apportions His distinctions with the unerring decision of perfect Love and perfect Justice.

"If you make it a rule to say sincerely the first verse of the Ordination Hymn every morning without failing, it will in time do more for you than any other prayer I know, except the Lord's Prayer." They were the words of one who had a right to speak from experience, and who has now gone to his rest.

> "Veni, Creator Spiritus,
> Mentes Tuorum visita,
> Imple supernâ gratiâ,
> Quæ Tu creasti pectora."

Certainly this prayer does not take long to say; and perhaps, fifty years hence, in another state of existence, some of us will be glad to have acted on the advice.

SERMON VI.

GROWTH IN THE APPREHENSION OF TRUTH.

HEB. vi. 1.

Therefore leaving the principles of the doctrine of Christ, let us go on unto perfection.

HERE we may see the germ of what afterwards became at Alexandria and elsewhere the catechetical system of the Primitive Church. When adult converts to Christianity were the rule, it was necessary to protect the Sacrament of Baptism against unworthy reception by a graduated system of preparation and teaching, each stage in which represented an advance in moral and intellectual truth. Hence the several classes of catechumens; the hearers, who were allowed to listen to the Scriptures and to sermons in church; the kneelers, who might stay and join in certain parts of the Divine service; and the elect, or enlightened, who were taught the Lord's Prayer,—the language of the regenerate, and the Creed,—the sacred trust committed to the regenerate—since they were now on the point of being admitted by Baptism into the Body of Christ. Then at last, when baptized, as the τέλειοι, or perfect, they entered on the full privileges of believers; they learnt all that was taught respecting the great doctrines of the Trinity, the Incarnation, the Atonement, and the Eucharist, and were thus placed in possession of the truths and motives which shape most powerfully Christian thought and life.

This was the system elaborated by great minds who successively taught or ruled at Alexandria, and whose influence spread so widely throughout the East. But its principle had been already sanctioned in the Apostolic age, and in the Epistle to the Hebrews we see it in its earliest form. In this Epistle we have before us two stages of teaching and two classes of learners.

There is, first of all, the initial or rudimentary stage of Christian teaching, which the sacred writer describes sometimes as "the elements of the beginning of the oracles of God,"[1] sometimes as the "first discourse about Christ,"[2] sometimes by metaphors, familiar to St. Paul, intended to point out its facility of comprehension or its early place in a system of Christian teaching, such as "milk"[3] or "the foundation."[4] The later and complete stage of Christian teaching is designated as the "discourse of righteousness,"[5] as "the solid meat,"[6] in contrast with "milk," or, as in the words before us, as "perfection."[7] The Christians who are receiving elementary instruction are termed babes, $\nu\eta\pi\iota\omicron\iota$;[8] they cannot understand, much less utter, the "discourse of righteousness." The Christians who have received the higher instruction are the "perfect;"[9] they can digest the solid food of Christian doctrine; their spiritual senses have been trained by habit to appreciate the distinction between the good and the evil, which in this connection are only other names for the false and the true.[10]

The readers, to whom all this is addressed, are themselves in an equivocal position. It is a long time since they were

---

[1] Heb. v. 12, τὰ στοιχεῖα τῆς ἀρχῆς τῶν λογίων τοῦ Θεοῦ.
[2] Heb. vi. 1, τὸν τῆς ἀρχῆς τοῦ Χριστοῦ λόγον.
[3] Heb. v. 13, γάλακτος.   [4] Heb. vi. 1, θεμέλιον.
[5] Heb. v. 13, λόγου δικαιοσύνης.   [6] Heb. v. 14, ἡ στερεὰ τροφή.
[7] Heb. vi. 1, τὴν τελειότητα.   [8] Heb. v. 13.
[9] Heb. v. 14, τελείων.   [10] Heb. v. 14.

first converted, so long indeed, that they ought ere now to be busily teaching other converts.[1] But, in fact, they still need to be taught themselves. They do not know what the rudiments of "the discourse about Christ" really are. They ought to be among "the perfect;" they are only "babes." They have gone backward instead of going forward,[2] and indeed because they have not gone forward; and, if the Apostolic writer is to continue the high argument of his Epistle with any hope of their accompanying him intelligently, they must at this point make a serious effort, or rather they must surrender themselves to impulses and a guidance which will carry them onward, if they will. Therefore, he exclaims, leaving the principles or the first discussion about Christ,—let us go on, or be "borne on," unto perfection.[3]

Perfection! what does he mean by it? Certainly not here moral perfection, the attainment of conformity to the will of God in general character and conduct. For this would be no such contrast to the first principles of the *doctrine* of Christ as the sentence of itself implies: the perfection must itself be a doctrinal perfection, in other words, the attainment of the complete or perfect truth about Christ, as distinct from its first principles. Of these first or foundation principles six are enumerated;[4] and they are selected for the practical reason that they were especially needed by candidates for Baptism. First come the two sides of the great inward change implied in conversion to Christ; repentance from all such works as are "dead," because destitute of a religious motive, and faith resting upon God as revealed in His Son. Then follow the two ordinances whereby the converted soul enters upon the

---

[1] Heb. v. 12.   [2] Heb. v. 11, νωθροὶ γεγόνατε.
[3] The whole passage, Heb. v. 11—vi. 20, is a digression, by which the argument respecting Christ's Melchisedekian priesthood is interrupted. It is resumed at vii. 1.   [4] Heb. vi. 1, 2.

privileges of full communion with Christ; the doctrine about Baptism, which distinguishes the Christian sacrament from the mere symbols of purification insisted on for proselytes by the Baptist and by the Law, and the laying on of hands in what we now call Confirmation. Finally, there are the two momentous truths which from the first must be motive powers in the life of a sincere believer; the coming resurrection of the dead, and the judgment whose issues are eternal. These three pairs of truths are precisely what the writer of the Epistle to the Hebrews meant by the first principles of the doctrine of Christ. And therefore by "perfection" he meant something beyond these truths. He meant no doubt a great deal else, but he was referring specifically and at the moment to the doctrine of Christ's Melchisedekian priesthood, in its majestic contrast to the temporary and relatively inefficient priesthood of Aaron, and with its vast issues in a Mediatorial work, whether of atonement or of sanctification, as carried out, the latter to the very end of time, by the Great High Priest of Christendom.

I.

Now the point on which the text insists is the duty of going forward from the first principles to the truths beyond —εἰς τὴν τελειότητα φερώμεθα. What are the intrinsic reasons which point to this? Undoubtedly the first is that a Christian, as such, believes himself to be in possession, partly or altogether, of a Revelation which God has made to man. Revelation is one of those momentous words which has lost its edge in these later times through being used by accommodation in new connections. No Christian can be concerned to deny what St. Paul teaches, that God has of old instructed all men through nature and conscience,[1] and that, as a consequence, elements of Divine truth are embedded, in different degrees of purity, in the various beliefs of the heathen world. But, the moral nature of man being what it is, there is a veil in all heathen religions over the face of God and the true meaning of human life. And the true Revelation is distinguished from these surrounding conglomerates of little truth and much error by a twofold note : as it comes to us from God it is without any accompanying error; and its arrival is certificated by miracle, which proclaims the identity of the Author of Nature with the Ruler of the Moral World speaking in the Revelation. Ask yourselves, brethren, what we of to-day can do, what others have done, and are doing, if Revelation be discarded. What, indeed, but enter on a weary round of guesses and retractations? Whence do we come ? Whither are we going ? Why are we here at all ? These are irrepressible questions, to which Reason does her best, from age to age, to furnish replies : but at her best she hesitates, she falters, she contradicts herself, she is perpetually discouraged by the sense of her powerlessness, she hastily affirms, and then forthwith she is frightened at her affirmation, she sinks back in perplexity and silence. So it was among the cultivated heathen before Christ came ; so it is still where modern thought has rejected Christianity. Agnosticism is not a term of reproach to those whose opinions it describes ; yet what is it but a confession of their impotence, face to face with the most vital problems that can engage the mind of man ? And therefore—to quote language which is not strictly theological, but which may be taken to represent the broad aspects of the fact before us—" Divine Providence, in compassion to the frailty, the imperfection, and the blindness of human reason, hath been pleased, at sundry times and in divers manners, to discover and enforce its laws by an immediate and

[1] Rom. i. 19, 20.

direct Revelation. The doctrines thus delivered we call the Revealed or Divine Law, and they are to be found only in the Holy Scriptures."[1]

With those who dispute the fact that God has spoken thus to man, not merely through nature or conscience, or both, but through His Son Jesus Christ, and through other teachers on whom Christ set the seal of His Divine authority, I am not for the moment disputing. Enough to say that the supreme certificate of the reality of the Christian Revelation is the fact that Christ rose from the dead. Deny this fact, and—forgive a stern word for the sake of its truth—the moral consistency of Christ, no less than His redemptive power, must forthwith disappear from earnest thought. Admit this fact, and the religion which it attests must mean not only much more than, but something altogether distinct in kind from, the highest lessons God has ever taught to the best heathen through nature and conscience;—you are in presence of a supernatural Revelation.

And if such a Revelation, as we Christians maintain, has indeed been given, then man's wisdom and business is to make the most of it. If such a body of truth is really within our reach, it is of importance, not merely to theologians, but to human beings as such; it cannot be neglected with impunity. As knowledge it is worth more than any other knowledge. It enables us to know a Being Who is infinitely greater, wiser, more powerful, and more nearly related to us than any other being. It touches us more closely in our deepest and most lasting interests than any other department or kind of knowledge. Surely if God speaks, reverence bids us listen until we have heard all that He is saying. Surely if God speaks, the common sense which He has given us bids us listen until we know what is the bearing of His utterance on ourselves. The

[1] Blackstone, *Commentaries on the Laws of England*, Introduction, § 2.

man in the parable who sells all that he has that he may buy the field in which the treasure is hid, will surely do his best to appreciate the treasure when he has found it.[1] If it was prudent to make the original effort, it is prudent to follow it up: if it is our wisdom to be Christians at all, it is not less our wisdom to make the most we can of the Creed of Christendom.

This then is a first reason for going on to what the text calls "perfection:" everything in a Revelation which comes from God must, from the nature of the case, be worth the best attention that we can give it. But another reason will be found in the nature of Revealed Truth itself. Revealed Truth is not a series of propositions, having no relation to each other, and out of which the human intellect may take its choice. It is not like a scrap-book, made up of extracts from all the religions of the world, which have been brought together by some master of eclectic industry. Nor is it like a museum of statues, in which each composition is complete and has no necessary relation to the figures around it. It is an organic whole, every portion of which is as perfectly connected with the rest as are the limbs of a living creature with its trunk and heart. Thus there is a *nexus* between all truths which fairly belong to the substance of Revelation; a relationship at once so intimate and so persuasive that the believing soul cannot but be drawn onward from truth to truth. The vital principle of a Divine authority which belongs to each truth is common to all; the intrinsic dependence of each truth upon the others is profound and reciprocal: and thus a believer passes from one truth to another, not by a fresh intellectual jerk or effort, but in obedience to a sense of sequence which he cannot resist.

Yes! It is on this account that the believing soul, clinging to the first principles of Christian doctrine, must needs

[1] St. Matt. xiii. 44.

advance to perfection. The Apostolic writer does not say, "Let us go on unto perfection;" he does say, "Let us be borne on,"—φερώμεθα. He does not say, "Be courageously logical: push forward your premises to their last conclusions." He does say, "Let us all, teachers and taught, trust ourselves to the guidance of such truth as we already hold,"—φερώμεθα. It will carry us on as we try to make it our own: it will lead us to the connected and derived truths which expand, explain, support it. We cannot select some one shred of this organic whole, baptize it by such names as "primary" or "fundamental," and then say, "This, and this only, shall be my creed." If the metaphor be permitted, the trunk whose limbs are cut off thus arbitrarily will bleed to death. Where spiritual life depends on spiritual activity, *non progredi est regredi*; and they who shrink from Apostolic perfection will forfeit their hold, sooner or later, on Apostolic first principles.

Let us trace this somewhat more in detail.

II.

We have seen what were the six first principles insisted on among the first readers of the Epistle to the Hebrews. They belonged to the disciplinary system of the Church, and were selected on practical rather than theological grounds. But what would probably be the first principles of an inquirer feeling his way upwards towards the light under the circumstances of our own day? What would be the truths that would greet him on the threshold of faith, as the catechumen of our time, whom conscience and thought are training for the full inheritance of believers?

They would be, in all probability, first—belief in a moral God. The inquirer discovers within himself an indestructible sense of the value and beauty of holiness, of justice, of truth, of love. He admires these excellences in others even when he is conscious of being himself without them; and he rises out of himself to conceive a Being in Whom they exist as in their source, and in an undimmed perfection. It is something to believe in a Cause Who is the cause of all that is besides Himself. It is more to believe in an Intelligence, the parent of all other intelligences. But religion properly begins when a man bows before One Who, being boundless Power and Wisdom, is also Justice, Sanctity, and Love.

At the same time the modern catechumen would probably be attracted by the character of Jesus Christ as it lies on the surface of the Gospels. He need not yet be a believer in order to discover that in the Gospels the human soul meets with that which it meets nowhere else—an ideal of moral beauty at once so winning and so awful as to command its homage. Renan will tell him that Jesus will never be surpassed;[1] and Goethe, that Jesus is the type and model for all men;[2] and Rousseau, that if the life and death of Socrates are those of a sage, the life and death of Jesus are those of a God.[3] A working carpenter, Who dies when He is thirty-three years old; Who has neither education, nor patronage, nor wealth at his command; Who lives, let us note it once again, poor, as it seems, inexperienced, unknown, unbefriended, yet speaks to the conscience of all time, and offers an example before which even those who reject His claims are silent,—awed into involuntary reverence, almost into love.

These, we will suppose, are the inquirer's two first principles, the goodness of God, and the perfection of Christ's character. They are now beyond controversy, at least for him. They seem to be all that he needs; and he says to himself that a simple faith like this, which perhaps he will be told is Christian Theism, is a working faith. He can at least live it, or try to live it, and leave the spheres of abstract

---

[1] *Vie de Jesus*, p. 325. [2] *Dial. with Eckermann*, vol. iii. [3] *Emile*, l. vi.

and metaphysical controversy to those who like to explore them.

But if he thinks, a time will come when he finds that he must go forward if he is not to fall back. For he observes, first of all, that this world, the scene of so much wickedness and so much suffering, is hard to reconcile with the idea of God, All-good and All-powerful, if indeed He has left or is leaving it to itself. If God is All-good, He surely will unveil Himself further to His reasonable creatures; nay, He will do something more, His revelation will be, in some sense, a cure. Exactly proportioned to belief in the morality of God is the felt strength of this presumption in favour of a Divine intervention of some kind: and the modern catechumen asks himself if the Epicurean deities themselves would not do almost as well as a moral God, Who yet, in the plenitude of His power, should leave creatures formed by Himself to think and to struggle without the light or the aid they so greatly need.

This is a first observation, and a second is that, if the character of Jesus Christ be attentively studied, it implies that His life cannot be supposed to fall entirely within the limits or under the laws of what we call "nature." For if anything is certain about Him, this is certain, that He invited men to love Him, trust Him, obey Him even to death, and in terms which would be intolerable if after all He was merely human. Human nature has had time to take the measure of itself, and it knows what is compatible with the just limits of its pretensions. Christ, as judged by His claims on others, is very much more than a mere man, or it is impossible to maintain that He was a good man. And therefore our modern catechumen feels that it is not enough to admire, even warmly, the character of Christ; a necessity, moral as well as logical, is laid upon his apprehension of it; he must let himself be borne on to a perfection that yet awaits him; he must ascend to a higher truth beyond.

Nor is this advance inevitable, only on account of the claims which Christ makes upon mankind. It is made necessary by His sayings about Himself. Thus, He expressly foretold that He should be crucified and should rise from the dead.[1] As a matter of fact, the Christian Church exists at this hour because it has been believed for eighteen centuries and a half that His words were verified by the event. Had He been crucified, only then to rot, whether in an undistinguished or in a celebrated grave, the human conscience would have known what to say of Him. It would have traced over His sepulchre the epitaph "Failure;" and it would have forthwith struck a significant balance between the attractive elements of His character and the utterly unwarranted exaggeration of His pretensions.

But our modern catechumen's reflections could not end here. For the character of God, and of Jesus Christ in the Gospels, is in one respect like the old Mosaic law; it provokes a sense of guilt by its revelation of what righteousness really is. The more we really know about God,—about our Lord, the less can we be satisfied with ourselves. It is not possible for a man whose moral sense is not dead only to admire Jesus Christ as if He were an exquisite creation of art,—a painting in a gallery or a statue in a museum of antiquities,—and without the thought, What do His perfections say to me? For Jesus Christ shows us what human nature has been when at its best; and in showing us this He reveals us individually to ourselves. Of His character we may say what St. Paul says of the law, that it is a schoolmaster to bring us to Himself. It makes us dissatisfied with our own attainments, if anything can do so: it forces us to recognise the worthlessness and

[1] St. Matt. xxvii. 40, 63. St. Mark xiv. 58. St. John ii. 19. St. Luke xi. 29, 30. St. Matt. xx. 19.

poverty of our natural resources; it throws a true, though it be an unwelcome light upon the history of our past existence; and thus it disposes us to listen anxiously and attentively for any further disclosures of the Divine Mind that may be either in store for us or already within our reach.

In this way the "first principles" which we have been attributing to an inquirer of our day may prepare him for truths beyond themselves. That Divine Goodness, those perfections of the character of Christ, bear the soul onwards towards Christ's true Divinity, and, as a consequence, to the atoning virtue of His death upon the Cross. These momentous realities rest on grounds of their own: but they bring satisfaction, repose, relief to souls who have attentively considered what is involved in such truths as those which lie on the threshold of the life of faith. They proclaim that God has not left men to themselves: that He does not despise the work of His own hands. They unveil His heart of tenderness for man. They justify the language which Jesus Christ used about Himself, and His claims on the faith and the obedience of mankind. And they enable us to bear the quickened consciousness of personal sin which follows upon true insight into His human character, because we now know that, in the garden of the Agony and on the Cross, "He was made to be sin for us Who knew no sin, that we might be made the righteousness of God in Him."[1]

But does the advance towards perfection cease at this point? Surely not. Where so much has been done, there is a presumption in favour of something more, if more be needed. The Divine Christ has died on the Cross a Victim for the sins of the world: what is He doing now? Did His redemptive love exhaust itself in the days of His flesh? The past has been forgiven; but has any provision been made for the future? Have we been reconciled to

[1] 2 Cor. iii. 9.

God by the death of His Son, but is there no salvation through His risen life?[1] May not reconciliation itself be almost a dubious boon if it be followed by an almost inevitable relapse?

Here, therefore, the soul makes a further stage in its advance to perfection. Its eye opens upon the work of the Holy Spirit, Who conveys to man the gift of that new human nature which is for ever united in Jesus Christ to the Person of the Eternal Son. It is mainly through the Christian Sacraments that the Spirit unites us to the perfect Manhood of the Redeemer. And it is by a consequence as natural as that which leads from Christ's character to His Divinity and Atonement, that we pass on from His Atonement to the sacramental aspects of His mediatorial work. He bestows the New Nature in Holy Baptism; "As many as have been baptized into Christ have put on Christ."[2] He strengthens the New Nature in the Blessed Eucharist; "He that eateth Me, even he shall live by Me."[3] This crowning gift does but complete what was begun when He became first our Example, and then the Propitiation for our sins. And the reality of this gift is guaranteed by a divinely-instituted organization; so that the threefold Apostolic ministry, to which the dispensation of the Word and Sacraments is committed, is an integral part of that perfection of truth to which intelligent faith conducts the soul. In other words, the Epistles to the Ephesians, to Timothy, and to Titus, contain teaching as essential to the completeness of the Gospel system as are the arguments in the Epistles to the Romans and the Galatians; and the Christian Creed has not said its last word to the soul of man until, besides assuring his reconciliation and peace, it has satisfied his desire for assured union with the Source of Life.

[1] Rom. v. 10.   [2] Gal. iii. 27.   [3] St. John vi. 57.

III.

But at this point we are asked a question which it is impossible to ignore. "Where are you going to stop? Is not your principle likely to carry you further than you mean? Has not the Church of Rome, too, her interpretation of what is meant by theological perfection, and is not the tendency of your argument to lead us to accept it?"

Here it is natural to recall the boldest work of that remarkable man, to whom many of us can never be slow to confess our obligations, whose name will always be associated with Oxford, and whose recent elevation to a place of honour in the Roman Church has commanded the attention and interest of the world. His Essay on the Development of Christian Doctrine presents this among other aspects; it is a theological confession. It is a confession that the creed of the modern Church of Rome cannot be said to be strictly identical with the creed of the Apostles; that at the best they are linked with each other by a law of substantial growth, as is the oak with the acorn; and even that Roman Catholicism in its full development contains elements which have no germinal counterpart in the age of the Apostles, since they have come to it by accretion from without. Bellarmine and Bossuet had supposed that the Roman faith in the sixteenth and seventeenth centuries respectively was exactly the faith of the Apostolic and Primitive Church. But, writing in the nineteenth, Möhler and Newman knew too much to entertain such a supposition. There were patent differences which had to be accounted for in some way; and there were tendencies in modern thought not unlikely to suggest or to recommend the method that actually presented itself. The theory of development, in its English form, was the most striking apology that could be made for a step to which its author was led by independent considerations; but it is an apology which would serve other causes, ancient and modern, at least as well as that of the Church of Rome. The ingenious Gnostics against whom St. Irenæus wrote, as well as some modern philosophical theorists of a different stamp, were also developmentalists; we know how much it is proposed to explain in morals not less than in physics or psychology by the kindred and more familiar formula of evolution. And St. Irenæus' position still holds good. The Church cannot know more than was known by the Apostles; and anything which men might claim to know which was unknown to the Apostles is not Apostolic doctrine, but something else.

"Go on unto perfection." Yes: but the Hebrew Christians are not bidden to create, but to explore. They are to explore a faith which was once for all delivered to the saints, and the several parts of which are organically connected with each other. They are not to assist in the production of substantial additions to this original deposit, as if they were themselves the organs of a continuous revelation.

Take one illustration out of several. Let us suppose that we are travelling during the month of August, and that we find ourselves within the walls of some foreign cathedral on the great festival of the Assumption. Everything betokens an occasion of the highest order of religious importance; the attendance of the people and the character of the services are exactly what they would be on Easter Day. And if we examine the Service-books we observe that there is no appreciable difference in the amount of new matter proper to the festival; it is, in liturgical language, a "double of the first class." And perhaps the choir sings in our ears, "Exaltata est sancta Dei genitrix super choros angelorum ad cœlestia regna;" and the preacher enlarges on the glories and prerogatives of Mary as the Queen of

Heaven. In short, nothing is wanting that can arouse or direct devotional enthusiasm; and the natural inference is that the event commemorated must be among the truths that lie closest to the heart of the believing and adoring Church.

But on what does it all rest? The question will surely present itself when we return to our homes. Certainly on nothing in Holy Scripture. There is indeed a passage in the Apocalypse which has been referred to Mary after her death,[1] but by a method of interpretation scarcely less fanciful and arbitrary than are those by which controversial imagination has read the institutions and history of the Roman Church herself into the darker imagery of this mysterious book. The fact is that Scripture says nothing on the subject, and Antiquity, properly so called, is no less silent. It is first hinted at in two apocryphal writings, attributed to St. John and to Melito of Sardis,[2] but belonging, it would seem, to the beginning of the fifth century: it is a pious supposition of a later age, without any proof of a real historic basis. And when well-informed divines are pressed they admit, that though it is treated in the public Service as if it were as certain as the Resurrection of Christ, it is not a matter of faith at all; that the Church of Rome has never said authoritatively that the body of Mary left its grave, whatever may have been taught by poets and painters and preachers; and that what we have witnessed and listened to on this great festival is

[1] Rev. xii. 1-6. In *Adv. Hær.* lxxviii. c. 11, St. Epiphanius only says that this passage may perchance have been fulfilled in Mary: he adds, οὐ πάντως δὲ ὁρίζομαι τοῦτο. He hesitates to say whether Mary did or did not die. Holy Scripture is intentionally silent on the subject of her death: ἐν μετεώρῳ εἴασε, διὰ τὸ σκεῦος τὸ τίμιον καὶ ἐξοχώτατον. In Origen's day it was sometimes inferred from St. Luke ii. 35 that the Blessed Virgin had died a martyr's death. Cf. *Hom. in Luc.* xvii.

[2] That attributed to St. John is styled εἰς τὴν κοίμησιν τῆς ὑπεραγίας δεσποίνης; that to St. Melito, "De transitu Mariæ." Cf. Herzog, *Encyc.* vol. ix. p. 92.

merely the expression of a pious opinion. And since, moreover, no intrinsic necessity can be shown for supplementing the confessed and altogether unique glory of the Mother of the Incarnate Son by the hypothesis of her bodily reception into heaven, it follows that when instructed faith, accustomed to the aspects and to the frontiers of Apostolic teaching, encounters this hypothesis, it recoils as from a block of foreign and intrusive matter; it whispers to itself, "By God's help I will live and die in the complete circle of truths unveiled by the Apostles, but I cannot be wiser than they."

To many minds the question now presents itself, whether acceptance of such materials of religious thought and life as we have been considering can properly be described as being borne forward to perfection. Certainly the process by which we accept them is fundamentally different from that by which we accept the true Divinity of our Lord, or the efficacy of His atoning Sacrifice, or the grace of the Sacraments, or the Apostolic structure of the Church. For these truths have, each and all of them, their place in the Apostolic mind and writings: and later definitions, such, for example, as are those contained in the Creeds, do not really add to the sum or extent of things to be believed; they only re-state in language which new intellectual circumstances have rendered necessary what was believed by the first Christian teachers. Yet how can this be said of pious but unattested conjectures which have gradually come to be treated as if they were established facts? In such a subject-matter as that of faith, so altogether transcending the limits of human thought, you cannot infer the truth of the unrevealed, though you may discern the necessary connection between one revealed truth and another. A very serious line of demarcation is passed when, from considering religious truths resting on Apostolic or Divine authority, we pass to the contemplation of pious surmises, or, as is not impossible, of unsubstantial legends. Must not the crisp and jealous sense of truth be impaired when the soul accepts with equal facility that which is certain and such portions of the imaginary as it may conceive to be probable; and when the truths for which Apostles gave their lives are practically correlated with stories which, in an age like ours, bring the whole faith into discredit and, for too many souls, into danger?

The Reformation cost much. It broke up, at least in the Western Church, visible unity, so dear to all Christians who believe that our Lord uttered the intercessory prayer in St. John, and that the Epistle to the Ephesians is the Word of God.[1] Whatever may have been the case in England, it became elsewhere religious revolution; and it produced not a few reckless experimentalists, who were the enemies of faith and charity and order. But, notwithstanding, it saved the cause of religion in Western Europe, by dissociating Christianity from the entail of legend which had gathered around it. The Roman Church herself, as any student of the earlier sessions of the Council of Trent may discover, has profited by the Reformation within such limits as were possible; and no believer in Christ can cease to hope, though it be against appearances, that a day may come when she, the largest division of the Christian Church, may yet more widely profit by it; that she may virtually abandon untenable positions, without forfeiture of her historic continuity, and that she may thus undertake to reunite the scattered worshippers of the Redeemer in one visible fold.

IV.

But meanwhile there can be no doubt that the dread of Roman exaggeration prevents many Christians in our day and country from embracing the unmutilated faith of the

[1] St. John xvii. 21. Eph. iv. 3-6.

Apostles. And there are two other causes at work which lead to the same result. Of these the first is the spirit of negative criticism. Criticism has its great duties and its ascertained rights. It is not necessarily the foe of religion: it may brace the air which religion breathes; it may sweep the home which she tenants. But criticism is not religion, nor is she always the servant of religion; and when, as is sometimes the case, criticism virtually usurps the place of faith, the soul is starved even to death upon the dry husks which are all that are offered for spiritual nutriment. Who of us living here in Oxford does not know the truth of this? It is not what has been said against the truths of faith; it is the haunting suspicion that something may be said which has not been said yet that is so fatal to any robust conviction, and as a consequence to all generous effort or self-sacrifice. Every truth in turn seems to be permitted to enjoy at the best an hypothetical existence; and souls are bidden rise to God out of an atmosphere of universal suspicion. What wonder if they sink down to earth and if heaven disappears from their sight?

The other cause to which I am referring is the vague but creditable desire for fellowship in religious sentiment which belongs to our time. Remark that it is religious sentiment, rather than religious truth, which is to be the bond of peace in most of the religious alliances of this age. The desire for spiritual fellowship is undoubtedly Christian in its origin and spirit; and it is aided by the great facilities for intercommunication which characterize our modern life. But when this desire becomes practical what is it that too frequently happens? The smallest of several co-operating creeds becomes of necessity the basis of their co-operation; its mutilated and impoverished contents are assumed, with whatever amount of hardihood, to contain the whole essential substance of Revelation; and men talk of "our common Christianity," when they mean only a fragment of the Christian Faith; a fragment, the variations of which are determined from time to time by petty local controversies. As each applicant for admission to the alliance comes bringing with him a smaller and yet smaller creed, the process of minimizing necessarily goes forward, and in the end it seems to be supposed that a service is somehow done at once to Christ and to Christians if the Christian religion can be shown to cover very little ground indeed.

It would seem that some among us have practically substituted for the Apostolic injunction, " Therefore leaving the first principles of the doctrine of Christ, let us go on unto perfection," the exhortation, " Therefore leaving the creeds of the Apostolic Church, let us do what we may to reduce the Christian faith to a working minimum." One after another the truths of Revelation are discarded, on the ground that they occasion differences; men retain that only in which for the moment they agree. And so it is that we are sometimes told that the Fatherhood of God and the character of Christ are the only permanent elements in Christianity; and we find ourselves exactly where we were when we started, in the company of the modern catechumen,—the first step in synthesis being in analysis the last.

But surely such a Christianity as this, if it could be allowed to deserve the name, is in reality open to at least as many critical objections as are the larger creeds which it is meant to supersede. Who does not see that our Lord's human character can only be described as perfect if His right to draw attention to Himself, in terms which befit only a superhuman person, be frankly conceded? Who does not know that the existence of a moral God, the Maker and Ruler of this universe, is at this moment more fiercely contested by a large class of materialist writers than any subordinate or derived truths whatever, and that, whatever may have been the case in the last century, a naked and shadowy Theism is in our own day even more earnestly rejected than are the specific doctrines of Apostolic Christianity?

Surely, then, it is our wisdom, as Christian believers, while life lasts, to make the most, and not the least, of the truth we hold. What must not He to Whom it refers think—and surely He is thinking on the subject now—of those many magnificent intellects which He has endowed so richly, and to which He has granted such opportunities of exercise and development, and who yet, living here in Oxford, know scarcely more about Him than do the children in our national schools, and make no effort to know more? All else is studied with eager enthusiasm, all forms of created life, all the resources of nature, all the intricacies and laws of human thought; but He, the Author of all,—He, the Infinite and the Everlasting,—is, it seems, forgotten. It was not always so in Oxford; it will not, it cannot, always be so.

> "Dies venit, dies Tua,
> In quâ reflorent omnia,
> Lætemur et nos in viam
> Tuâ reducti dexterâ."

And meanwhile, those who have this hope in them will do what they may to forward it. It is not much to ask of any serious Christian that he should endeavour each day to take possession of some little portion of that highest knowledge, which, in the light of the eternal world, will assuredly seem incomparably more precious than any other. Half an hour a day costs something in the life of a hard-worked man; but it will not be held to have involved a very great sacrifice, when we are at length face to face with the unchanging realities, and know in very deed what is meant by Perfection.

SERMON VII.

THE LIFE OF FAITH AND THE ATHANASIAN CREED.

ST. JOHN iii. 36.

He that believeth on the Son hath everlasting life; and he that believeth not the Son shall not see life; but the wrath of God abideth on him.

ARE we listening to St. John the Baptist, or to St. John the Evangelist? To answer with positiveness is, to say the least, difficult; but probabilities are in favour of the opinion that the Evangelist is here following out, in the full light of the Apostolic age and inspiration, the train of thought to which the Baptist's earlier proclamation of the greatness of Jesus Christ naturally led him.[1] Where, then, does the report of the Baptist's words end, and where does the inspired commentary on them begin?[2] Here, again, we must confess to the presence of difficulty. For there is no abrupt break in the order of thought; there are no marks of quotation which distinctly transfer the attention from the last words of the text to the first words of the commentary. We pass almost insensibly from what is plainly the Baptist's rebuke of a querulous jealousy excited in his disciples by the increasing popularity of the new Teacher, to words which sound like an Apostolic

---

[1] So Olshausen, Tholuck, Klee, Kuinoel. On the other side, cf. Meyer, *Evangelium des Johannes*, p. 140.

[2] Cf. Lücke, *Ev. Johannes*, i. p. 566.

warning respecting the privilege of possessing by faith the life-giving and manifested Son, and the danger of rejecting Him by unbelief. There is a somewhat similar difficulty about determining to whom the verses are addressed which immediately follow St. Paul's account of the dispute at Antioch in the Epistle to the Galatians. Is St. Paul still remonstrating with St. Peter in the whole paragraph which extends from the narrative itself to the end of the second chapter?[1] Or is he now reasoning with the Galatian Judaizers, and only taking his brief reply to Peter as the text of his remonstrance? Certainly the latter would appear for various reasons to be, on the whole, the truer answer; and yet, if it be accepted, where does the reply really end, and the inferential commentary upon it begin? The difficulty of answering this question is not inconsiderable. It might seem as if, in some passages, Holy Scripture, or rather its Divine Author, purposely disappointed our attempts to apply our wonted critical procedures of method and analysis. Perhaps He would teach us that where all is of enduring and Divine authority, the question of human authorship or immediate purpose is relatively unimportant: that we are to believe St. Paul, whether he is addressing himself to a Church of disciples or to a brother-apostle; that we are to believe the Holy Ghost, whether He speaks through St. John the Baptist or through St. John the Evangelist.

I.

"He that believeth the Son hath everlasting life." It is not too much to say that the purpose of St. John's Gospel is condensed into this sentence. The Evangelist tells his readers that his book was written " that they might believe that Jesus is the Christ, the Son of God, and that

[1] Gal. ii. 15-21.

believing they might have life through His Name."[1] And St. John does but echo the fuller declarations of his Lord; " God so loved the world, that He gave His only-begotten Son, that whosoever believeth on Him should not perish, but have everlasting life."[2] So our Lord warns the Jews: " Ye will not come unto Me that ye might have life."[3] He assures the disciples that " this is the will of Him that sent Me, that whosoever seeth the Son, and believeth on Him, hath everlasting life; and I will raise him up at the last day."[4] And He promises that " he that eateth My Flesh, and drinketh My Blood, hath eternal life, and I will raise him up at the last day."[5] Of Himself He says, " I am the Bread of life."[6]

What is life? Who, indeed, shall attempt to answer? We recognise it by its symptoms: what it is in itself we know not. We can only apprehend its presence, as we apprehend simple ideas; as we apprehend facts which we cannot take to pieces and explain; there it is;—a matter of experience. Its inner nature we cannot analyze; its existence we cannot dispute.

What is life? Looking at it, as we must look at it in other beings, from without, and speaking roughly and popularly, we may say that its presence is intimated by two symptoms, by movement and by growth. Whether life be vegetable or animal, whether intelligence or spirit, it exhibits in varying degrees one or both of these characteristics—growth and movement. The mineral does not live; it exists. It only exists because it neither grows nor moves. The tree grows; its growth is its movement; it grows until it dies; growth is a condition of its existence;

---

[1] St. John xx. 31. The immediate reference is to the selection of miracles ($\sigma\eta\mu\epsilon\hat{\iota}\alpha$, verse 30) made by the Evangelist, but in effect the words refer to the drift of his whole Gospel.

[2] St. John iii. 16.   [3] St. John v. 40.   [4] St. John vi. 40.
[5] St. John vi. 54.   [6] St. John vi. 35, 48.

it ceases to live when it no longer grows. We speak of a vital fluid which circulates through the plant; but what do we mean by calling a fluid vital? Within each plant there is some mysterious property or power, the nature of which is as entirely beyond our capacities for investigation as is the life of an archangel, but the reality of which is at the same time strictly a matter of observation.

In the animal the presence of life is more manifest. The animal also grows; it grows until it has attained the normal proportions of its kind; it grows to repair the waste of nature. But in the animal movement is not generally identified with growth; if we except zoophytes on the very confines of the vegetable world, the animal moves with unchecked freedom from place to place. The animal has, moreover, an immaterial sphere of its life; its senses, instincts, feelings, are constantly developing, constantly playing upon external nature with free, varied, subtle, unceasing movement; and thus, in a far higher sense of the word than can be said of the tree, it lives.

Nor is it otherwise with the natural intellect of man. It, too, grows, even in the most uneducated; it grows as a condition of its existence. If it be not growing, it will be shrivelling and withering away; with it, too, not to make progress is to fall back. And it grows by movement; by reiterated exercise; by examining again and again the sources of its knowledge; by testing the processes whereby it reaches its conclusions; by cross-questioning the teachers who have led it on to its existing attainments; by analyzing the ideas which illuminate or control its efforts; by actively welcoming all real additions to its existing possessions. In a word, its movement is its life; the mind which stagnates is on the way to ruin. In order to hold its own against the numbing influences of animal habit, of social routine, of material pressure from without, of softness and indolence from within, the mind must be constantly rousing itself to exertion, like a traveller who is overtaken by night upon the ice, and who knows that although the temptation to sleep is almost overpowering, his safety altogether depends upon his being able to resist it. And this is intellectual life. It is at once growth and movement, whatever be the level of its attainment, whatever the subject-matter upon which it is exercised. Such a life it is ever a main business of an University—with all its apparatus of libraries and teachers, with all its inspiring traditions and associations, with its many separate departments of earnest study, with its many broad and deep currents of conflicting speculation and opinion—to excite and to sustain, if it may be, in every single student who finds a home within its walls.

But beyond the life of the understanding there is a still higher kind of life. It is that through which man enters into communion with a spiritual world; it is the life which belongs to man as a personal spirit, recognising his own awful immortality, and recognising the existence of his God. It is true that natural thought and feeling may and must be exercised upon these tremendous subjects. But spiritual life is a distinct thing from active intelligence. And it is a higher thing. Spiritual thought can see farther and more clearly than can natural thought: spiritual feeling is purified from the selfish alloy which mingles with natural feeling.[1] And the fruits of the Spirit are such as do not come to us as natural men, they are "love, joy, peace, long-suffering, gentleness, goodness, faith, meekness, temperance."[2]

In this, the highest sphere of life, it is not less true than elsewhere that life is known to exist by growth and by movement. What in itself it is we know not. "The wind bloweth where it listeth, and thou hearest the sound thereof, but canst not tell whence it cometh or whither it goeth: so is every one that is born of the Spirit."[3] Most assuredly

[1] 1 Cor. ii. 14, 15. [2] Gal. v. 22. [3] St. John iii. 8.

"the peace of God which passeth all understanding," and which is its choicest gift, is not spiritual stagnation. It is indeed a repose of conscience which ensues, when all the faculties of the soul are felt to centre upon their true and legitimate Object; but this repose is like that of the awful beings around the Throne who "rest not day and night, saying, Holy, Holy, Holy."[1] Created life at its highest summits does not really issue in what would be practically death. And the true life of souls here below consists in a continuous growth in the mastery of moral and spiritual truth; it is perpetual movement onwards and upwards towards the Perfect Being Who is so altogether beyond us. We are to "grow up into Him in all things, Who is the Head, even Christ,"[2] and "when Christ, Who is our life, shall appear, then shall we also appear with Him in glory."[3]

Certainly this life is ever moving and growing in those who possess it; but when, it may be asked, does a man who lives it feel that he lives it? In a certain sense, it must be answered, always. At the bottom of his thought and feeling about himself, there is the habitual, unsuspended consciousness that he is a personal spirit, whose real home is not within this world of sense, since he lives face to face with the Eternal God. Every good action, undertaken for the sake of God and without any lower selfish aim, is immediately rewarded by a new pulse of spiritual vigour; and it is felt in the quickened consciousness of spiritual immortality. But it is in prayer that this consciousness is roused into its greatest activity. Prayer is the act by which man, detaching himself from the embarrassments of sense and nature, ascends to the true level of his destiny. In prayer man puts aside the lower forms of life which belong to his complex existence, his vegetative, his animal, even his intellectual life; as a spirit, he seeks the Father of Spirits;

[1] Rev. iv. 8.   [2] Eph. iv. 15.   [3] Col. iii. 4.

and he reflects back upon his bodily form, upon his social relations, upon his place and work in the world of sense, something of the lustre of a purely supersensuous being who already knows by insight that the "things which are seen are temporal, but the things which are not seen are eternal."[1]

How is this life secured? Not, it must be answered, by any force latent in human nature. There is enough in us to show that we were destined for such a life; enough to prompt the aspirations which, in the noblest members of our race, have struggled again and again to compass it. It has been sought,—it has not been reached,—by the quick intelligence of Greece, which failed to understand its moral and purifying power, and by the seductive mysticisms of India, too dreamy to seize its practical force. If we seek for it, where it is really to be found, in the Sacred Books and history of Christendom; if we study its code of action in the Sermon on the Mount, or its deepest and highest consciousness, as in our Lord's Last Discourse; or its practical results upon vigorous natural characters, in such a career as was St. Paul's; or its many-sided relations to thought and to society in the Apostolic Epistles; we must admit that it is in itself something beyond nature—beyond the scope of natural genius to have sketched in outline, or of natural effort to attain in practice.

And there is a reason for this. If man looks within himself he must perceive two things; a law of right, and that which it condemns. The law of natural conscience, illuminated, it may be, in a greater or less degree by Divine Revelation, and constantly confronted by moral evil, whether coarse and revolting, or subtle, refined, spiritual:—this inward anomaly explains to us why, of ourselves, we cannot, in the highest sense of the word, live. We read within ourselves a sentence of death; we have light enough to

[1] 2 Cor. iv. 18.

know, if we will, what manner of beings we are;—that is all. For moral evil is weakness, numbness, death: it is in varying degrees, darkness in the understanding; it is coldness in the affections; above all, it is enfeeblement and warping of the will; it paralyzes the faculty upon which the destiny of the soul mainly depends. If man is to be helped out of such evil; cleansed from its traces in the past, invigorated so as to resist it for the future; if he is to rise to a life which cannot but be its antagonist and its cure; he must seek the feet of One Who, of His free love and bounty, is ever willing to "take up the simple out of the dust, and lift the poor out of the mire, that He may set him with the princes, even with the princes of His people." [1]

Yes,—"he that believeth on the Son hath everlasting life." One has in very deed appeared in human history, Who could promise and bestow this life of eternity which begins in time, this highest life of which man is capable. A Galilean peasant, as He seemed, He left an impression, He gave an impulse, from which—it is a simple matter of historical fact—the human soul dates a new era in its history. From the first, He was felt to be a new and unique force in humanity; to say this is to say the least that a bystander could say about His work. But when He died in pain and shame, His death was declared and known to have a purifying and sacrificial power, and to re-establish a lost relationship between earth and heaven. The days have passed when a sterile criticism could attempt to represent St. Paul as the real author of Christianity; the Apostle's indignant question to the Corinthian sectarians, "Was Paul crucified for you?" was a sufficient answer.[2] St. Paul himself knew, as each who shares his faith knows, that "the life which I now live in the flesh I live by the faith of the Son of God, Who loved me and gave Himself

[1] Ps. cxiii. 6, 7.   [2] 1 Cor. i. 13.

for me."[1] For this life, this truly soul-transforming impulse, this immense moral encouragement and relief, this sense of reanimated freedom, and hope, and power, did not die away with a single generation. It lived on still when Apostles had left the earth. It lived on in its first freshness, because it was in reality the widening personal influence of an ever-present Master; because He Who was its Source and Author had not really gone. It lived to attract and enlist in His service minds of great originality and power; it lived to robe the young, the weak, the timid, the very poor, with the high moral dignity of confessorship and martyrdom; it breathed a new spirit into art and literature, and social intercourse, and, though after long delay, into the very structure of society; it changed the character and habits of entire classes, populations, races; and finally, if it did not destroy the great pagan empire, which would fain have strangled it in its birth, it at least followed hard on the steps of the real destroyers, to create a new and healthier civilization which might fill the void.

Nor is this force spent in our own day. Whatever may be the discouragements of the modern Church; however Israel may seem at times to be finally falling back before the hosts of Syria; grievous as are the divisions, the corruptions, the many inevitable sorrows of a perplexed and enfeebled Christendom; still "he that believeth on the Son hath everlasting life." It is a matter of experience. Again and again, thank God, we see men, like the noble Prelate who has recently been taken from us in South Africa,[2] in whom everything natural is sensibly elevated by some unearthly force; men, of whom, if we knew nothing more, we should know that they had felt the present power of something higher than a beautiful literature, or a great memory; that some invisible Friend must have

[1] Gal. ii. 20.
[2] The Most Rev. Robert Gray, Lord Bishop of Cape Town.

looked upon them with favour, and changed them from their old selves and made them what they are.

II.

Some may ask, if not in words, yet in their secret hearts, Why cannot the text stop here? Why is it not enough to proclaim the blessedness of those who possess life in possessing Christ? Why should anything be added as to the loss of those who do not possess Him? Why is it also said, "He that hath not the Son shall not see life," and still more, that "the wrath of God abideth on him"?

This question would be more difficult to answer, if Christianity were only a philosophy, and of human growth. The business of a philosophy is to say what it can in order to recommend itself; to fight its way, if possible, by reason and argument, to intellectual empire; to show that the systems of thought which oppose it are without foundation, or at least that they rest upon considerations of inferior weight to those which it can produce on its own behalf. A philosophy is, however, always more or less a guess at truth; it is a happy speculation, on great topics if you will, but still a speculation; and as such it is, and knows itself to be, in some degree provisional and tentative. If it were to announce that serious consequences would follow upon its being rejected, it would be guilty of an immodesty, which the reason and conscience of its most attached disciples would forthwith condemn.

Doubtless Christianity may throw itself into a philosophical form for missionary purposes; it may descend into the lists, and borrow the language of its adversaries, as it did so well at Alexandria in the second and third centuries; as it has done since, in more places and at more times than one. But although Christianity may be presented as the highest philosophy, it is also much more: it is nothing, if it is not much more; if it is not in very truth a Revelation. In the last resort it claims to have come, not from man, but from God; and when addressing itself to man it has a corresponding character of imperative urgency. Further, its object is not merely or chiefly to enlighten man's understanding by the offer of a new and attractive and well-attested theory of destiny, but to change, purify, elevate, his entire being by the infusion of a new principle of life. And if man rejects it, he rejects not merely so much information upon the highest topics, but conditions of moral and spiritual renovation, which are not, as it maintains, to be found elsewhere. In the language of the first Christians, "Neither is there salvation in any other; for there is none other Name under heaven given among men whereby we must be saved."[1]

Indeed all knowledge that is based on fact, all assertion of truth that is positive, and not merely hypothetical or speculative, must insist upon the mischief of neglecting or rejecting it with an earnestness corresponding to the dignity of its subject-matter. This law does not merely hold good of spiritual truth. Do teachers of physics admit that the ascertained laws of nature—of health for example—can be neglected with impunity? Do economists allow that the ascertained laws of production, of population, of supply and demand, can be ignored without social and political mischief? Not to insist upon a truism; is it not, I ask, of the very nature of truth that its acceptance is compulsory in a degree proportioned to its importance; so that acceptance of the highest truth is therefore in the highest degree compulsory? There may be truths so insignificant in their bearings upon thought and life, that it is hard to say what does depend upon our accepting them beyond the moral strength which inevitably accompanies all recognition of fact in all directions. But no spiritual

[1] Acts iv. 12.

truth, if it be truth, is of this order; even although we may be ourselves unable to trace the importance of a particular truth, or to receive it for the time being, except upon authority.

Every Theist must admit this respecting the first and greatest of all truths. If, of course, a man regards God as only an hypothesis by which to account for the existence of the visible universe, no harm will, in his opinion, happen upon denying God's existence, beyond the intellectual embarrassment of suggesting any reasonable counter-hypothesis to take His place. But if it be known to be a fact that there does exist One Being, the Parent of all besides, the Ruler of all besides, before Whom all besides are as less than nothing, yet to Whom all and each are objects of the deepest, tenderest love; it cannot be possible to reject this fact as you would reject an hypothesis, or indeed, without loss—certain, awful, immeasurable. Loss to the intellect, but still more to the affections and the will; loss here, presaging only too clearly, in the case of an immortal being, loss hereafter. To insist upon this would be beside my present purpose, and unnecessary, it might be hoped, under any circumstances, within these walls; but especially when an essay of great power and beauty on "the Moral Significance of Atheism" has been recently in the hands of many of us, and will have suggested to those who have read it all that a preacher could wish to say.[1]

And as with Theistic, so with Christian truth. If Christ be indeed the Son of God, through and in Whom the Perfect Moral Being has spoken to His creatures—to reject Him is to reject God. "He that hateth Me hateth My Father also."[2] If to believe Him is life, to have known and yet to reject Him is death. There is no middle term or state between the two. And this rejection of the Son

---

[1] Cf. *Essays, Theological and Literary*, by R. H. Hutton, M.A., vol. i., essay I.   [2] St. John xv. 23.

incurs the wrath of the Father, Whose Image and Counterpart He is; so that God's righteous displeasure with a rebel against His authority rests upon the rejecter; "the wrath of God abideth on him." The man enters of his free will into a state of moral being which is uncheered by the smile of God, and which, after death, is fixed and irretrievable. The Absolute Religion can claim no less than this; it cannot dare to represent its acceptance as other than a strict moral necessity for those to whom it is offered. In fact, this stern, yet truthful and merciful claim, makes all the difference between a Faith and a theory.

III.

A statement of this truth in other terms is at present occasioning a painful controversy, which it would be better in this place to pass over in silence, if too much was not at stake to warrant a course from which I shall only depart with sincere reluctance.

Need I say that I allude to the vexed question of the Athanasian Creed? Certain clauses of that document are so unwelcome in some quarters, and all of it in others, that men have gravely proposed either to omit large portions of it, or to banish it altogether from the service of the Church. The good taste of scholars, and a fitting sense of the immodesty and grotesqueness of any pretension on the part of a merely National Church to alter the terms of a document of world-wide authority, will probably save the Athanasian Creed from the various current schemes for mutilating it. But the proposal to expel the Creed from its place in our public worship may even yet, unhappily, receive much consideration and support; nay, its eventual success is far too possible to be safely disregarded.[1]

---

[1] Since this sermon was preached, the author's fears have been, alas! too accurately justified in Ireland.

Here let me endeavour to anticipate an objection which will occur to many who may have accompanied me thus far without difficulty, but who feel that at this point they must take up an attitude of criticism, if not of opposition.

"We admit," you say, "that to reject Christ wilfully is to forfeit everlasting life. We do not shrink from the awful words of Apostles and Evangelists about the obligations of faith. But then it appears to us that the faith which is required in Scripture is faith in a Person, and not faith in a series of dogmatic assertions. We can understand that to refuse to put faith in our Lord's Person may incur even eternal loss; but it is a very different matter to attribute this consequence to the rejection of certain abstract propositions such as are those of the Athanasian Creed."

Here, then, let me join issue by asking, What is meant by faith in a person? You reply that faith in a person is an instinct rather than a judgment; that it is an act of the heart rather than of the intellect, or at most a combined act of heart and understanding moving together. Very well: you do not then mean to say that faith in a person is altogether irrational; you mean that it depends upon reasons which can be produced, if need be, but which the heart would rather keep in the background, if only from the natural disinclination to discuss that which we love. This, indeed, is the case with our trust in the relatives and friends of early life. Few men have drawn out into a formal theory their deepest grounds of confidence in a father or in an elder brother, or in a very wise and revered adviser; to do this would be like exposing to the rays of the sun the roots of a very tender plant. Still the time may come when you will have to do this at all costs. If, for instance, you are told that the object of your trust is not what he appears to be; that he is insincere, or selfish, or otherwise unworthy of the confidence which you place in him, from that moment forth you are obliged to consider *why* it is that you trust him, and whether it is reasonable to continue to do so. You have no choice about it. From that moment forth, if your trust survives the early shock of hostile controversy, it necessarily assumes the form of deliberate assent to a proposition or to a series of propositions; it becomes, whether you will or not, something like a formal creed. It takes the shape of assent to the propositions that your friend *is* sincere; that he is unselfish; that he is all which it was suggested he was not; that he is, in short, worthy of the confidence you have placed in him; and this personal or domestic creed of your heart has its warning, yes, if it must be so, its damnatory clauses behind; it affirms that to deny your friend's sincerity or unselfishness is to forfeit all the happiness that this precious trust in his character implies. Some who are here may possibly have known the agony of moments when faith in an old friend has been assailed by some insinuation or controversy; and when the instincts of love and loyalty have had to throw themselves into a harsh logical form, if the heart was not to be left in the outer darkness of a lifelong disappointment.

Thus, if we may compare small things with great, it has fared with the faith of Christendom in Him Who is the adored Master of every truly Christian soul. At first faith in Him was an instinctive trust; it was the trust of the weak, the sickly, the poor, the wandering, the bewildered, in One towards Whom they were drawn as if fascinated by some power which they did not analyze, yet could not but obey. So it was doubtless with the men and women who sought His blessed feet and hung upon His words in the villages and lanes of Galilee. He was surrounded from the first by the deep fervid homage of human hearts. But even within the Apostolic age the grounds of this homage were challenged. Was He indeed what He claimed to be; was He the Teacher, King, and Judge of men? Was He what His followers said of Him? Was He not in reality much less than this, if not, indeed, as the Jews alleged, something utterly different? These questions could not be declined; and an Apostle insists upon the necessity of "giving a reason" for the hope with which Christians had been endowed by Christ.[1] The Christian heart might still pour out its ceaseless tide of adoration and trust; but the Christian intellect must the while be able formally to proclaim why the Object of that homage was rightfully entitled to it. Faith in Jesus Christ had already passed from the region of pure moral instincts into the atmosphere of dialectics. The transition, however unwelcome, was, from the nature of the case, inevitable; but the logical form which was thus given to the tenderest spiritual judgments of the earliest Christendom did not really forfeit their inner character.

For it was asked whether Jesus Christ was really justified in using the language which He did use about Himself. Was He really able to fulfil the promises which He made so profusely, and which His Apostles made in His Name and with His authority? Who was He then, in His deepest personality, that He should speak sometimes as if He were Monarch of two worlds; sometimes as if His aims and interests were strictly identical with those of God; sometimes as if His human countenance and form was but a veil of a Being Who did not really belong to the sphere of sense and mortality and time? If men were to cling to His pierced hands, protesting that they could trust Him not merely in life, but in death—not merely for time, but in eternity; what was the justifiable basis and explanation of this unique and altogether extraordinary trust? It was a vital question; which, having been once

[1] 1 St. Pet. iii. 15.

raised, could not be evaded, at least if Christianity was to live.

Not to dwell here upon the answer to this question which we find in the Apostolic writings, let us observe that, in the three Creeds which the Church proposes for our acceptance, we see three sections of that answer thrown into the forms which it has assumed for all time.

The "Three Creeds"[1] are not a fortuitous collection of dogmatic formularies. They represent—not indeed the successive inventions or speculations of an accretive doctrinal development, but—three answers to the three stages of the great question which is proposed to every Christian thinker. And they meet this question which could not but be asked with replies which had been from the first included in the teaching of the Apostles.

When it is inquired, "Why Jesus can save us to the uttermost from our most formidable enemies, in life and in death; why He can give us, now and hereafter, everlasting life?" the Apostles' Creed replies that He is the "Only Son" of "God the Father Almighty." To the natural rejoinder, "What do you exactly mean by the 'Only Son of God the Father Almighty;' is He some unique and extraordinary man, or is He altogether above the level of humanity?"—the Nicene Creed answers that He is "God of God, Light of Light, Very God of Very God, of one substance with the Father, Begotten not made." To the further and not less inevitable question, How do you propose to reconcile this very serious assertion either with the truth of the Divine Unity or with the Gospel record of a truly Human Life? the Athanasian Creed,

---

[1] Art. viii. To refer to the "Quicunque" as a Psalm may be only a pedantic crotchet. But if it is intended to imply that as a Psalm the Quicunque is not properly a Creed, this is to contradict the formal language of the Church of England both in the Articles and the Prayer Book.

and it alone, furnishes a full and elaborate reply. "The Catholic Faith is this: that we worship One God in Trinity, and the Trinity in Unity." For associated with the Son and the Father in the unity of an undivided substance, is that Divine and Glorious Person, Who in the mystery of the Divine Existence is their eternal bond,—the Ever-Blessed Spirit. And "such as the Father is, such is the Son; and such is the Holy Ghost:" Each uncreated, Each illimitable, Each eternal, Each almighty, Each Lord and God: while the Son is not only " Perfect God, but also and as truly Perfect Man, of a reasonable soul and human flesh subsisting; equal to the Father as touching His Godhead; but inferior to the Father as touching His Manhood; Who, although He be God and Man, yet is not two, but one Christ." And, we may not shrink from the conclusion, that to deny the doctrine thus stated, is to give up the very warrant and basis of our trust in Him. The several propositions of the Creed, looked at separately, may wear the appearance of "hard, abstract, unfruitful dogma;" in combination with the rest, each statement is seen to be an indispensable part of a living and integral body of truth, whereby the two terms of our faith, the perfectness of our Lord's human character, regarded in the light of His self-assertion, and the Unity of the Godhead, are brought into fundamental harmony. It is the trustworthiness of Jesus which is the master-truth asserted by the Athanasian Creed. In the last analysis it will be found impossible to justify the promises which He held out to the human race, and the language which His Apostles used about Him, except upon such grounds as those which are taken by the Creed. Men may wish that it were otherwise; but we can no more reverse the underlying laws or the providential conditions of religious truth, than we can change the past course of history. To discard the Creed, and imagine that we can go back intellectually to days when the questions which are here answered had not yet been asked, may suggest the proceedings of a statesman who should wish to reorganize English society upon the legislative basis of the Heptarchy. For these questions thus authoritatively decided in this Creed, will be asked by the restless mind of man even to the end of time; and the answer which is before us is that of the Church of Christ, reasserting, in new terms, the original meaning of the faith which she guards, and in the spirit of a true charity for souls, bidding us receive these her explanations as surely involved in that act of perfect trust in the Son of GOD, which is the earnest of true spiritual life.

The disuse of the Athanasian Creed has been recommended by reference to the case of the State Services,[1] which were abandoned a few years ago. Such a parallel would almost seem to imply a dulness or a levity unworthy of the subject.

Doubtless, as involving an acknowledgment of God's governing Hand in our national life and history, these Services had a religious value; and in the century which created them they may well have been justified, if not in all their expressions, yet at least in their general drift, by crimes and dangers which are happily remote from ourselves. But there was much to be said against perpetuating in our sanctuaries the echo of political passions which belonged to another, and in civil matters, a less favoured age. And the Services in question, originally deficient in ecclesiastical sanction, disappeared from among us, without any action on the part of the Church, without any general protest against their disappearance, and with some confessed sense of relief. It does not follow that because such a liturgical representation of a particular view of portions of our national history could be disused without grave offence, it would be easy to discard or to mutilate one of these solemn

[1] For Nov. 5, Jan. 30, and May 29.

documents in which, using not merely the language of our own Communion, but language adopted by the Church of Christ at large, we tell out before God and man the revealed facts of God's inner Being, and the Incarnation and Work of our Divine Redeemer. To presume this was surely to mistake the relative importance of the matters in question, and the mistake is as inconsistent with statesmanlike insight into existing convictions as it is unintelligible in the judgment of serious faith.

For on the very face of the matter, to disuse or to mutilate the Athanasian Creed involves the first great step in a theological revolution. It involves the public abandonment of a position with relation to the claims of Christian truth which the Church of England deliberately accepted at the Reformation, and which, by the mouth of her best and wisest, she has ever since maintained. The use of this Creed in our Services cannot be described as a foreign element which survives the wreck of a discarded system through having in some way escaped the jealous eye of liturgical reformers. The Quicunque was indeed transferred from the Latin Breviary, as were the Apostles' Creed, the Te Deum, or the Benedicite. But one of the most deliberate acts of the leaders of the Reformation, when editing the Prayer Book of 1552,[1] was to double the number of days on which this Creed was to be used; and this measure is probably attributable to Cranmer's apprehensions of the Arian opinions which had made themselves felt in England, not long after the publication of the earlier Book in 1549. Within the sixteenth century, the use of the Creed is defended by Hooker against Cartwright, on the

[1] In the First Prayer Book of Edward VI. (1549) the Creed is ordered to be said on the Feasts of Christmas, the Epiphany, Easter, the Ascension, Pentecost, and Trinity Sunday. In the Second Prayer Book (1552) the following days were added: St. Matthias, St. John Baptist, St. James, St. Bartholomew, St. Matthew, St. Simon and St. Jude, St. Andrew. These thirteen days were retained in 1559, 1604, and 1662.

practical ground of existing experience. Hooker, having in his mind the then recent histories of foreign Reformed bodies, Zwinglian, Calvinistic, Moravian, Bohemian, Polish, and the acts and words of Socinus, of Gentilis, of Francis David, of Blandrata,—writes that "the blasphemies of Arians, Samosatenians, Tritheites, Eutychians, and Macedonians (he is quoting in part the very admissions of Beza himself), are renewed by them who, to hatch their heresy, have chosen those Churches as fittest nests where Athanasius' Creed is not heard."[1] The murmurs of the early objectors died away; and the Creed has maintained its position through successive periods of change. It survived the Hampton Court conference, the Savoy revision, and the abortive Commission of 1689. It outlived the hostility of popular latitudinarianism as represented by Tillotson, and the acute philosophical Arianism of Dr. Samuel Clarke, of Westminster, and the frank and coarse scorn of Priestley. Is it left for this generation to surrender what our forefathers have preserved to us at the cost of so much effort, often of so much obloquy? Are the labours and judgment of Hooker and of Waterland to be set aside at last, and in the interest of theories which until the present day have never found a home within the Church of Christ? Is it now at length certain that our future happiness does not depend upon our rightly believing the central truths of the Christian faith? or has the Church failed to define those truths accurately in the language of the Quicunque vult?

Let it not be thought that the disuse or mutilation of a Creed is any mere question of literary, or professional, or antiquarian feeling. What would be the practical effect of such disuse upon the people? Theologians might remark that the Creed was still preserved among the Thirty-nine Articles; but the question would be asked again and again,

[1] *E. P.* v. xlii. p. 188.

Why was it deposed from its old position? If the answer should be that the Creed was liable to being misunderstood, it would be rejoined that the 109th Psalm, in the popular use of which the risks of grave misunderstanding are at least greater, was still used by the Church twelve times a year. If it were argued that the Athanasian Creed required too much explanation, it would be asked in turn whether the Collects, the Prefaces in the Communion Service, nay, the other Creeds, suggested no serious questions which needed explanation. If it were pleaded that the origin of this Creed was obscure, or of a comparatively late age, or that it was not really written by the great Father whose name it bears, it might be urged with greater reason that the origin and composition of the Apostles' Creed is not less obscure, its growth even more gradual, its title to the name which we give it more difficult of strict justification. If the argument should be advanced that no Œcumenical Council had sanctioned this Creed, or that its place in the Services of the Eastern Church is doubtful or insignificant,[1] it could be replied that the Apostles' Creed, too, could point to no formal œcumenical decision in its favour; and that it also is unrecognised in the public prayers of the Oriental Church.

The broad common sense of the people would argue that the Creed was discarded because it was imagined to be wholly or partly untrue; untrue enough, it would be observed, to be discredited as a formulary for general use, although not sufficiently untrue to be unfitted for solemn clerical subscription. The fact would remain patent to all men that, after using this Creed for the last three centuries on all the greatest festivals of the Christian year, the English Church had deliberately abandoned it; and the friends and foes of faith would alike draw their own

---

[1] The Athanasian Creed is found in Eastern Service-Books. Cf. Ὡρολόγιον, p. 495, ed. Venice, 1868. After τὸ Πνεῦμα τὸ ἅγιον ἀπὸ τοῦ Πατρὸς, the Western clause referring to the Son is omitted.

conclusions as to the meaning of such a step.[1] It would be inferred that the Church of England no longer held belief in the doctrines of the Holy Trinity and of our Lord's Incarnation, as taught by the Church Universal, to be necessary to salvation; and that she admitted herself to have erred in affirming this necessity since the Reformation, not less than before it.

But the Creed would be really rejected because it is too faithful an echo of that Gospel which men do not venture openly to reject. "This is life eternal, that they may know Thee the only true God, and Jesus Christ, Whom Thou hast sent."[2] Eternal life consists in a practical knowledge of God the Holy Trinity, and of Jesus, God and Man. And thus " he that believeth the Son hath everlasting life, but he that believeth not the Son shall not see life, but the wrath of God abideth on him." Nothing can be urged against the principle of the warning clauses which is not equally applicable to the principle of such a passage as this. The Bible and the Creed alike imply the moral character of faith, the connection which exists between right belief and moral wellbeing, the consequences which must follow upon the rejection of known truth from perversity of will. But does Holy Scripture, or do the warning clauses of the Creed condemn those who have never heard of the faith? Certainly not: the Church, like the Apostle, cannot " judge them that are without."[3] Do these clauses or does that text condemn those who have had to contend with difficulties which God knows to have been insurmountable, but who have sincerely sought the truth which the Creed in its integrity asserts? Again, I say, surely not. " Nemo tenetur ad impossibile" is a first maxim of natural morals. The violent interpretation which would press

---

[1] The congratulations which were addressed by the Socinians of Belfast to the revisers of the Irish Prayer Book had a painful significance.
[2] St. John xvii. 3.
[3] 1 Cor. v. 12.

these general statements so literally as to admit of no limitations would be no less fatal to the general assertions of Holy Scripture, or indeed of any treatise on morals and conduct. No human judgment can safely rule the fearful question, to what individuals these clauses do apply? He only knows Who sees us as we are. But we are not justified in silencing the proclamation of a great law of the kingdom of souls, for the reason that, except in our own case, we cannot accurately determine the range of its application.

"Surely," it may once more be said, "the Life of which the text speaks as being possessed by the believer in the Eternal Son, is much more than a correct logical apprehension of His place in the scale of being." God forbid that I should for one moment deny it. Undoubtedly, truth is apprehended vitally, if at all, by the spiritual eye; it is embraced, if to any real purpose, with the energy of the moral nature. With the heart, now as of old, man believeth unto righteousness;[1] now as of old, a living faith means much more than an intellectual assent, however perfect, to a Creed, however true. But the intellect also has its office towards religious truth; it contributes an important element in the complex act of faith; and the right discharge of this office is itself moral; it is a most serious department of Christian duty; it is a work incumbent on us in exact proportion to the gifts of knowledge and thought which we have severally received.

The controversies of our day may do us lasting harm, if they lead us to adhere to our own opinions only because they are our own; if they estrange from each other hearts which should, in the holiest of causes, be one, and weaken by dividing moral forces, which when

---

[1] Rom. x. 10, καρδίᾳ. The word means here, as generally in the New Testament, not merely the seat of affection, but the centre point of the whole inward life. Cf. Delitzsch, *Bibl. Psych.* iv. § 5.

united are none too strong to cope successfully with the energies of evil around us. But if we should have been endowed in any degree with the high and rare grace of intrepid loyalty to known truth allied to an unselfish spirit, we, too, may "take up serpents, and if we drink any deadly thing it shall not hurt" us.[1] Nay, more: to be forced back upon the central realities of the truth which we profess; to learn to know and feel better than ever before what are the convictions which we dare not surrender at any cost; to renew the freshness of an early faith, which affirms within us clearly and irresistibly that the one thing worth thinking of, worth living for, if need were, worth dying for, is the unmutilated faith of Jesus Christ our Lord;—these may be the results of inevitable differences, and if they are, they are blessings indeed. In these, as in other ways, God "maketh the wilderness a standing water, and watersprings out of the dry ground." Truth has her sterner responsibilities sooner or later in store for those who have known anything about her; but they are also the responsibilities of a pure and fearless love to God and man, and when honestly met, they are blessed proportionately.

[1] St. Mark xvi. 18.

SERMON VIII.

CHRIST'S SERVICE AND PUBLIC OPINION.

GAL. i. 10.

If I yet pleased men, I should not be a servant of Christ.

ST. PAUL is noticing a taunt which had been levelled at him by some opponents of his authority in the Galatian churches. They were bent upon making certain Jewish observances obligatory upon Christians. But while engaged in this enterprise they were met by the objection that the Apostle to whom the faithful in Galatia owed so much was altogether opposed to them. St. Paul's opposition could not be ignored; but then St. Paul was at a distance, and it was thought that the great weight of his judgment might be lessened by a twofold process. His opponents suggested first of all that he was no such true apostle as were the Sacred Twelve: he had not been taught and sent as they had been, by our Lord Jesus Christ Himself.[1] How completely he disposed of this objection it is no part of our present business to consider;[2] but the Galatian teachers had another weapon in reserve. Whatever St. Paul's authority might be, he was, they contended, a man of such facile and

[1] Gal. i. 1, 11, 12.   [2] Gal. i. 12—ii. 19.

plastic temper, that when once he had satisfied himself of the popularity of the new tendency in the Galatian churches, he might be confidently expected to withdraw any serious opposition. His large sympathies would ensure his acquiescence in all that the new teachers had at heart; his popular instincts, they may have hinted, were likely to prove stronger than his attachment to any given religious theory or to any single religious truth.

Some language of this kind must have found its way across the sea to the ears of the great missionary during his three months' visit to Corinth. Had it only touched his personal credit, he would have left it, we may be sure, unnoticed. He does notice it, because it could not remain unchallenged without injury to his Master's work. After the apostolical greeting[1] which opens his letter to the Galatian churches, he has none of the usual congratulations, no warm expressions of sympathy and interest for readers who have so largely surrendered themselves to an imposing falsehood. He wonders at their swift transfer to another gospel; no, it is not another, since there is only one.[2] He glances in anger at the teachers—he will not name them—who were troubling the principles and faith of his own spiritual children; they were men who would so alter the Gospel of Christ as to give it a totally new direction.[3] But the matter before him is no merely personal question; it is a question of principle. Though he himself or an angel from the skies should preach a gospel contradicting that which he had preached, let the preacher be anathema, let him be sentenced by God to eternal ruin.[4] His readers might suppose that he was using words which were the result of a momentary irritation and in excess of his real meaning; but as he has uttered these words deliberately on some former occasion, he will deliberately repeat them. "As we have said before, so say I also

[1] Gal. i. 1-5.   [2] Gal. i. 6.   [3] Gal. i. 7.   [4] Gal. i. 8.

K

now again, If any man preach any other gospel unto you than that ye received at first, let him be anathema."[1] Now, at any rate, there could be no room for mistake as to the course he would adopt towards the new teaching in Galatia; and every reader of his epistle must have known, at least by name, the men whose conduct had incurred this solemn and authoritative condemnation. So for the moment, before pursuing his general subject, the Apostle justifies his severity. He would not have uttered these stern and unsparing sentences if his first object had been popularity among men instead of the approval of God. "Do I now," he asks, "win over to myself men or God? Or am I seeking to be an object of man's goodwill? No: and there is a decisive reason against any such efforts. If I were still pleasing men, if I had not resigned the hope of human favour and of human approval, I should not be the slave of Christ."[2]

I.

The title which the Apostle thus gives himself, of servant or slave of Christ, is adopted by him, and in a more formal manner, on other occasions.[3] It expresses, we may be sure, no mere acquiescence in a current fashion of Eastern speech; but an aspect of his life and conduct which he desires to keep before himself and others. St. Paul belonged to two worlds, the Jewish and the Greek; and in this title, as in much else that he says and does, he has both worlds in view. In the language of the Hebrew Scriptures every Israelite is, as such, a servant of the Lord;[4] and to the collective people, viewed in its separate

---

[1] Gal. i. 9. [2] Gal. i. 10.
[3] Rom. i. 1. Phil. i. 1. Tit. i. 1. Cf. St. James i. 1. St. Jude 4. 2 St. Pet. i. 1. Rev. i. 1.
[4] Ps. lxix. 37; cxiii. 1; cxxxiv. 1; cxxxv. 1; cxxxvi. 22, etc. Isa. lxv. 8, 9, 13, 14.

and consecrated life, it is said, "Thou Israel, art My servant.... Thou whom I have taken from the ends of the earth, and called thee from the chief men thereof, and said unto thee, Thou art My servant; I have chosen thee."[1] Besides this general and ethical meaning, the title had a technical, almost an official force. Any man who was marked out from among his fellows as having a special work to do for the Lord and for Israel was regarded as taken into the service of the Invisible King; in the eyes of his countrymen he was robed in God's livery, by the drift of events, or by the acts and tenor of his life. Legislators such as Moses, soldiers such as Joshua, rulers such as David, or Eliakim,[2] or Zerubbabel,[3] are called in Scripture servants of the Lord;[4] nay, the title is given to pious men dwelling on the very frontiers of heathendom, whose experience teaches the people of Revelation some much-needed lesson, such as was Job,[5] or even to pagan monarchs, intrusted by Providence with some stern mission to Israel, as was Nebuchadnezzar.[6] In this sense, too, every member of the order of prophets came in time to be termed a servant of the Lord;[7] and the title reached its highest significance when, in the later writings[8] of Isaiah, it was used of the King Messiah, Whose future humiliations and glory there mingle indistinctly with the nearer although still distant sufferings and deliverance of the martyr-people in Babylon.

When, then, St. Peter and St. Jude, writing to Churches mainly or entirely of Jewish origin, style themselves

---

[1] Isa. xli. 8, 9.   [2] Isa. xxii. 20.   [3] Hag. ii. 23.
[4] Deut. xxxiv. 5. Josh. i. 1, 13, 15; xxiv. 29. Ps. xviii. title; xxxvi. title; lxxviii. 70; lxxxix. 3, 20. Jer. xxxiii. 21.
[5] Job i. 8; ii. 3; xlii. 8.
[6] Jer. xxv. 9; xxvii. 6; xliii. 10.
[7] Amos iii. 7. Jer. vii. 25; xxv. 4, and often. Dan. ix. 6. Isa. xx. 3.
[8] Isa. xlii. 1-7; xlix. 1-9; l. 4-10; lii. 13; liii. 11.

servants of Jesus Christ, it is probable that these Apostles understand the title chiefly, if not exclusively, in the traditional and narrower Hebrew sense. But when St. Paul, writing to the Roman or the Philippian Church, calls himself, or himself and Timothy, servants of Jesus Christ, it is difficult to suppose that he does not read into the title the meaning which his readers would naturally find there. In these Churches, consisting altogether or predominantly of converts from heathendom, the phrase would rather suggest the ordinary slave of the Græco-Roman world than the inspired or distinguished servant of the Hebrew theocracy. That uncounted population of human beings, which worked and suffered in silence, which tilled the fields, which manned the fleets, which constructed the palaces and bridges of the world; which supplied to those who had property and power their cooks, carpenters, painters, astronomers, doctors, copyists, poets, valets, gladiators, buffoons; which ministered to the refinement, to the intelligence, to the luxury, to the passions of the wealthy; which by its ceaseless and almost unnoticed waste of unregretted life, satisfied the requirements or helped to fill the coffers of the State;—the great class of slaves was often the most conspicuous, as it was always the saddest element in the old pagan society. In the view of antiquity the slave was but an "animated instrument;" a mere body which chanced to be endowed with certain mental capacities. There was at Athens, says Hesychius, an enclosure where they sold σκεύη καὶ σώματα—utensils and bodies. In the eye of the law the slave was not a person; he was classed by the jurists with goods or with animals. He was sold; he was bequeathed by will; he was lent to a friend; he was shut up; and until later ages he was killed at the discretion of his owner. He had no rights whatever before the law; "servile caput nullum jus habet;" so said the lawyers. Cato advised an economical householder to sell off his old cattle and his sick slaves. Pliny speaks of the slaves as a class of men who were habitually desperate. Seneca, writing on the tranquillity of the soul, mournfully reflects that he must avail himself of the services of persons who are miserable and who cannot endure him; "flentium detestantiumque ministeriis utendum est." [1] And the best word of counsel which the Stoic philosophy could give to inquiring despair was suicide. "Wherever," says Seneca, writing to a person about court in a servile and degraded position—"wherever you turn your eyes, you see the possible end of your sufferings. Here is a precipice; you may descend it to liberty. There is the sea, a river, a well; freedom is at the bottom. Yonder is a tree; liberty hangs from its branches. Here is your throat or your heart; pierce them and you are free. Are such deaths as these too painful; do they demand too much of your strength and resolution? Would you travel towards liberty by an easier path? Then every vein in your body may open the way to it." [2]

The slave of Jesus Christ! Yes; it was in the Greek as well as in the Hebrew sense of the term that St. Paul would describe his relationship to the Divine Redeemer. He was not simply a servant holding an honourable post in the Kingdom of Heaven, which he might relinquish at pleasure: he was a slave. And in this abandonment of all human liberty at the feet of Jesus Christ; in this utter surrender of the right to dispose of his intelligence, of his affections, of his employment of time and property, of his movements from place to place, except as his Master might command, St. Paul found the true dignity and the true happiness of his being. His sense of justice was satisfied by this as by no other relationship to Jesus Christ. For him our Divine Saviour was not merely a sinless and incomparable Person, Whom it was a pleasure

[1] *De Tranquillitate Animi*, c. 9.   [2] Senec. Cons. *ad Marciam*, 20.

and an honour to approach and to obey; the relations between them were more urgent and exacting. St. Paul was already a moral slave when Jesus Christ found him, subject to the power of sin and death; and out of this slavery he too had been bought by the ransom paid for all the world upon the Cross of Calvary. Of the three aspects under which the Atonement is presented to us in his epistles, as a propitiation for sin,[1] a reconciliation with God,[2] and a redemption from captivity to evil and to death,[3] it is the last which sinks most deeply into the heart of the Apostle, and which shapes most decisively the features of his life. He belonged to Jesus Christ, not by any original or voluntary act of his own, but because, as he could not but acknowledge, Jesus Christ had paid for him. Jesus had bought him at an incalculable cost out of a slavery which was misery and degradation, into a service which, whatever its outward aspects, he knew to be freedom indeed. As he said to his own children in the faith, "Ye are bought with a price; become not the slaves of men;"[4] "Ye are bought with a price, therefore glorify God in your body and in your spirit, which are God's;"[5] so, for himself, he exultingly counted the scars which he had received at the hands of pagan persecutors as so many "marks" of the Lord Jesus which he was privileged to bear in his body; just as the slaves in the Roman workhouses were branded with a hot iron that there might be no legal questions about their ownership.[6] Not for all the world would he have had it otherwise: not for all the liberties that man could conceivably enjoy apart from Christ, would he surrender the privilege of complete enslavement in thought and conduct to This Most Gracious and Best

---

[1] Rom. iii. 25.   [2] 2 Cor. v. 19. Rom. v. 10.
[3] Gal. iii. 13.   [4] 1 Cor. vii. 23.   [5] 1 Cor. vi. 20.
[6] Gal. vi. 17, τὰ στίγματα τοῦ Κυρίου Ἰησοῦ ἐν τῷ σώματί μου βαστάζω.

of masters.[1] "The love of Christ constraineth us," he said: "because we thus judge, that if He died for all, then were all dead: and that He died for all, that they which live should not henceforth live unto themselves, but unto Him Which died for them, and rose again."[2]

II.

The dignity of service, like the dignity of labour, is a moral fact which the world is slow to understand. To us of this generation it is obscured or rather banished from sight by an obtrusive counter-ideal; need I name the supposed dignity of independence or of self-dependence? Here, as elsewhere, our theories of religious relations have been shaped, and not for the better, by the disturbing influence of political ideas. We have never traced, or we have forgotten, the real origin of our habits of thought; and we ascribe them to Revelation, much as country-people search their Bibles for oft-quoted texts which have, in reality, quite another and a very homely origin. Doubtless, if we look only to the creatures around and below us, we may for a moment suppose that we are meant not to serve but to command. Compared with them, we cannot but recognise in ourselves the possession of powers which ensure superiority. They may, indeed, excel us in swiftness, in strength, in keenness of ear or of eye, in far-reaching and varied subtlety of instinct; but there is that in man before which they fall back and quail as before a higher power. Man is a spirit, conscious of its existence, capable of reflecting on it, of measuring it, and of forming an estimate of all around it. And thus God has "made man to have dominion over the work of His hands, and has put all things in subjection under his feet; all sheep and oxen, yea, and the beasts of the

[1] Phil. iii. 8.   [2] 2 Cor. v. 14, 15.

field; the fowls of the air, and the fishes of the sea, and whatsoever walketh in the paths of the sea."[1] Among the lower creatures man is made for command; and he has had some thousands of years in which to strengthen and extend his empire. But does it therefore follow that there is none above man to whom he stands in a relation somewhat analogous to that in which the lower animals stand towards himself? Is he to suppose that the hierarchy of beings which rises by such gradual steps from the lowest zoophyte to the race of Newton and Shakespeare does in very truth rise no higher; that it stops abruptly at the link which he himself forms, between an animal organism and a personal spirit? Is it not more reasonable to suppose that the upward series continues, and that above man there are beings stretching, in rank beyond rank of ascending excellence, upwards towards the throne of the Uncreated and the Eternal? And supposing such beings to exist, as Revelation says they do exist, is it not at least conceivable that they do in sundry ways limit our independence, just as we, on our part, interfere with that of creatures below us? Say, if you will, that this is only a speculation; but what is to be said of man's relations to that Being of beings Who is separated from the highest archangel by a measureless interval? Is it possible that, face to face with God, man can claim to be independent or self-dependent? We owe, each of us, to God the original gift of existence. We owe to God the continuance of this gift, moment by moment, as we exist. When He thinks well, and at a moment which He has already determined, our present existence will end; and it will end in some manner which He has willed, and of which we know nothing. Independence in the sense contemplated is an impossible theory of life for any man who believes seriously in the existence of a Supreme Being.

[1] Ps. viii. 6-8.

And therefore service is the true law, the true dignity of man's existence. Service is written everywhere, for those who have eyes to see, on the face of creation. The service of unconscious law; the service of sentient life; the service of rational and free beings; the service of the splendid and illuminated intelligences around the Throne, —these are the steps in the ascent. But between the purely material bodies to which God has given a law that it should not be broken, and those majestic and spiritual ministers of His who do His pleasure in the highest realms of created life, there is the bond of this universal and constraining law, which holds all created things in subjection to the Will of the Great Creator. The same witness is borne by the faculties of the soul of man. Man is free; but he can only preserve his true freedom by a voluntary service. His reason, his affections, his will cannot dispose of themselves capriciously with entire impunity. Truth, beauty, goodness, these are the objects of their rightful service; and what are these but aspects of the Eternal God? Believe that all truth is unattainable; and the ruin of the understanding is only a question of time. Treat moral beauty as a mere fancy; and the degradation of the affections must quickly follow. Decide that right and wrong are only phases of human feeling; and the unnerved will must ere long forfeit all that gives it directness and strength. It is only in the service of high ideals that the soul of man can attain its excellence; and when these are renounced, man does not escape from service, he only changes masters, and that for the worse. He falls back under the empire of sense or of nature, and he finds in the depths of his degradation the justification of the law against which he has rebelled.

Nay more, all the apparent superiorities among men are really forms of service. What is government but service, not indeed of the follies and passions, but of the true interests of the people? The highest in rank knows that he consults his real dignity most effectively when he professes himself the obedient humble servant of a rival or an inferior. The head of a great hierarchy, in whom its power is absolutely centred, appears before the Christian world on occasions of critical solemnity as Servant of the servants of God. Whatever inconsistencies may be involved in the use of such conventional language, it is an act of homage to a truth which no man with an eye for moral beauty will dispute; it proclaims that service, so far from involving degradation, is an ornament of human nature, a true patent of nobility. For Christians, indeed, this greatness of service is beyond discussion. He Whom we worship and love, as the Prince and Flower of our race, has, by His words and His example, set the seal of His high approval on this distinctive excellence of man. He, the Object of our service, is also its Model. He has taught us, by a parable for all time, how to serve Himself in the service of others. The form, indeed, which at His Incarnation He took on Him was the form of a servant. The life which He lived on earth was a life of service. Again and again He verified His own words; He was among men as One that serveth, but never more markedly than on the solemn evening which He passed with His disciples before He died. Note how the Evangelist who describes the scene contrasts the high and ever-present consciousness of a superhuman greatness with the lowly bearing of the Servant of men. "Jesus, knowing that the Father had given all things into His hands, and that He was come from God, and went to God; He riseth from supper, and laid aside His garments; and took a towel, and girded Himself. After that He poureth water into a bason, and began to wash the disciples' feet, and to wipe them with the towel wherewith He was girded."[1]

[1] St. John xiii. 3-5.

III.

There are many hindrances to this service. The Apostle notes one. "If I yet pleased men, I should not be the servant of Christ."

St. Paul is distinguishing between giving men satisfaction and doing them essential good; between action which is popular and action which is wise and conscientious. He is probably thinking of such words of our Lord as that "no man can serve two masters;"[1] and that the man of whom all speak well on earth is very far indeed from being entitled to the congratulations of heaven.[2] St. Paul had known what it was to "please men," and to succeed by doing so. He had enjoyed great consideration among all classes in Jerusalem; and he may have reconciled himself with some difficulty to the realities of his new life. A man of his strong affections and simple purpose might have hoped to live down opposition, to reconcile to himself even the fiercest prejudices, to combine some measure of toleration and approval on the part of his old friends, with loyalty to the creed of his conversion. To a character so sympathetic, so sensitive as his, it would have been painful in no ordinary degree to have to acquiesce in the conviction, that if he was to do his duty, he must incur the permanent enmity of large bodies of his fellow-men. Yet already, when he wrote his first Epistle to the Thessalonians, he had learned this truth; he had preached the Gospel to them with much contention,[3] and "not as pleasing men, but God, Which trieth our hearts."[4] And in both his Corinthian letters we see how entirely he takes it for granted that the servant of Christ in the Apostolate will not be an object of general goodwill, but of much bitter calumny and suspicion; he must approve himself a minister of God in much patience;

---

[1] St. Matt. vi. 24.
[2] St. Luke vi. 26.
[3] 1 Thess. ii. 2.
[4] 1 Thess. ii. 4.

he is to make his way by evil report and good report; he is to pass as a deceiver, and yet be true;[1] he is "in stripes above measure," "in prisons more frequent" than others.[2] It seems to him, he says, that "God has set forth the Apostles last, as it were appointed unto death; for they are made a spectacle to the world, and to angels, and to men; they are fools for Christ's sake, . . . they are weak, . . . they are despised, . . . they are made as the filth of the world, and are the offscouring of all things unto this day."[3]

It was his own doing after all; had he so chosen it might have been otherwise. He might have kept on good terms with that powerful Jewish society in which he was brought up, and in which he had excellent connections— that Jewish society then, as ever, so wealthy, so widespread, so shrewd and practical, so familiar with all that commands political influence and personal self-advancement, so able to bestow prosperity on talent that is loyal to it, and that can help it in turn. He might have succeeded Gamaliel as President of the Sanhedrin, to enjoy Hillel's reputation for mild wisdom, or to be the subject of mysterious traditions such as those which surround Jochanan ben Zaccai, or to become a fierce politician like Rabbi Akiba, with happier results it may be to his country and himself; he might even have attained an earthly immortality, such as could have been conferred by some honourable association with the wisdom and the follies of the Talmud. Even after that memorable occurrence on the road to Damascus all was not forfeited; a return to the Synagogue was more than possible. Could he only have consented to treat his conversion as an impression unaccountably created by a thunderstorm, as a psychological illusion, or as a trick of the evil one; could he only have once more cursed the Crucified Nazarene, and undertaken the work of officially persecuting His worshippers, everything might have been his, in the way of

[1] 2 Cor. vi. 4, 8.   [2] 2 Cor. xi. 23.   [3] 1 Cor. iv. 9-13.

wealth, respect, influence. He would have escaped the hatred of an entire people; a hatred, deadly, implacable; a hatred which would dog his steps from city to city, which never would rest till it had punished his apostasy as such an apostate deserved. He might have escaped the stripes, the plots, the stonings, the prisons which awaited him at Cæsarea, and at Rome; but then, "had he pleased men, he would not have been the servant of Christ."

He had broken with the Synagogue; but he had a second chance in life; he was already, by his education at Tarsus, half a Greek. The life and culture of the Greek world, its political ideas, its public amusements, its popular literature, its modes of thought, were far from unfamiliar to him. Settled at Alexandria, or wherever contact with Greek civilization was most natural and easy, he might have platonized what remained of his early modes of thinking, and have passed with distinction into the intellectual and social life of the Græco-Roman society. But then Greek opinion was fastidious, and to keep on good terms with it required caution and flexibility. Had Paul sought to please the Greeks, he would not have provoked their cultivated levities by any such doctrine as that of the Cross; he would not have opposed to the vague spiritualism of their better philosophy his own unalterable faith in Christ's literal resurrection from the dead; he would not have roused their jealousies of race by an ostentatious zeal for the very countrymen who were even then seeking to take his life. If he had really "pleased men" generally at Athens or at Corinth, he would have ceased to be a servant of Christ.

Certainly it was strange that the Galatian leaders did not know the man with whom they had to deal. They probably fell into the common mistake of confusing courtesy with weakness, and indifference to what is accidental with a compromise of principle. They thought that the Apostle, who to the Jews could become as a Jew that he might save the Jews,[1] would become a Judaizer with the Judaizers that he might be popular with the Judaizers. They knew that he could be made all things to all men,[2] but they forgot that it was upon the condition of serving Christ by saving some of those for whom He died.

IV.

Under what form does this temptation to please men at the cost of a higher sense of duty especially present itself to ourselves?

When, in the early years of manhood, we first try to take the measure of the world in which Providence has placed us, nothing is more calculated to arrest our attention than that most energetic of all abstractions, public opinion. Public opinion is that common stock of thought and sentiment which is created by human society, or by a particular section of it, and which in turn keeps its authors under strict control. It is a natural product; it is a deposit which cannot but result from human intercourse; no sooner do men associate with one another than a public opinion of some kind comes to be. And as civilization advances, and man multiplies the channels whereby he ascertains and governs the thoughts of his fellow-man, public opinion grows in its strength and in its area; and men voluntarily, or rather instinctively, abandon an increasing district of their understandings and of their conduct to its undisputed control. It varies, in definiteness and in exigency, with the number of human beings which it happens to represent: there is a public opinion proper to each village or town, to each society or profession, to a country, to a civilization, to the world; but between the most general and the narrowest forms of this

---

[1] 1 Cor. ix. 20.   [2] 1 Cor. ix. 22.

common body of thought and sentiment there are bands and joints which weld the whole into substantial unity.

And in modern times public opinion has taken a concrete body and form, such as two centuries ago was undreamt of; it lives and works in the daily press. In the press we see, visibly embodied, this empire of opinion, with its countless varieties and subdivisions, and its strong corporate spirit and substantial unity. We all live face to face with the press; and every man who hopes, I will not say to do much good to his fellow-men, but to keep his own conscience in moderately good order, knows that in this servant of public opinion he encounters a force with which, sooner or later, on a large scale or a small, before the world or in the recesses of his own conscience, he may have to reckon; whether, like St. Paul, he bears a commission from heaven, or whether he only endeavours to be loyal to such truth as he knows of, chiefly or altogether concerning the things of earth.

What is the duty of a Christian towards this ubiquitous and penetrating agency? Is he to ignore or despise it, in the spirit of some Stoic of the earlier school? Assuredly not. St. Paul was respectful even towards heathen opinion; he bids Christians do nothing recklessly to forfeit its favourable judgment;[1] he shapes his phrases, not seldom, as would a man who is guided by this instinctive deference. For, always and everywhere, public opinion must needs contain certain, perhaps considerable, elements of truth. Those great moral ideas of righteousness and retribution, which are to human conduct what its axioms are to mathematical science, and which have their attestation or their echo in the depths of every human soul, do, more or less, enter as ingredients into all forms of public opinion; they secure to it a claim on respectful attention; they preserve it from the rapid

Col. iv. 5.   1 Thess. iv. 12.   1 Tim. iii. 7.

disintegration which, without them, could not but overtake it. They may be grossly misapplied, or associated with wild profanity and folly; but they forbid us to treat any public opinion as wholly worthless or erroneous; they secure to it an element which is certainly from above, and which may partly shape the baser material in which it is imbedded.

Are we then to place ourselves trustfully in its hands, to defer to, and to obey it, at least in a Christian country, and in an age of enlightenment and progress? Is it to furnish us, in the last resort, with a rule of conduct or with our standards of moral and religious truth?

Again, assuredly not. For consider how this public opinion is formed: it is practically the result of a general subscription; it is the workmanship of all the human beings who go to make up society or a section of society. Certainly the wise, the experienced, the conscientious, the disinterested, contribute towards it, each in proportion to his weight and influence. But as certainly, also, the reckless, the unprincipled, the foolish, the selfish, have their share in producing it; a larger share, the world being what it is, than their nobler rivals. In public opinion power often counts for more than character; Nero could shape opinion at Rome more effectively than Seneca. Genius which holds itself bound by moral considerations is often less influential, at least for a time, than genius which mocks jauntily at the simple distinctions between right and wrong. Public opinion is, in point of fact, a conglomerate; it is a compromise between the many elements which go to make up human society, a compromise in which all are represented, but in which, upon the whole, the lower and selfish elements of thought and feeling are apt to preponderate. And therefore, while it is always a matter of high interest to ascertain what is the verdict of public opinion on a given question, both because it represents so much, and because it can do so much, this verdict will never be received by Christians as an absolute guide to truth, though it may well be a subject for respectful attention.

The same conclusion is suggested by a consideration of the vicissitudes to which public opinion is liable. It is liable to the action of disturbing causes, which betray it, upon occasions, into wild inconsistencies with itself. The panic produced by an unforeseen catastrophe, the fascination exerted by a brilliant writer or speaker, the apparent coincidence between some suspicion entertained by a long-cherished, perhaps unexamined prejudice and some trivial discovery or occurrence;—these things will sometimes rouse into desperate energy some one element of passion latent in the vast body of general opinion, so that it breaks with all that has hitherto restrained and balanced it, and precipitates a society upon some course of conduct altogether at variance with its better antecedents. And this liability of powerful sections of opinion to suffer from the disturbing effects of panic, must needs unfit them for the duties of guides in matters of religious and moral truth. In truth, common opinion is too wanting in patience, in penetration, in delicacy of moral touch and apprehension, to deal successfully, or otherwise than blunderingly and coarsely, with questions like these. It cannot be right to cry

"Hosanna!" now, to-morrow "Crucify!"[1]

to applaud in Galilee that which is condemned in Jerusalem; to sanction in this generation much which was denounced in that; to "adore what you have burned, and to burn what you have adored," with conspicuous versatility; merely because a large body of human beings —the majority of whom, it may be, are quite without particular information on the subject—love to have it so. To

[1] *The Christian Year*, Advent Sunday.

attempt to please men in this sense is most assuredly incompatible with the service of Christ.

Whatever evils were bound up with the old order of things in France, every generation reads with fresh interest the tragic story of the fate of the Monarchy; and the unfortunate king, confined with his family in the prison of the Temple, and exposed to the coarse insults of his fanatical enemies, extorts a tribute of sympathy, and of admiration which is independent of any political convictions. But with that group of high-born sufferers there is another figure upon whom, as it seems to me, a Christian moralist must bestow something more than a passing thought. The devoted servant who had waited on his sovereign in the old days of feudal splendour, found his way, at the risk of his life, to the tower in which the royal family was confined, and remained to the end, only narrowly escaping his master's fate. He has left us a diary of three weeks of suffering; a simple unaffected narrative, without pretensions to literary finish, and in the pages of which it is impossible to trace any thought of winning glory for himself.[1] Yet, as we follow it, we find our interest divided between the royal prisoners and their faithful attendant, whose conduct, had he feared or courted the opinion of Revolutionary Paris, would never have illustrated so persuasively, because so undesignedly, the moral glory of a generous service. For some of us it may be impossible to read his pages without a sense of self-reproach, which the thought of a Master Who has none of the weakness of Louis XVI., and Who has often to encounter among those whom He would save a more enduring and implacable hostility, may, alas! too well suggest.

[1] Journal de ce qui s'est passé à la tour du Temple pendant la captivité de Louis XVI., Roi de France. Par M. Cléry, valet de chambre du roi. A Londres, 1798.

Doubtless it may be more difficult to avoid renunciation of Christ's service when importuned by intimate and trusted friends than when pressed by a strong public opinion. Those whom we have always known, and with whom we wish to stand well, have an undoubted title to influence our thoughts and conduct; and yet it is possible that they too may one day ask us to sacrifice our sense of moral right or of religious truth to the claims of party or to the claims of friendship. They may be moving into regions of conviction where we cannot follow them; or they may refuse to accompany us when our sense of what is right and true obliges us to go forward. And then there is an inward struggle, or perhaps a "parting of friends," which leaves heartaches for life, but which is inevitable if there is not to be a violence to conscience. To men of affectionate tempers these are among the very sternest trials in our whole probation: to prefer the friendship of truth to that of Plato makes a greater demand on a generous nature than any choice between loyalty to duty and physical pain. But a Christian is governed by a revelation of truth which sets him above the claims of friendship and the exigencies of opinion; there are times when in this sense too " he that is spiritual judgeth all things, yet he himself is judged of no man."[1] He will not, indeed, break with either one or the other lightly or wantonly; he will look once and again to be sure that he is not himself deceived, if not in his principle, yet in its application. But when this point is once clear, he will resolutely go forward. There is no improving on the old adage, "Quodcunque agis, respice finem." Look to the end; look onward to those last hours of sunlight and of responsibility, when life will be sensibly ebbing away, and another world almost breaking upon the view. In hours such as those men live, they say, quickly; a life is compressed into minutes, into sentences. The mists which

[1] 1 Cor. ii. 15.

had hung about questions of duty then roll away, and, like other things, public opinion is stripped of any fictitious value which may once have clung to it, and is resolved into its real ingredients. "The loftiness of man shall be bowed down, and the haughtiness of men shall be made low, and the Lord alone shall be exalted in that day."[1] To plant our feet upon the Rock; to give to Him Who is the Eternal and the True the best homage of heart and mind and purpose will surely be the effort—it may be a feeble or a failing effort—of a time like that. "Quodcunque agis, respice finem." Look to the end; and resolve to make the service of Christ the first object in what remains of life, without indifference to the opinion of your fellow-men, but also without fear of it.

[1] Isa. ii. 17.

SERMON IX.

CHRIST IN THE STORM.

St. Mark iv. 38.

And He was in the hinder part of the ship, asleep on a pillow: and they awake Him, and say unto Him, Master, carest Thou not that we perish?

THE event here referred to must have occurred in the late evening of the day on which our Lord pronounced the series of Parables of the Kingdom of Heaven.[1] The multitudes lingered round Him; and He determined to cross to the Peræan side of the Sea of Tiberias. The passage was only in part accomplished, when one of these sudden and dangerous squalls to which inland seas in mountainous districts are exposed swept across the waters. The ship which carried our Lord and His disciples was in the utmost peril. "The waves," says St. Mark, "beat into the ship, so that it was now full."[2] It was not the excited imagination of landsmen, but the common sense of hardy and experienced fishermen, which told the disciples of their danger. They already knew enough of their Master's power to seek His help; but, while they were expecting instant death, He "was in the hinder part of the ship, asleep on a pillow."[3] We feel a solemn irony in this contrast between the majesty of His unruffled repose, and the wild confusion, alarm, agony,

---

[1] St. Matt. xiii. 3-50. St. Mark iv. 2-34.   [2] St. Mark iv. 37.
[3] St. Mark iv. 38.

which prevailed around Him; and the disciples cannot have felt it less than we. But if they gazed at Him for a moment in hesitating wonder, their anguish was too strong for a silent reverence. They broke in upon His rest with cries of terror; "Master, Master, we perish;"[1] "Lord, save us: we perish;"[2] even with the half-reproachful "Master, carest Thou not that we perish?"[3] Then He arose and "rebuked" the winds and the sea; as if to imply that disorder in the material world may sometimes be due to the malignant will of a personal agent. Yet to Him the raging waters were of far less concern than the state of the souls around Him; so He proceeded to notice in sterner terms the want of faith in Himself, of which His disciples had just given proof. "Why are ye so fearful? how is it that ye have no faith?"[4]

Undoubtedly their cry of agony had a double aspect. It was, on the one hand, an act of faith in our Lord's Power: they would not have roused Him, at least in such terms, had they deemed Him as resourceless as themselves. But, on the other hand, their appeal to Him was an act of impatience, and of that particular kind of impatience which implies that ordinary grounds of confidence are giving way, that faith is dashed by some serious hesitations. To have trusted Him perfectly would have been to have been silent. Silence would have meant a conviction that all would yet be well, let the winds roar and the waves toss as they might, while He, the Lord of the waves and the winds, slept on upon a pillow in the hinder part of the ship.

I.

It is natural to compare this miracle with others which define our Lord's relation to the physical universe, and to

---

[1] St. Luke viii. 24.
[2] St. Matt. viii. 25.
[3] St. Mark iv. 38.
[4] St. Mark iv. 40.

examine the estimate of His Person which such a relation necessarily suggests. But there is another line of thought which we may follow to-day. Is this narrative only an appropriate incident in a Life which so wonderfully blends the miraculous and the moral? Has it no permanent significance? no wider bearing upon the history of Christendom? upon the vicissitudes of the Church? upon the trials of the soul?

Now, to answer this question as it would have been answered by all the exegetical schools of ancient Christendom; by literalists as well as by allegorizers and mystics; by Antioch as well as by Alexandria; by St. Chrysostom and Theodoret, no less than by Basil, Ambrose, and the Gregories, is to incur, on the very threshold, the charge of fancifulness. In this application of an event of our Lord's life to the subsequent history of His Kingdom a particular class of minds can see nothing but the levity of an untrained imagination. "Why," they ask, "should there be any discoverable relation whatever, such as is here presumed, between an event in the life of Christ, and events which can only bear to it a distant, if any, analogy, in the Christian history of after ages? No one has perceived an occult reference to the later history of the Cæsars, in the conquest of Vercingetorix, or in the invasion of Britain, or in the passage of the Rubicon, or in the first triumvirate. No writers, not even the Platonic and Stoic allegorizers of the Greek mythology, have supposed the vicissitudes of a philosophical school to be anticipated, however indistinctly, in this or that incident of its founder's life: and it is difficult to see why the Author of Christianity should be held to stand in so unique a relation to Christendom, which thus invests the incidents of His earthly career with a quasi-prophetical character."

There is a valuable warning implied in this objection. As with Origen, so in some modern methods of interpretation, the reality of the literal narrative may be denied or forgotten in an allegorizing treatment. And, to take instances when this is far from being the case, no one, probably, would now indulge in the exuberant mysticism of the school of the St. Victors, or even, *pace tantorum nominum*, of some greater and older writers, such as the author of the Magna Moralia on Job. But with principles of interpretation, as in other matters, it is true that *usum non tollit abusus*. In the present case we have to consider, first, that the very scene was, to a mind trained in the school of the Old Testament, full of moral meaning. In the Hebrew Scriptures, as in the apprehension of the early Christian Church, nature is treated as a sacrament of the moral world; it is the outward sign of truths which altogether transcend itself. Its various moods of calm and storm answer to the varying movements of the soul or to the incidents of history. Secondly, to an Eastern apprehension our Lord's action would have been, naturally and as a matter of course, pregnant with significance. To the Eastern mind action is ever eloquent; in the East action is language in a degree unknown to us of the West. The solemn prophetical actions of Isaiah, Hosea, and others recognise and illustrate the Oriental way of looking at such subjects; and our Lord addressed Himself to it in more than one of His miracles, by gestures which were, we may venture reverently to say, unnecessary to the execution of His purpose, but full of meaning for the lookers-on. In ancient Palestine the acts of the Prophet of Nazareth would have had, and would have been designed to carry, a meaning beyond themselves; and when He rose in the boat to rebuke the elements on the Sea of Galilee, He was proclaiming His power over elements of another order in distant scenes, and in centuries yet to come.

But, undoubtedly, the question whether our Lord's act

has this kind of significance will be chiefly determined by our belief about His Person. If, while admiring some moral elements in His teaching, and the literature which embodies it, we yet think of Him as only one of the race of men who appeared eighteen centuries ago, and who has passed away, it may be, into a world of conscious shades, or into torpor, or into annihilation; then, indeed, it would be absurd to endeavour to extract from this narrative any typical relation to history. We do not suppose that John Howard continues from his place in the eternal world to further, by some energetic pressure or interference, that noble work of benevolence for which many a generation will honour and bless his name; for we do not ascribe to him any such relation, whether towards that world or this, as would enable him to mould events here below. But if, looking to the evidence of Christ's Resurrection from the dead, to the general effect of His miracles, to the unique outline of His character, to the attitude which He instinctively assumed in dealing with others, above all to His constant language about Himself, we cannot but form a very different idea about His present relation to the world from that which we assign to any other of the sons of men; if we believe that His announcement of a day on which He would judge the world was warrantable, that His Promise of His Presence with His followers to the end of time was not a misleading and empty consolation, and that this Presence was to be, not, as Mahomet's might have been, a presence in memory, but an actual nearness and encompassing of His personal Being, whether it were felt by His Church or not: if, in short, we believe Him to be what His first followers believed, the Eternal Son of God, Who rules men and events with an arm of power; then it is not any wantonness of fancy which sees in His earthly actions the models and presentiments of His later providences. If we truly hold that He is now what He was then; that He is consistent with Himself from age to age; that He means us to learn from what we read about Him then something of that which He is actually now; then we may reverently connect the incidents of a day in His earthly life with the turning-points of Christian history, and the fortunes of a ship's company with that of a divinely-organized society, and deliverance from physical dangers with deliverance from evils which may assault and hurt the soul.

II.

It is, then, no freak of fancy to see in this narrative an acted parable, if you will, an acted prophecy. Again and again the Church of Christ has been all but engulfed, as men might have deemed, in the billows; again and again the storm has been calmed by the Master, Who had seemed for awhile to sleep. Often has Christianity passed through the troubled waters of political opposition. During the first three centuries, and finally under Julian, the heathen state made repeated and desperate attempts to suppress it by force. Statesmen and philosophers undertook the task of eradicating it, not passionately, but in the same temper of calm resolution with which they would have approached any other well-considered social problem. More than once they drove it from the army, from the professions, from the public thoroughfares, into secrecy; they pursued it into the vaults beneath the palaces of Rome, into the catacombs, into the deserts. It seemed as if the faith would be trodden out with the life of so many of the faithful: but he who would persecute with effect must leave none alive. The Church passed through these fearful storms into the calm of an ascertained supremacy; but she had scarcely done so, when the vast political and social system which had so long oppressed her, and which by her persistent suffering she had at length made in some sense her own, itself began to break up beneath and around her. The barbarian invasions followed one upon another with merciless rapidity; and St. Augustine's lamentations upon the sack of Rome express the feelings with which the higher minds in the Church must have beheld the completed humiliation of the Empire. Christianity had now to face, not merely a change of civil rulers, but a fundamental reconstruction of society. It might have been predicted with great appearance of probability that a religious system which had suited the enervated provincials of the decaying Empire would never make its way among the free and strong races that, amid scenes of fire and blood, were laying the foundations of feudalism. In the event it was otherwise. The hordes which shattered the work of the Cæsars learnt to repeat the Catholic Creed, and a new order of things had formed itself, when the tempest of Mahommedanism broke upon Christendom. Politically speaking, this was perhaps the most threatening storm through which the Christian Church has passed. There was a time when the soldiers of that stunted and immoral caricature of the Revelation of the One True God, which was set forth by the false prophet, had already expelled the very Name of Christ from the country of Cyprian and Augustine; they were masters of the Mediterranean; they had desolated Spain, were encamped in the heart of France, were ravaging the seaboard of Italy. It was as if the knell of Christendom had sounded. But Christ, "if asleep on a pillow in the hinder part of the ship," was not insensible to the terrors of His servants. He rose to rebuke those winds and waves, as by Charles Martel in one age, and by Sobieski in another; it is now more than two centuries since Islam inspired its ancient dread. The last like trial of the Church was the first French Revolution. In that vast convulsion Christianity had to encounter forces which for awhile seemed to threaten its total suppression. Yet the men of the Terror have passed, as the Cæsars had passed before them; and like the Cæsars, they have only proved to the world that the Church carries within her One Who rules the fierce tempests in which human institutions are wont to perish.

Political dangers, however, do but touch the Church of Christ outwardly; but she rests upon the intelligent assent of her children, and she has passed again and again through the storms of intellectual opposition or revolt. Scarcely had she steered forth from the comparatively still waters of Galilean and Hellenistic devotion than she had to encounter the pitiless dialectic, the subtle solvents, of the Alexandrian philosophy. It was as if in anticipation of this danger that St. John had already baptized the Alexandrian modification of the Platonic Logos, moulding it so as to express the sublimest and most central truth of the Christian Creed; while, in the Epistle to the Hebrews, Alexandrian methods of interpretation had been adopted in vindication of the Gospel. But to many a timid believer it may well have seemed that Alexandrianism would prove the grave of Christianity, when, combining the Platonic dialectics with an Eclectic Philosophy, it endeavoured in the form of Arianism to break up the Unity of the Godhead by making Christ a separate and inferior Deity. There was a day when Arianism seemed to be triumphant; but even Arianism was a less formidable foe than the subtle strain of infidel speculation which penetrated the Christian intellect in the very heart of the Middle Ages, that is to say, at a time when the sense of the supernatural had diffused itself throughout the whole atmosphere of human thought. This unbelief was the product sometimes of a rude sensuality rebelling against the precepts of the Gospel; sometimes of the culture divorced from faith which made its appearance in the twelfth century; sometimes, specifically, of the influence of the Arabian philosophy from Spain; sometimes of the vast and penetrating activity of the Jewish teachers. It revealed itself constantly under the most unexpected circumstances. We need not suppose that the great Order of the Templars was guilty of the infidelity that, along with crimes of the gravest character, was laid to their charge; a study of their processes is their best acquittal, while it is the condemnation of their persecutors. But unbelief must have been widespread in days when a prominent soldier, John of Soissons, could declare that "all that was preached concerning Christ's Passion and Resurrection was a mere farce;"[1] when a pious Bishop of Paris left it on record that he "died believing in the Resurrection, with the hope that some of his educated but sceptical friends would reconsider their doubts;"[2] when that keen observer, as Neander terms him, Hugh of St. Victor, remarks the existence of a large class of men whose faith consisted in nothing else than merely taking care not to contradict the faith—" quibus credere est solum fidei non contradicere, qui consuetudine vivendi magis, quam virtute credendi fideles nominantur."[3] The prevalence of such unbelief is attested at once by the fundamental nature of many of the questions discussed at the greatest length by the Schoolmen, and by the unconcealed anxieties of the great spiritual leaders of the time.[4] After the Middle Ages came the Renaissance. This is not the time or place to deny the services which the Renaissance has rendered to the cause of human education,

[1] So Guib. Abb. *De Vitâ suâ*, iii. 15, quoted by Neander, *Ch. Hist.* v p. 451.
[2] In 1198; cf. Rigord, *de gestis Philippi*, quoted by Neander, ub. sup. p. 432.
[3] *De Sacr. fidei*, lib. i. c. 4, quoted by Neander, p. 454.
[4] The Abbot Peter of Cluny composed a tract to prove that Christ bore witness to His own divinity, in order to meet the doubts of some of his monks.

and indirectly, it may be, to that of Christianity. But the Renaissance was at first, as it appeared in Italy, a pure enthusiasm for Paganism, for Pagan thought, as well as for Pagan art and Pagan literature. And the Reformation, viewed on its positive and devotional side, was, at least in the South of Europe, a reaction against the spirit of the Renaissance: it was the Paganism, even more than the indulgences of Leo X., which alienated the Germans. The reaction against this Paganism was not less vigorous within the Church of Rome than without it; Ranke has told us the story of its disappearance.[1] Lastly, there was the rise of Deism in England, and of the Encyclopedist School in France, followed by the pure Atheism which preceded the Revolution. It might well have seemed to fearful men of that day that Christ was indeed asleep to wake no more, that the surging waters of an infidel philosophy had well-nigh filled the ship, and that the Church had only to sink with dignity.

Worse than the storms of political violence or of intellectual rebellion, have been the tempests of insurgent immorality through which the Church has passed. In the ages of persecution there was less risk of this, although even then there were scandals. The Epistles to the Corinthians reveal beneath the very eyes of the Apostle a state of moral corruption, which, in one respect at least, he himself tells us, had fallen below the pagan standard.[2] But when entire populations pressed within the fold, and social or political motives for conformity took the place of serious and strong conviction in the minds of multitudes, these dangers became formidable. What must have been the agony of devout Christians in the tenth century, when appointments to the Roman Chair itself were in the hands of three unprincipled and licentious women;[3] and when the

---

[1] *Hist. of Popes*, vol. i. [2] 1 Cor. v. 1. 2 Cor. vii. 8-11.
[3] Möhler, *Kirchengeschichte*, ii. p. 183.

life of the first Christian Bishop was accounted such that a pilgrimage to Rome involved a loss of character. Well might the austere Bruno exclaim of that age that "Simon Magus lorded it over a Church in which bishops and priests were given to luxury and fornication;". Well might Cardinal Baronius suspend the generally laudatory or apologetic tone of his Annals, to observe that Christ must have in this age been asleep in the ship of the Church to permit such enormities.[1]

It was a dark time in the moral life of Christendom: but there have been dark times since. Such was that when St. Bernard could allow himself to describe the Roman Curia as he does in addressing Pope Eugenius III.; such again was the epoch which provoked the work of Nicholas de Cleargis, "On the Ruin of the Church." The passions, the ambitions, the worldly and political interests which surged around the Papal Throne, had at length issued in the schism of Avignon; and the writer passionately exclaims that the Church had fallen proportionately to her corruptions, which he enumerates with an unsparing precision.[2] During the century which preceded the Reformation, the state of clerical discipline in London was

---

[1] Möhler has endeavoured, but not very convincingly, to minimize the stern judgment of Baronius.—*K. G.* ii. pp. 186-191.

[2] To this may be added the remarkable report on abuses in the Roman Church which was drawn up and published by order of Pope Paul III.; Consilium delectorum Cardinalium et aliorum Prælatorum de emendandâ ecclesiâ, S.D.N.D. Paulo III. ipso jubente conscriptum et exhibitum, 1537. Among the nine signataries are Cardinals Pole, Contarini, and Caraffa. They trace the evils of the Church to the fact "quod nonnulli Pontifices tui prædecessores prurientes auribus, ut inquit Apostolus Paulus, coacervaverunt sibi magistros ad desideria sua, non ut ab eis discerent quod facere deberent, sed ut eorum studio et calliditate inveniretur ratio quâ liceret id quod liberet." Presently they add, "Ex hoc fonte, Sancte Pater, tanquam ex equo Trajano, irrupere in Ecclesiam Dei tot abusus et tam gravissimi morbi, quibus nunc conspicimus eam ad desperationem ferè salutis laborâsse vel manâsse harum rerum famam ad infideles usque."

such as to explain the vehemence of popular reaction; and if in the last century there was an absence of grossness, such as had prevailed in previous ages, there was a greater absence of spirituality. Says Bishop Butler, charging the clergy of the Diocese of Durham in 1751—
"As different ages have been distinguished by different sorts of particular errors and vices, the deplorable distinction of ours is an avowed scorn of religion in some, and a growing disregard to it in the generality."[1] That disregard, being in its essence moral, would hardly have been arrested by the cultivated reasoners, who were obliged to content themselves with deistic premises in their defences of Christianity: it did yield to the fervid appeals of Whitfield and of Wesley. With an imperfect idea of the real contents and genius of the Christian Creed, and with almost no idea at all of its majestic relations to history and to thought, these men struck a chord for which we may well be grateful. They awoke Christ, sleeping in the conscience of England; they were the real harbingers of a day brighter than their own.

For if the question be asked, how the Church of Christ has surmounted these successive dangers, the answer is, by the appeal of prayer. She has cried to her Master, Who is ever in the ship, though, as it may seem, asleep upon a pillow. The appeal has often been made impatiently, even violently, as on the waves of Gennesaret, but it has not been made in vain. It has not been by policy, or good sense, or considerations of worldly prudence, but by a renewal in very various ways of the first fresh Christian enthusiasm which flows from the felt presence of Christ, that political enemies have been baffled, and intellectual difficulties reduced to their true dimensions, and moral sores extirpated or healed. Christianity does thus contain within itself the secret of its perpetual youth, the certificate of its indestructible

[1] *Works*, vol. ii. p. 312.

vitality; because it centres in, it is inseparable from, devotion to a living Person. No ideal lacking a counterpart in fact could have guided the Church across the centuries. Imagination may do much in quiet and prosperous times; but amid the storms of hostile prejudice and passion, in presence of political vicissitudes or of intellectual onslaughts, or of moral rebellion or decay, an unreal Saviour must be found out. A Christ upon paper, though it were the sacred pages of the Gospel, would have been as powerless to save Christendom as a Christ in fresco; not less feeble than the Countenance which, in the last stages of its decay, may be traced on the wall of the Refectory at Milan. A living Christ is the key to the phenomenon of Christian history. To Him again and again His Church has cried out in her bewilderment and pain, "Up, Lord, why sleepest Thou? awake, and be not absent from us for ever."[1] And again and again, in the great thoroughfares of Christian history, He, her Lord, to borrow the startling image of the Hebrew poet, has "awaked as one out of sleep, and like a giant refreshed with wine,"[2] to display Himself in providential turns, whether in the world of events or in the world of thought, on which no human foresight could have calculated. And what has been will yet be again. There are men who can say to Him only, "Thou, O Christ, art the most exquisite work of chastened imagination, of purified moral sense, that our race has known: in that Thou art our highest ideal of human goodness, Thou art truly Divine; we cannot rival, we cannot even approach, we cannot, if we would, forget Thee." But if this were the highest language towards Him that is honestly possible, whatever else He might be, He would not be "our hope and strength, a very present help in trouble."[3] He would only be precious as a poem or a piece of sculpture is precious; just as beautiful

---

[1] Ps. xliv. 23.   [2] Ps. lxxviii. 66.   [3] Ps. xlvi. 1.

perhaps, but just as helpless an object, rendered into the finer forms of the world of thought. But we Christians have cried to Him in one form of words or another for many a century—" Thou sittest at the Right Hand of God, in the Glory of the Father. We believe that Thou shalt come to be our Judge. We therefore pray Thee, help Thy servants, Whom Thou hast redeemed with Thy precious Blood." And in His being what this language implies lies the recuperative power of the Church; it lies in faith's grasp of the fact that Christ really lives and rules in earth and heaven, and that He may still be appealed to with success, even though men dare to exclaim, "Master, carest Thou not that we perish?"

III.

This power of resistance and recovery inherent in Christianity may be looked at from another side; that of the profound impression it has made on the soul of man. The Christian Creed has brought all the activities of which the human soul is capable into active exercise. It has been charged against our Divine Redeemer that He has so exhausted the religious instincts and energies of man as to make it impossible to establish at all permanently and generally, in lands and among populations which have owned His sway, any tentative religion of the future, such, for instance, as a philosophical Deism. We may admit the charge; indeed we ought not to be surprised at it. For in truth Christ has so taught His people to explore the heights and depths of the spiritual world, the resources and capacities of the soul, its treasures of feeling and passion, its powers of resolution, as well as its subtlety and strength of thought, that after Him all else must needs pall and be uninteresting. Men do not voluntarily recede from the sunshine to the twilight; from civilization to semi-barbarism;

from the advanced prosecution of a science to the study of its elementary truths. And it is because Christianity cannot be superseded by any strong positive religion on its own ground, except indeed through the extermination of Christians, that the Christian faith is constantly renewing itself. The religious sense, roused from a temporary torpor, moves again along the lines of the Christian Creed: and religious thought makes the grand tour of comparative theology, to discover that the extremest limits of experience and speculation have been already anticipated by the Creed which was learnt in childhood.

Surely, brethren, some of ourselves must know something of this power of recovery of Christian faith and life, of this practical inaccessibility to danger which is guaranteed by the Presence of Christ. Have not we, too, had our days of darkness; our days of outward trial; our days of conscious weakness, of inward misgiving and fear? Have not we, too, known what it is to have doubts hushed, and dangers averted, and temptations overcome, at the rising, as if from sleep, of that most sacred Presence, which is enshrined in every Christian soul, to rebuke, or to encourage, or to protect? Our inward heaven, it may be, was so overcast that we could not see Him—

> "When looks were strange on every side,
> When, gazing round, I only saw
> Far-reaching ways on every side,
>   I could but nearer draw.
> I could but nearer draw, and hold
> Thy garment's border as I might."

But that was enough. When the time came He spoke and the trial passed. And there is a correspondence between the larger organism and its component particles, between the Church and the soul; what passes within the soul is an interpretation to those who have felt it of much that belongs to the history of the Church. "Through Thy commandments," each may say, "I get understanding," not merely of the preciousness of moral truth, but of the philosophy of sacred history.

The subject suggests, among others, two reflections in particular.

And, first, it is a duty to be on our guard against panics. Panics are the last infirmity of believing souls. It is of course easy to denounce them from the standpoint of a philosophical unconcern as to all religious interests; calmness is a cheap virtue when you have, or when you suppose yourself to have nothing really at stake. It is not, in this sense, that panics are to be deprecated; the most irrational panic of an unlettered peasant who believes that his creed is imperilled, is, beyond all comparison, a nobler thing than the tranquil indifference of a Talleyrand. But panics are to be deprecated, not because they imply a keen interest in the fortunes of religion, but because they betray a certain distrust of the power and living Presence of our Lord. Granted that materialism rears its crest more boldly than of yore; that a section of modern democracy threatens to break up all public institutions that assert the supernatural; that one branch of the Church of Christ has added to existing difficulties by burdening its official Creed, for the while, with an unhistorical absurdity; that our English Church is embarrassed and enfeebled by misbelief and divisions. Yet it does not follow that the life of particular Churches is imperilled, much less that Christianity is doomed. Science may for the moment be hostile; in the long run it cannot but befriend us. We may have to surrender misapprehensions or to make explanations along the frontier where the Faith touches on the province of physics: science will help us, if she forces us to surrender the untenable.

Criticism may have done us an ill turn in unkindly or unskilful hands; but it has more weapons to place at the disposal of the Faith than opportunities of wounding it. Popular agitators may mean mischief; but we should do ill to fear the people whose best interests are our own. The Church of this country has everything to gain by throwing herself on the classes to which the Gospel was preached at first; for the Church is the real mistress of that social science which either makes want and suffering more than endurable, or which relieves and assuages it. An ecclesiastical absolutism may rule abroad; a sour fanaticism may endeavour to proscribe faith and reverence nearer home; but the eccentricities of human error pass and are forgotten, while Christianity remains. It remains in that breadth of compass, in that common substance of absolute Truth, in that unconquerable strength which resists not merely attacks from without, but grave corruptions and usurpations within; the waves do not merely lash the ship, they wellnigh fill it; yet it does not sink. It does not sink, because He is with it, Who has spoken as none other has spoken to the human soul; Who has opened to man the Eternal World, and revealed to man his own boundless capacities for bliss or for woe. It was accounted something in days of old to carry Cæsar. And He Who is with us in the storm is most assuredly beyond the reach of harm: to be panic-stricken is to dishonour Him. Brethren, let us beware of panics. Panics are the work of timid men, and they make men timid. And if a man has power, timidity will make him cruel; if he is impotent, it will make him foolish.

A second reflection is this: a time of trouble and danger is the natural season for generous devotion. They say that young men who in quiet days, when there was little work and no controversy, and no peril to position and endowments, would have taken Holy Orders, are not ordained now. It may be so. If it be, the Church is not the weaker for the loss of those who would seek her ministry, not for her Lord's sake, but for their own. To generous minds a time of trouble has its own attractions. It enables a man to hope, with less risk of presumption, that his motives are sincere; it fortifies courage; it suggests self-distrust; it enriches character; it invigorates faith. The storm may rage without, the flood may rise within, but while the Lord of the soul and of the Church is here, though it be "asleep in the hinder part of the ship," all must in the end be well. Things would not have been better than they are for martyrs and confessors, if, in their day, the sea had been calm and the waves unruffled. For them, long since, the winds and waves of life have been stilled, and Christ has brought them to the haven where they would be. "Sit anima nostra cum sanctis:" with them, if He wills, in the fellowship of their sorrows; with them, through His Mercy, as sharers of their everlasting rest!

SERMON X.

SACERDOTALISM.

2 Cor. v. 18.

But all things are of God, Who hath reconciled us unto Himself, through Jesus Christ, and hath given unto us the ministry of The Reconciliation: to wit, that God was in Christ, reconciling the world unto Himself, not imputing their trespasses unto them; and hath given unto us the word of The Reconciliation.

THE First Lesson for this morning's Service[1] describes an event which is presupposed by these words of the Apostle. The doctrine or fact of the Fall of Man is the key to the Christian estimate of human nature. Instead of looking upon man as a creature who, in the course of a long series of ages, has struggled upwards out of some lower form of animal existence, by a continually ascending progress, until he has reached his present attainments in conduct, thought, and civilization, the Gospel teaches that man once was in possession of capacities and glories which have left their traces upon his life, but which, while he remains in his natural state, are no longer his. At the present day these two conceptions of man's early history divide the world of thought between them; and the Apostle's expression in the text—to cite no other passages from his writings—shows which side he would take in the controversy, if he were to appear among us.

[1] Sexagesima Sunday, Gen. iii.

I.

Reconciliation, the exchange[1] of enmity for friendship, points by implication to a friendship which had once existed, and had been subsequently lost. Man, St. Paul maintains, at the earliest period of his history was on good terms with his Creator. No disturbing influence was there to mar the harmony of created and uncreated life, in their mutual relations of sovereignty and dependence. But the Apostle insists that there has been a break of moral continuity, which we read in man's present inward ruin and disorder, and the work of which is only repaired by Christ. "By one man sin entered into the world."[2]

If the question be asked, what are the evidences of the Fall? the reply is not far to seek. We trace it in those many precautions which are taken by human society for its self-defence, and which imply that man's nature has something of the wild beast in it, so that it must be watched and held down, if it is not to do man himself a mischief. Then there is the cynical estimate of human motives and character which is almost a matter of course in literature, whether of ancient or modern times, although such cynicism in many instances is guilty of extreme injustice. But, not to dwell on these less direct indications, the Fall has left its mark partly on man's understanding, and partly on his will.

Deep in man's natural intelligence is the idea of God; an idea which is the product of man's survey of nature, accompanied by his introspection of conscience. The Author of Nature identifies Himself with the Legislator of Conscience in the inmost recesses of the soul of man; and yet man, while he is yet unrestored by Christ, is positively impatient of this truth, from which he can never perfectly escape. Thus man is constantly endeavouring to account

[1] $\kappa\alpha\tau\alpha\lambda\lambda\alpha\gamma\acute{\eta}$, Rom. v. 11. [2] Rom. v. 12.

for nature without attributing it to an Author, and to account for conscience as a mere conglomerate of antique prejudices. These efforts, although incessant, have no permanently widespread result. Apart from the teaching and influence of Revelation, the thought of God is too intimately bound up with the highest and deepest life even of fallen human beings, to be really set aside by any destructive eccentricities, whether of physical science or of mental philosophy. It resists the solvents which are so constantly applied to it; it tenants the human soul, if seriously impaired, yet never altogether obliterated; for it is the shadow and the representative of One Who, as we know, sits high above the water-flood of human passion and human thought, in the unassailable majesty of His self-existent Life. And yet, when man cannot escape from God, he shrinks from Him. He can attach himself easily to any created form; to a flower, to a prospect, to an animal, to any concrete representation of beauty or of force. But God, the source of all beauty, the concentration of all force, is, it seems, a Being from Whom man would fain conceal himself. There is something in man's own nature which whispers to him that between himself and God there is a lack of harmony: being such as he is, he would rather keep out of God's way, if it be possible to do so; he hears the voice of the Lord God walking in the garden in the cool of the day of life, and he forthwith seeks to hide himself as of old from the presence of the Lord God among the trees of the garden.[1]

Nor is it otherwise with man's moral nature. Man is born into the world with the idea of right and wrong. There it is; so deep in his soul, that when wellnigh all else has been destroyed, this remains. There may be disputes, in different ages and countries, as to what is right and what is wrong. But the belief that there is a right, and that there

[1] Gen. iii. 8.

is a wrong, is as wide and as old as the race of man, and the broad lines which mark off right from wrong in detail are almost universally recognised. And yet, in presence of this great conviction, what is the average bearing, the historical conduct, of the human will? On the one side, it displays a marked incapacity for virtue. The difficulty of virtue, that is, of living according to the rule of right, the true rule of human life, is a well-worn topic with heathen moralists. Virtue is an effort of strength; the very word implies as much. It is not the easy spontaneous product of our nature. It is the force which we exert when we are at our best. On the other hand, vice, condemned by the human conscience, needs no effort whatever in order to produce it. It springs up in the soil of human nature as do the weeds in a deserted field or garden. It flourishes side by side with man's noblest achievements in the world of thought and in the realm of nature; it is cradled with literature and with science, as having a copartnership in the empire of man; and conscience waits hard by, distressed but powerless, while her clearest and most imperative commands are disregarded. "Video meliora proboque, deteriora sequor." —" The good that I would I do not, but the evil which I would not that I do."[1] Thus speaks fallen human nature at its best; and conscience lingers on, like the dishonoured and pathetic representative of some decayed family splendour, to witness that it was not always thus with man; to whisper to him, as occasion may present itself, that after all he is not really an improved brute, that he once wore his Maker's likeness, and that he still retains some traces of its glory, though dimmed by accompanying weakness and shame.

Such is man, as his first father has left him. Adam could not transmit what he had lost; and his children remain alienated from the Source of Life, shrinking from

[1] Rom. vii. 19.

God, disobeying Him, yet haunted in their inmost being by His frown or His smile; unable to expel Him altogether, whether from their understandings or from their wills. That man should raise himself was, in the moral order, just as impossible, as it is physically beyond the power of the most accomplished athlete to lift himself from the earth by the waistband. If man is to be restored, a power greater than himself, independent of himself, must needs restore him. Accordingly, "after that the kindness and love of God our Saviour towards man appeared, not by works of righteousness which we have done, but according to His Mercy He saved us."[1] What we could not do for ourselves, our Divine Saviour did for us, and in us. There is One Mediator between God and men;[2] a Mediator in His acts, because, first of all, a Mediator in virtue of His twofold nature. On the one hand, He is very God; on the other, He is of the race of man; and thus simply by being what He is, He bridges over the chasm which the Fall had opened between earth and heaven. He acts for God upon mankind; and He acts for men towards God. As the Perfect Man, He represents mankind in the Eternal Presence; while, since in Him dwelleth all the fulness of the Godhead bodily, He is also the channel through which the Divine Life flows down into all those members of the human family who are in real contact with Himself. As the sinless representative of the race before the awful Sanctity of God, He atones for all who are one with Him; God sees us sinners in Him, our sinless Brother; the Father beholds, in His supreme act of self-sacrifice upon the Cross, that absolute moral elevation of which we in our weakness and isolation could never have been capable; and thus we are "accepted in the Beloved,"[3] Who becomes "a propitiation for our sins,"[4] and buys us back from slavery to sin and to its penal consequences.[5] And,

---

[1] Titus iii. 4, 5.   [2] 1 Tim. ii. 5.   [3] Eph. i. 6.
[4] Rom. iii. 25. 1 St. John ii. 2; iv. 10.   [5] 1 Cor. vi. 20. 2 St. Pet. ii. 1.

as representing God to us, He bestows upon us the gifts of which we fallen men stand so greatly in need—grace and truth. Truth, to restore to the intelligence that clear, undimmed perception of Him Who is the Source and End of Life, and in the knowledge of Whom standeth the true life of the human intellect itself; and grace, or, in modern language, force, that practical favour of God which is something more than kindly feeling, and which invigorates and braces the will, and makes it really capable of virtue. Thus the light of the knowledge of the glory of God is given in the face of Jesus Christ.[1] Thus we can do all things through Christ that strengtheneth us.[2] Thus our complete reconciliation with God is achieved, not without our co-operation, but certainly not in virtue of it, through the bounty and compassion of God in Christ.

St. Paul adds, " He hath committed unto *us* the word of the Reconciliation." Is the Apostle speaking here in the name of the whole Christian body? This can hardly be maintained, if we look at the context, in which St. Paul refers to this very commission as a warrant for addressing his readers; as furnishing him, in fact, with his credentials as an ambassador from God. He hath committed unto us— the sentence is twice repeated—the ministry or word of the Reconciliation. " Now, then," he adds, " we are ambassadors for Christ, as though God did beseech you by us; we pray you in Christ's stead, be ye reconciled to God."[3] Nor is there anything to imply that St. Paul is restricting his language to himself personally, or to the other Apostles, or to the circumstances of the first Christian age. The embassy from heaven which he describes was surely not less necessary to mankind in the second or third Christian centuries than it had been in the first. And when we find the Apostle in the Pastoral Epistles engaged in providing for the perpetuation of a ministerial institute

---

[1] 2 Cor. iv. 6.   [2] Phil. iv. 13.   [3] 2 Cor. v. 20.

in the Church of Christ,[1] and giving rules for its action and its guidance,[2] we are justified in concluding that his own claim to be Christ's ambassador of reconciliation among the Corinthians would be repeated by remote and undistinguished successors, who in distant ages and countries would still carry on, in their several scenes of duty, his own life-absorbing work.

Now, so far as we can see, without some such provision, the work of Reconciliation would have been incomplete. For this Reconciliation between God and man, achieved by Christ, is first of all a truth to be recognised by the understanding, and then a fact with which each soul must be placed in actual contact. When the Mediator had withdrawn from sight, how was the truth of the Mediation to be kept alive and propagated in the souls of men, unless some organized machinery for securing this were authoritatively provided? Hence the institution of the Christian Ministry. The ministers of Christ are not a body of lecturers, whose business it might be to investigate a subject which is imperfectly understood, and to make periodical reports of their successive investigations. The first duty of the Christian ministry is to witness persistently to the fact, that in Christ Jesus, God and Man, mankind and God are really reconciled. But this is not its highest duty. Since the Reconciliation is of no avail except to those who are actually reconciled, it is not enough for a man to learn that it has been made; he must know how he personally may reap its benefits. Thus the Christian ministry is a ministry of grace as well as of truth; it bids every man, on the one hand, hold out the hand of faith that he may receive God's gifts; while, on the other, it is itself a means whereby the grace or invigorating force of Christ, conveyed by His Spirit, and reaching man by the certificated channels of His ap-

[1] 2 Tim. ii. 2. Tit. i. 5.   [2] 1 Tim. iii. 2-12. Tit. i. 7-9.

proach, makes us "one with Christ, and Christ with us."[1] The "Word of Reconciliation," taken in its broad sense, includes all the powers[2] of the Gospel age, which enable Christ's ministers to do their Master's work. And thus, at this hour, the commission still runs—" Be thou a faithful Minister of the Word of God, and of His Holy Sacraments, in the Name of the Father, and of the Son, and of the Holy Ghost."[3]

II.

Here we encounter the watchword of an objection, perhaps I ought rather to say, of a state of feeling, which, under present circumstances, if it is to be noticed at all, requires on all hands a serious effort of forbearance. A label is not an argument, properly speaking; it may represent the effort of a busy age to dispense with argument, and to record its judgment in a compendious form; it is sometimes the instinctive language of far-sighted justice; but not less frequently is it the verdict of onesidedness or of passion. In religious matters men have always been prone to affix labels to forms of belief or thought of which they feel more or less suspicious; and this not always ill-naturedly, or with the view of disabling an opponent by imprinting on him a stigma, but in order to make their own way clear to themselves under perplexing circumstances. For the mass of men are secretly but profoundly conscious of their real indistinctness of vision, even when their language is boisterously positive. As they feel their way doubtfully along the frontier which separates the seen from the unseen world, they are often more ready to welcome, or even to set up guide-posts, than to inquire whether such erections are recommended by adequate authority, and whether the guidance which they offer is altogether accurate. And

---

[1] Communion Service, Exhortation.
[2] Heb. vi. 5, δυνάμεις μέλλοντος αἰῶνος.
[3] Ordination of Priests.

thus it has happened, that fearing some very possible and some quite impossible dangers, certain persons have lately raised a prominent notice-board close to the district of thought which we are now considering; and, on looking up, we find traced across it, in characters that compel the attention of the world, a formidable word, harmless in itself, but surrounded with very invidious associations; the word "Sacerdotalism."

Now, a popular judgment, such as this word represents, is not by any means to be at once set aside, as if it were only the product of ignorance or injustice. A certain element of justice, it is at least probable, underlies all such public judgments; and those whom they may seem to concern do well, while recognising this, to analyze them, and to separate the element which is dictated by a true insight or feeling from the element which is supplied by vulgar prejudice. This word Sacerdotalism is intended to disparage what we know to be a great and solemn truth; but it is also employed to describe traditional habits of thought or a professional temper, which are really due to human weakness, and which are not untainted by human sin. Let us begin with the truth which those who employ it would ignore or set aside.

Here the maintenance of positive truth has been made more difficult than it might be, by later accretions gathered round the deposit which comes down to us from the early Church. When, for instance, the New Testament speaks of an authoritative "word of reconciliation,"[1] or of "the keys of the kingdom of heaven,"[2] or of a "stewardship of the mysteries of God,"[3] men think of claims which have been made to dispense with the Divine Law, or to depose monarchs from their thrones; and they reflect that such claims do undoubtedly threaten the wellbeing or even

---

[1] 2 Cor. v. 18, 19.   [2] St. Matt. xvi. 19. Cf. Isa. xxii. 22. Rev. iii. 7.
[3] 1 Cor. iv. 1.

the independence of civil society. And yet, if we are to give up all truths that have been exaggerated into errors, all institutions that have swerved from their original purpose to become the instruments of ambition or worldliness, it is easy to see that much will not be left of the best blessings which God has given us. Not that, in the case before us, it is necessary to enter at length upon a minute discussion of the exact powers involved in the Apostolic ministry, in contrast to exaggerations on this side, or to negations on that. For the popular brand of Sacerdotalism knows nothing of these distinctions; it does not generally attach itself to one particular conception of the Christian ministry and spare the rest; it would have been just as freely used of St. Paul " magnifying his office "[1] as the Gentile Apostle, as it is used of those who advance pretensions which he never thought of, and even of others who ostentatiously disclaim powers which he fearlessly asserted. Nay, a living writer has not scrupled to describe our Lord Himself as a sacerdotalist. By sacerdotalism, then, something is meant of a broad and general kind which underlies specific forms of the idea, and with this conception of what sacerdotalism is, it is, on every account, important to reckon if we can.

It would appear that the etymology of the word is no real guide to us. The Jewish priest was pre-eminently a sacrificer; he had a commission from above to put animals to death in expression of a religious faith. In other priesthoods other powers have been more prominently claimed than sacrifice; but it is not any one pretension or endowment which rouses the feeling which the word " sacerdotalism " now represents.

That which is really objected to would seem to be the claim to speak and act in the things of God under a Divine commission; to have been put in trust with the Gospel, not

[1] Rom. xi. 13.

of man, but by Jesus Christ; to be part of the Divine plan of reconciliation, as actually given to the world, however humble and subordinate a part; to be an integral element of the Divine Constitution of the Church, in such sense that the Church would be something else than the Church of the Apostles if it were omitted. In this broad sense "sacerdotalism" is charged against a serious Presbyterianism as well as against Episcopacy;[1] against the Westminster Assembly not less than against the Savoy Conference. From this point of view new Presbyter is but old Priest writ large; and not merely the English Clergy, but the Wesleyan Conference, are said to be "inclined to sacerdotalism." All thoughtful Christian ministers know that they need a Divine warrant for their momentous work; rightly or wrongly, they all, in some sense, claim it; and it is the claim to have such a warrant which is resisted, because it involves on the part of others a certain dependence upon the man or order which possesses it. Whether one ministerial power only is claimed, or others also, does not here matter; what is objected to is the assertion that a man is in any way dependent upon the intermediate agency of his brother man for obtaining any of the Redemptive Blessings which have been won by Christ.

---

[1] For an old illustration of this see "Rome ruined by Whitehall; or The Papall Crown Demolisht: containing a Confutation of the three Degrees of Popery, viz. Papacy, Prelacy, and Presbitery; answerable to the Triple Crown of the three-headed Cerberus, the Pope, by John Spittlehouse, Assistant to the Marshall-General of the Army under the command of his Excellency the Lord General Fairfax. London, Paine, 1650." In his preface, addressed "to the Commons assembled in Parliament," Mr. Spittlehouse assures them that they "are the men whom God intends to honour as His Instruments to pluck up Antichrist, root and branch." He prays them "to delay not time, but with a Christian courage resolve to act a full Reformation, which," he continues, "you will never effect so long as you support the Prelaticall *or* Presbiterian Clergy, either in office or maintenance, *that of Presbitery being a Romish Hierarchy as the other*, as in this insuing treatise is proved at large." Cf. ch. vi. pp. 244-7.

III.

What, let us ask, are the main currents of thought which underlie the feeling which raises the cry of "sacerdotalism"?

First of all, there is the doctrine of the original equality of man with man. This is a conception with which we are familiar in the sphere of politics. The assertion that spiritual blessings come to one man through the agency of another man, or order of men, appears to traverse the inherent equality of all men before their Maker. If there are no traces of this sentiment in the earliest ages of the Church, it is because then the Clergy, first in labour and first in suffering, were tribunes of the people, the working representatives of classes who groaned under the iron rule of the Cæsars. But with the Middle Ages, or rather before them, there came a change. It was a consequence, perhaps an inevitable consequence, of the conversion of the Empire. It was due, not to clerical ambition or greed, but to the nature of things, to the course of the Divine Providence. The Church became politically powerful; her chief ministers were often princes; they were still spiritual pastors, but they were also robed in earthly splendours. Now so long as the early feudal order of society held its place, the Church did not suffer from this association. But when that long series of struggles for a new political freedom set in, which began with the efforts of small townships to hold their own against the great territorial lords, and which have culminated in the revolutionary outbreaks of our own age, men could no longer distinguish between what belonged to this world and what to another in a feudalized clergy. Too often the Church's spiritual claims have shared in the hostility which her temporal power or wealth provoked. Presbyterianism, it has been said, was in its origin not so much an attempt to create a new kind of Church government supposed to be Scriptural, as a political protest against an aristocratic hierarchy. And thus it has come to pass that there is a modern feeling against any ministerial order claiming a Divine commission, as being an indirect violation of the civil rights of man; and as threatening a relapse into social conditions from which the modern world is happy to think that it has finally escaped.

And yet, brethren, is it true that any such equality of man with man, as this feeling really presumes, is possible? Doubtless, as simple souls divested of all save that inalienable responsibility for all which each of us is and does, we are absolutely equal before the eye of God. No difference is possible before God, between king and subject, between priest and layman, between the unlettered and the learned, between the poor and the rich, save that which each for himself has made. But beyond this point inequalities—so far as we can see, inevitable, irremoveable inequalities—at once begin. Modern experiments have done much for liberty; something here and there for fraternity; but even when, as in France, they have effaced nearly all that is beautiful in the civilization of a thousand years, they have achieved for real equality absolutely nothing. There is no making head against the nature of things, against the structural laws of common human life. And thus in natural society we still see on all sides, men and classes of men, with whom we cannot ourselves dispense; we trace a series of hierarchies, upon which we are dependent for moral, mental, physical blessings, whether we will or no.

There are the priests of wealth. Wealth is not, and it cannot be, distributed among men, as the apostles of an absolute human equality would desire. Proclaim a general confiscation of property to-day; and wealth will begin to concentrate itself anew in a few hands to-morrow: there are economical laws which make this concentration imperative. And if this be so, what are the holders of wealth but its priests; the guardians of its great shrines; the dispensers of material blessings which are unattainable without it;—priests of wealth, having the power of the keys and the power of sacrifice, as a priesthood should ?

Again, there are the priests of knowledge; the priests of the most enterprising forms of modern knowledge, of physical science. What a hierarchy is this; how brilliant, how enthusiastic, how powerful! How does the modern world hang breathless on its dogmatic utterances; how does our freshest and most promising talent throng its temples! It may take liberties, this priesthood, such is its power; it may unsay to-day what yesterday it affirmed very positively; and yet it does not imperil its influence, or risk our allegiance; we are altogether dependent on it; we cannot do without it if we would. It is the herald of a revelation, the revelation of nature; and we, children of nature as we are, cannot deny its capacity for blessing us, or our powerlessness to do for ourselves what it undertakes so well. Every day it brings alleviation to individual suffering, or safeguards against public danger to health, or it opens out new and magnificent prospects for the bettering of the whole condition of our earthly existence; and as we observe, and listen, and reflect, we cannot but see in it an organ of God's Providence, an embassy from Heaven; we welcome in it a Priesthood which guards a truth that has claims upon us all.

Once more, there are the priests of political power. This, too, is claimed for every individual by current doctrines of human equality. And it has been, in point of fact, again and again distributed throughout vast populations, so that every man may, as the phrase goes, govern himself. But, practically speaking, what happens? If political power is to work as government, it must be resigned to some deputy; it must be concentrated in some person or body: if you have not a king, you must have a president, a directory, a convention, a parliament, perhaps a dictator. What is this after all but a hierarchy? And the gifts which fit men for this high service of the state are, as we have all been thinking lately, rare and often unshared; they are not secured by careful training; they cannot be conferred by vote; they belong to genius. Do what we will, we are their debtors and dependants; live when or where we may, we cannot dispense with them. This priesthood of the state, which in its way blesses, and absolves, and offers sacrifice, and instructs, is essential to society; and it guards, it does not confiscate, our individual rights.

In fact, look where we will in human life, we must recognise this great fact in God's providential government of the world. He does make large masses of men dependent upon the good dispositions as well as on the capacity of others; He makes a minority the guardian and trustee of the means of blessing the majority; He dispenses His gifts to us not immediately, but through the agency of our fellow-creatures. As far as we can see, this law of responsibility on one side, and of dependence on the other, does not belong to any particular stage of civilization; it may take different forms, it may be modified in many ways, but it is inherent in the nature of society. Society, made up as it is of human beings with different capacities, and of human beings who inherit the results of similar inequalities in past generations, will always present to the very end of time this aspect, against which abstract doctrines of an absolute equality among men must dash themselves in vain. And thus, in religion, a ministerial order illustrates and consecrates the general law; spiritual blessings depend, within limits, like other blessings, on human agency; and the agency which confers them has a Divine warrant in history as well as in the nature of things. Therefore, to say that such an arrangement is hostile to the rights of man as man, is to object to God's general plan of governing the world; a plan which makes every one of us depend upon the ability, the conscientiousness, the will of others, for the greater part of the blessings which we enjoy.

Next, the cry of "sacerdotalism" is raised on religious grounds: all Christians, it is said, are already priests. If anything is plain from Holy Scripture, it is that the sacrificial character of the Jewish priesthood was believed by the Apostles of Christ to be transferred to every member of the Christian body. St. Peter insists that Christians are an holy priesthood; appointed to offer up spiritual sacrifices, acceptable to God through Jesus Christ.[1] St. John, in vision, praises the Divine Redeemer for making us kings and priests unto God and His Father.[2] Where all are priests, it is asked, why should there be a ministerial order, since it can only discharge functions which are the functions of us all?

Certainly, if Christian laymen would only believe with all their hearts that they are really priests, we should very soon escape from some of the difficulties which vex the Church of Christ. For it would then be seen that in the Christian Church the difference between clergy and laity is only a difference of the degree in which certain spiritual powers are conferred; that it is not a difference of kind. Spiritual endowments are given to the Christian layman with one purpose, to the Christian minister with another: the object of the first is personal, that of the second is corporate.

Yes, the Apostles of Christ tell us all that we are priests. But do we take them at their word? Do we say to ourselves, except when we are dealing with one particular controversy, that their language is only metaphor, and forget

---

[1] 1 St. Pet. ii. 5-9.   [2] Rev. i. 6.

that every metaphor guards a truth? To the first Christians this lay priesthood was a reality. A Christian layman in the Apostolic age conceived of himself as a true priest. Within his heart there was an altar of the Most Holy, and on it he offered continually the sacrifice, the costly sacrifice, of his will, united to the Perfect Will of Jesus Christ, and, through this union, certain of acceptance in the courts of heaven. The Christian layman of early days was thus, in his inmost life, penetrated through and through by the sacerdotal idea, spiritualized and transfigured as it was by the Gospel. Hence, it was no difficulty to him that this idea should have its public representatives in the body of the Church, or that certain reserved duties should be discharged by Divine appointment, but on behalf of the whole body, by these representatives. The priestly institute in the public Christian body was the natural extension of the priesthood which the lay Christian exercised within himself; and the secret life of the conscience was in harmony with the outward organization of the Church. But a layman in our day is not necessarily a successor of the primitive Christian layman in anything but the name. He is not always a believer whose faith and humility shrink from the responsibilities of the ministerial office; he may be only a human being, whose convictions are doubtful, but who certainly is not in holy orders, and who sees in the Ministry of Christ chiefly a badge of social or political disabilities. Where there is no recognition of the priesthood of every Christian soul, the sense of an unintelligible mysticism, if not of an unbearable imposture, will be provoked when spiritual powers are claimed for the benefit of the whole body by the serving officers of the Christian Church. But if this can be changed; if the temple of the layman's soul can be again made a scene of spiritual worship, he will no longer fear lest the ministerial order should confiscate individual liberty. The one priesthood will be felt to be the natural extension and correlative of the other.

Lastly, when denouncing "sacerdotalism," men point to the Throne of the Great High Priest of Christendom. Since He died, rose, and ascended into heaven, is not, they ask, all Priesthood, all Ministerial Power, concentrated in Him? and must not any earthly order of priesthood incur some risk of obscuring these Solitary and Prerogative offices, which are our only assured ground of Christian life and hope?

Such language is too genuinely Christian to be disregarded; and yet, if it be pressed, it is fatal to the truth which was the basis of the previous objection. If all Christians are, in some sense, priests, Christ does, in some sense, give a share of His Priesthood to His brethren. And if He gives a larger share to some, and a less to others, for the good of the whole, the question between the opponents and advocates of a true ministerial commission is, in reality, a question of degree. When St. Paul bade Timothy see to it, that, in the Church under his care, intercessions[1] should be made for all men, he did not think that he was authorizing an invasion of the rights of the One Great Intercessor. And when at the altar Christ's Ministers plead His perfect Sacrifice before the Father, or bless His people, or announce His pardon, they act, not as His rivals, but as His representatives, empowered to share, at however vast a distance, in carrying forward His Mediatorial work.[2] It is with His Priesthood as with His other offices of King and Prophet. He is the Prophet of Whom Moses sang;[3] He is the King of kings and Lord of lords of the apostolic vision.[4] Yet He is not dishonoured, if His teaching office is exercised, however imperfectly, by human instructors; and the objection of the Fifth Monarchy men to an earthly sovereign would hardly be repeated at the present day. Nor is He less truly alone, as a Priest upon His heavenly

[1] 1 Tim. ii. 1. [2] 2 Cor. vi. 1. [3] Deut. xviii. 15. [4] Rev. xix. 16.

throne,[1] in His work of sacrifice and intercession, because there is a priesthood of the Gospel[2] commissioned by Himself here on earth, whose business it is, as ministering the Word and Sacraments, to bring His Mediation home to the souls of men. In short, He is Priest, Prophet, King, in an absolute and unique sense; all who bear these titles beneath His Throne are only holders of a delegated authority; but His rights are not compromised, His Majesty is not obscured, because He intrusts to a certain number of His servants this or that power for the good of all His brethren.

And yet, let us be sure, there is a certain justice in the popular cry which we have been considering. Let me address myself to those of you who hope, with God's assistance, to devote yourselves to His service in Holy Orders. Remember that prejudice is less often roused by a theory or doctrine about our office than by a temper, a bearing, a line of conduct. Men will not tolerate the love of spiritual power, as power, for its own sake; they expect us to bear in mind that spiritual power is only lodged in the hands of weak and sinful men for the purposes of Divine beneficence. They will not put up with what seems trivial or petty, where such great claims are made upon their thought and conscience. And their eyesight has been sharpened by our Divine Master's dealings with the Scribes and Pharisees; and the faults of the Scribes and Pharisees are faults to which a clerical order—such is human weakness—is always prone, and against which it must be constantly on guard, if it would not fail most miserably. To appropriate the high gifts of heaven, or the love, and trust, and dependence of human souls, which in some measure are the portion of every minister of Christ, for the promotion of some selfish object, is sufficiently easy; and yet it surely deserves the harshest judgment of a critical and hostile world. If the world tells us home

[1] Zech. vi. 13. [2] Rom. xv. 16, ἱερουργοῦντα τὸ εὐαγγέλιον τοῦ Θεοῦ.

truths in rough language, a true wisdom will forget the language, and will treasure the truth. When the Apostle says that the word of the Reconciliation has been committed to us, he tells us that we are trustees; and our safety consists, perhaps, in dwelling on the responsibilities of a great trust, rather than any other aspect of our office. A conscientious trustee thinks first of the interests committed to him, next of the office which he fills as guarding them, least of all of himself. A conscientious clergyman will think more of his office than of his person, but he will also take less account of his office than of his work. After all, the first is only a means, the last is the end. Ministerial powers are given, not to confer importance on a man or on an order, but to promote a work; the highest work that can be carried on in time, and for eternity, among or by human beings. Such a work no doubt implies and requires great powers, but these powers, like the muscular action of the body, or like the finer capacities of the mind, are, it may be, better taken for granted than constantly discussed. Certainly, if their existence is challenged, it may have to be asserted. But even when such a vindication is required, there is always some danger of putting the means before the end, and of forgetting the claims of spiritual duty in the advocacy of a spiritual position. How slight indeed is the outward structure of the Church militant, framed though it were by the Pierced Hands of the Divine Redeemer, when we compare it with the vast object which it is designed to achieve; the working together with God for the reconciliation of souls to Him, the Source and End of created Life, through union with the One Mediator Jesus Christ! Only in a far-off eternity shall we understand the full scope of words like these; we come nearest to understanding them here, by never forgetting that they describe a work which infinitely transcends in its importance any other that can possibly engage our attention.

SERMON XI.

THE PROPHECY OF THE MAGNIFICAT.

St. Luke i. 51-53.

He hath showed strength with His arm: He hath scattered the proud in the imagination of their hearts. He hath put down the mighty from their seats, and exalted them of low degree. He hath filled the hungry with good things; and the rich He hath sent empty away.

THE Magnificat is tacitly recognised, by the judgment and by the heart of Christendom, as the noblest of Christian hymns. The occasion of its utterance was unique in Jewish, or rather in human history; it was such as to place Mary's Hymn in a higher category than those other evangelical canticles which, together with it, and with a view to illustrating St. Paul's teaching, are preserved by St. Luke. When Mary sang, she had received Gabriel's message, and she knew that her expected Child, conceived under circumstances altogether preternatural, would be greater than any of the sons of men. Her hymn, in fact, is presented to us in Scripture as the Hymn of the Divine Incarnation; and its contents, alike in their explicitness and in their reserve, are in keeping with its historical origin. It has indeed been suggested[1] that Mary, in visiting her cousin, would scarcely have broken out into a long canticle instead of engaging in the conver-

[1] Strauss, *Leben Jesu.*

sation which would be natural between relations after a period of separation. But it may be replied, first, that the Evangelist does not profess to report all that passed at the Visitation; and, secondly, that, even within the sphere of purely natural experience, there are moments when human feeling altogether refuses to submit to the ordinary restraints of homely intercourse, and when, under the stress of great joy or sorrow, we must either be silent, or express ourselves in a strain which to cool observers at the time, and to ourselves at other times, would appear to be unnatural. If, then, we reflect what, according to the Evangelist, the recent experience of the Virgin-mother had actually been, we must feel the impossibility of interpreting this utterance by the rules which govern our feelings and conversation in daily life. And, indeed, it is not difficult to imagine how our critic would himself have treated the report of a business-like discussion on family matters, interspersed with some pious reflections, if St. Luke could have bequeathed one. Nor is it possible to agree in the forced expression of surprise that a hymn emanating immediately from so high a source of inspiration "should not be more striking for its originality."[1] Certainly the modern feeling of anxiety to owe nothing to a literary predecessor finds no place in the sacred writers; prophets continually repeat, with new freshness and authority, the language of older men of God; and, to omit other examples, the holiest of all prayers is largely based on Rabbinical petitions which were in use when it was first prescribed. Yet in all such cases, new combinations, new associations, a new and all-inspiring purpose, do secure a true element of originality; for originality may be achieved not less perfectly by the effective use of old ideas and language than by the production of new material. Unquestionably Mary, in her hymn, does speak almost entirely in the sacred language of the past;

---

[1] Strauss, *Leben Jesu.*

two Books of the Law, a late Psalmist, two Prophets, and the work of the Son of Sirach are laid under contribution: above all, the Song of Hannah, to whose memory in her new circumstances Mary would not unnaturally have turned, supplies a large proportion, both of its language and its form, to the Hymn of the Visitation. And yet who would seriously compare the earlier with the later poem? Throughout the Magnificat, exclaims a living foreign Protestant divine, there reigns a truly royal majesty:[1] Mary passes from pouring forth the thankful joy of her heart to point with reverent awe at the Divine fact which was its provoking cause; and then, as if gazing from a lofty eminence, in the fulness of the prophetic spirit, she discerns the consequences of this fact in human nature and history; and the last strophe of her song dies away, as she owns in it, not simply a personal honour rendered to herself, but the supreme token of God's faithfulness and compassion towards the people of His choice.

I.

It is in what, if we were to write it out in its original Aramaic form, we should call the third strophe of the hymn[2] that Mary's feeling seems to attain its highest point of elevation; while yet the rising impulse of inspired passion is restrained by her observance of the law of poetic parallelism. Mary has already referred in tender, solemn, and reserved language to the great things which God has done to her. And now she is, as it were, looking out across the centuries at the mighty religious revolution which would date from the appearance of her Divine Son on the scene of human history. God, she exclaims, hath showed strength with His arm; He hath scattered the proud; He hath put down the

---

[1] Godet, *Comm. S. Luc, in loc.*   [2] St. Luke i. 51-53.

mighty; He hath exalted the humble; He hath filled the hungry; He hath sent the rich empty away. It is true that these are past tenses, and they might thus be referred to the triumphs and fortunes of Israel in bygone days; to that ancient discomfiture of the Egyptian power, which was scarcely ever absent from the memory and heart of Hebrew saints and patriots; to the dethronement of the Canaanite, the Amorite, the Amalekite kings who vainly endeavoured to arrest the advancing destinies of Israel; to the abasement of the pride of Moab and of the might of Babylon; to the restoration in splendour and in power of the chosen race, when it had been fast bound by merciless conquerors in misery and iron. Mary has been understood to mean that Israel, as a people, did, on the whole, even in its worst moments, more or less hunger and thirst after righteousness, and was rewarded by a long line of teachers of spiritual truth, culminating in the Greatest Teacher of all; while other peoples, rich indeed in natural endowments, but sated with the conceits of misdirected speculation, or with the cumbrous splendours of a mere material civilization, were sent empty away from the spiritual feast. But it seems that Mary is thinking less of the past than of the present, and of the future which lies in the womb of the present. So, after the manner of prophets, she does not anticipate that which is yet to come; she reads off what she sees intuitively, as if it were already history. He *hath* scattered the proud; He *hath* put down the mighty; He *hath* exalted the humble; He *hath* filled the hungry; He *hath* dismissed the rich. God's work is for Mary as if it were present or past, while, speaking historically, although on the point of beginning, it was still, in its richest and truest sense, altogether future. In her great hymn Mary stands, no doubt, between two histories, between two dispensations. They present many points of resemblance to each other, and she can hardly prophesy without describing, or describe without prophesying. But upon the whole she is looking forward rather than backward; she is prophetess rather than historian; and her language is to be interpreted less by the history of Israel after the flesh than by that of the New Kingdom of her Divine Son.

And here let us dwell more closely on Mary's words, to learn, if it may be, their interpretation in history.

Who are these — the "proud"[1] — claiming distinction beyond others on the score whether of influence, or accomplishments, or position, or virtue? There are critics who cannot think of Mary as more than a patriotic Jewess. Accordingly they see in this epithet only a reference to heathen pride, whether the pride of political power or the pride of culture and philosophy. This pride still lives in the pages of Tacitus, or Juvenal, or Lucian; lavishing its bitterness on the strange unaccommodating race, whose spirit it could not quell; despising its virtues not less than its vices, its intrepid loyalty to what truth it knew not less than its narrowness and superstition. But if the pride of heathendom was in the background of Mary's vision, there were, in the more immediate foreground, others than the heathen on whom her spiritual eye would probably rest. Unless we are to suppose that, deferring to a merely technical use or abuse of language, and in defiance of the moral facts of the case, she draws a sharp line between Jew and Gentile, making the first monopolize the graces of humility and meekness, and the latter the vice of pride, we must see in "the proud" a reference to the great Jewish sects, who, speaking historically, were the first opponents of the Gospel. There was the pride of the Sadducee; generally wealthy, sceptical, and conservative, tolerant of what he deemed fanaticism till it gave him trouble, or threatened the existing order of things, but

[1] ὑπερηφάνους.

regarding with serene contempt any serious proposal for extending the influence of religion, or for improving the condition of the people. And there was the Pharisee; aiming morally far higher than his rival, but ruining everything by his determined self-complacency, forgetting the motive in the act, the inward in that which meets the eye, the real in the conventional. And behind these were the Herodians; interesting themselves in the religious situation only so far as was necessary to make political capital out of it, but resenting with scorn any assertion of a spiritual claim or force which could not be made politically serviceable. These were the first opponents of the New Kingdom; and their discomfiture, when the Church of Christ burst the bonds of Jewish nationality, and spread out her arms to all the nations of the world through the ministry and by the voice of St. Paul, is the first stage in the great drama which Mary sees unfolding itself before her.

The second is wider in its range. He hath put down the "sovereigns,"[1] from their thrones. Here it is possible enough that Mary glances at the Idumæan ruler, whose presence, in the judgment of all Jewish patriots, casts a dark shadow over the city of David. But behind the throne of Herod is the more remote but more awful throne of his great patron, the throne of the Cæsar. Here the horizon has already widened too largely to permit us to think only of the fortunes of a local and dependent potentate. Mary is gazing at the head and centre of the ancient world, at the godless power which St. John in his Apocalypse describes as Babylon. When Mary sang, the Cæsars were at the head of their legions, and the world was at their feet. But pass a few centuries and the imperial name is but a shadow, and Rome has been again and again the prey of her barbaric enemies, and

[1] δυνάστας.

Goths and Huns, Vandals and Lombards, have shared her spoils. Doubtless the Christians were loyal to "the powers that be." But Christianity, as a principle, did, however involuntarily, contribute to the ruin of the Pagan Empire. Sooner or later the new wine of a Divine life must have burst the bottle of an effete civilization. An apostle had seen "another angel come from heaven, . . . and he cried mightily with a strong voice, saying, Babylon the great is fallen, is fallen."[1]

Yes! Gibbon felt the power of Mary's words, when, as he tells us in his autobiography, on the 15th of October 1764, he sat musing amid the ruins of the Capitol, while they were chanting the Vesper Service in what had once been the Temple of Jupiter; and the idea of writing the Decline and Fall of the city first presented itself to his mind.[2] That which met his eye was a comment on the language of the Magnificat, as it fell upon his ear: "He hath put down the mighty from their thrones." The great monument of historical genius which he was thus led to rear, is unrivalled to this day in its own field and province as a sample of literary method, and in many respects of actual information, although it is disfigured by features which all Christians must deplore. But do we not trace in it not merely a reaction from the thoughtless impulse which had hurried its author in early life into communion with the Church of Rome, but also, and much more, a sort of literary resentment, such as was seen more than once in the earlier days of the Renaissance against God's judgments manifested in history; a resentment which, by its very petulance, attests the completeness and the meaning of God's work? It was hard to confess—it was impossible to deny—that when Rome fell, God had put down the mighty from their thrones.

[1] Rev. xviii. 2.
[2] *Autobiographic Memoirs of Edward Gibbon*, p. 79 (ed. Warne).

The Empire has passed away, the horizon widens yet more, and Mary sees a new stage in the fortunes of the Church. "He hath filled the hungry with good things, and the rich He hath sent empty away." The old pagan civilization, sated with its luxury, sated with its false philosophy, was dismissed; and the young races beyond the Rhine and the Danube, hungering for a higher truth than as yet they knew, were filled with good things of the kingdom of Christ. Pagan Rome was succeeded by Christian Europe; and since that astonishing revolution, the last clause of this strophe of Mary's song has been continually fulfilling itself. The old civilizations of the East, but especially the races which have been petrified by the creed of Islam, and so believe themselves to have attained all that is needed for true human excellence, receive nothing, century after century, from the Master of the feast; while simple and comparatively rude peoples, such as the New Zealanders and the Melanesians, are brought into the fold of Christ, and filled with the good things of the everlasting Gospel.

Thus, then, Mary seems to imply a correspondence between the conditions of the Incarnation itself and its remote moral consequences in Christian history. As the Highest had regarded the low estate of His handmaiden, putting upon her, conceived though she was in sin, such altogether pre-eminent honour, that, from henceforth to the latest time, all the Christian generations should bless her name; so the chiefest blessings of that new order of things which was to date from the coming of the Lord Incarnate, would not belong to the qualities which might hitherto have seemed to enjoy a presumptive claim upon success. The kingdom of grace would have a history all its own. The self-assertion, the power, the wealth of the world would be at a discount; the men of low estate would be exalted, and the hungry would be filled.

II.

But while we may thus with fair probability connect these clauses of the Magnificat with successive stages in the history of the Church, it is unquestionable that they are or may be in course of fulfilment, at any one period and simultaneously; that each and all of them is or may be realized perfectly in every age. The "proud," the "mighty," the "rich" of the Incarnation Hymn are always here; to be scattered by the arm of God; to be put down from their thrones; to be sent empty away. This is true in the private and spiritual as well as in the political and public sphere. And the question arises, why *is* it true? Why is there this intrinsic antagonism between the Revelation of God on the one hand, and so much that is characteristic of human nature and energy on the other?

The answer to this question is, that Christianity presupposes in man the existence of an immense want, which it undertakes to satisfy. It further assumes that this want is so serious and imperative that all honest natures must crave for its satisfaction. Thus when St. Paul, in the greatest of his epistles, is about to explain how man attains to peace and reconciliation with God through faith in the mediatorial work of Jesus Christ, he prefaces this statement with an inquiry into man's actual moral circumstances. Having divided the human race for this purpose into Jew and Gentile, he shows how and why each section of mankind is guilty before God, as falling altogether short of the moral ideals which the law of nature and the law of Sinai respectively presented.[1] And here, of course, St. Paul is dealing with a matter of general experience. The ancients could be profuse in acknowledging the moral misery of human life. And if Rousseau

[1] Rom. i. 20-32; ii. 17-29; iii. 9-20.

traces this misery to a false culture, and would cure it by returning to a state of nature, and if Goethe, when he is writing about Winkelmann, permits himself to dream of the indestructible healthfulness of Greek heathenism, the first of these opinions may be profitably tested by almost any book of African or Pacific travel, while the second has only to be examined by the light of the best Greek writers. Indeed, wherever a *bonâ fide* law of moral truth, however imperfect, is recognised at all, St. Paul's position must be conceded.[1] And what he argues as to man's moral condition is true of his intellectual condition as well. When man is left to himself, all the great problems which surround human existence, man's origin, his relation to the world around him, the meaning and drift of his existence, his destiny, nay, the question what he himself is, whether only brute or embodied spirit, are either entirely unsolved or approached only in uncertainty and twilight. In short, a man does, as a matter of fact, need health and light from above; and these requirements have been met by what St. Paul calls the "goodness and philanthropy of our Saviour God"[2] in the Divine Incarnation.

There was, indeed, a great school of divines[3] in the Middle Ages, which, if it has few direct representatives, yet is not without some influence on modern theology, and which ventured, in the real or supposed interests of a comprehensive philosophy, to maintain that the Incarnation was not simply an answer to our needs; that it did not originally depend upon the lapse of our first parent, but only received a new shape and purpose in consequence; that "etiamsi non peccasset homo, Deus tamen esset incarnatus." Few would venture nowadays to affirm or to dispute so bold a thesis as that. All that we know is that the earliest intimations of God's gracious purposes towards us are linked to the first steps in the degradation of our race;

[1] Rom. iii. 9.   [2] Tit. iii. 4.   [3] The Scotists.

and we dare not speculate upon what He might have done with a sinless world, so utterly unlike that world of which we have actual experience. We know that "all have sinned and come short of the glory of God, being justified freely by His grace through the redemption that is in Christ Jesus."[1] We know that "because the children are partakers of flesh and blood, He also Himself likewise took part of the same; that through death He might destroy him that had the power of death, that is the devil; and deliver them who through fear of death were all their lifetime subject to bondage."[2] We know that He was made "sin for us Who knew no sin, that we might be made the righteousness of God in Him."[3]

Christianity, then, appeals to a matter of fact; it insists that the deficiencies of our nature are such as to require some moral and intellectual aid from heaven. There are many gifts of God which enrich human life, but which do not come to it as knowledge comes to those who are perishing through ignorance, or as medicine comes to those who are the victims of neglected disease. These gifts are embellishments of human life; they are not essential to its wellbeing. They do not fill up a gap; they only add to what was already in its way complete without them. Now that we enjoy them we know their value, and perhaps they have created wants which would beset us sorely if they were withdrawn; but at least we did not crave for them; we did not feel, until they were vouchsafed to us, that something of the kind was absolutely needed for the welfare of our race. Take, for example, two such gifts of God as poetry and photography; the one almost as old as the human family, the other a gift to this Western world within the lifetime of the present generation. No doubt poetry has its moral value, sometimes of a very high order; and a world from which it should be utterly banished would seem to many

---

[1] Rom. iii. 23, 24. [2] Heb. ii. 14. [3] 2 Cor. v. 21.

of us to be by comparison an impoverished and uninviting world. Still it would get on—this prosaic world—somehow, even without the poets; and as for photography, we remember that not many years ago the most civilized nations in Europe were not conscious of any vital deficiency in the absence of this beautiful and interesting art. And in like manner, although astronomy has enlarged our knowledge of God, perhaps, more than any other non-theological branch of human knowledge, and the use of steam-power has done more than any recent discovery to improve the conditions of man's physical life, yet the world did not yearn for a Watt or a Copernicus, however ready it now is to admit its indebtedness to them. And it may well be that in future years our children will have discovered powers in nature and made the most of them; —new gifts of God, which we do not look for, because we have no want which suggests even a suspicion of their existence.

With Christianity it is otherwise. It was vaguely anticipated by the thoughts and hearts of men for ages before it came. Not merely Judæa, but Athens and Alexandria—not merely the heirs of Abraham's promises, but heathens feeling after God, if haply they might find Him—expected Him to reveal Himself, listened for Him to speak. They looked out upon the old world, such as it was—a stage on which all the moral laws witnessed to by the natural conscience were perpetually violated; they looked up to the throne of heaven. "Surely," they said, "if there be a moral God He must interfere; sooner or later He will rend the heavens and come down; the clouds and darkness that seem to be round about Him will not always hide from our eyes the righteousness and judgment that are the habitation of His seat."

And now He has spoken, nay, He has come among us. And if a man is to accept Christianity, he must recognise in his own case, as well as generally, the force of the fact to which Christianity appeals; the fact that man needs it. If he has no appetite based on this sense of want; if he has never known that instinctive feeling after God which St. Paul ascribes to the old Gentile world;[1] if his conscience is treated as a mere bundle of associations, or at least has never been sufficiently active,

"Nocte dieque suum gestare in pectore testem,"

as it ranges over his past life; if he has been living, and still lives, as though the universe were self-existent, and there were no such thing as absolute moral truth; then, for him, the Gospel is of course unwelcome, if in no other sense, yet as being superfluous. It offers a supply where there is no demand, and it is naturally rejected. As our Lord said, with the tenderness of Divine irony, "They that are whole need not a physician, but they that are sick; I came not to call the righteous, but sinners to repentance."[2]

But this insensibility to the facts of man's existence will not always last. Sooner or later the truth will avenge itself. Happy they who in this world experience the sentence of the Magnificat; in whom pride and self-reliance is put down from its seat, and spiritual hunger is rewarded; who discover ere it is too late that, in Scripture language, they are poor and blind and naked, and who take the Divine counsel to buy raiment and fine gold and eye-salve from the Son of Man.[3]

Observe the bearing of this on a point which sooner or later has a practical meaning for most men, in days like ours.

When men get perplexed about the claims of Christianity, they are often led to complain that the evidences of Christianity are not more cogent than they are. They

[1] Acts xvii. 27. [2] St. Matt. ix. 12, 13. [3] Rev. iii. 18.

ask, "Why, if Christianity is true, and of such great importance to all of us, we cannot have mathematical demonstration of its claims? Why are we thrown back upon moral considerations, which confessedly present themselves so very differently to different minds? Does it not look as if the producible evidence was really unequal to the task required of it, and as if Christian apologists, conscious of this fact, were anxious to blunt the keenness of criticism by insisting that inquirers about Christianity should take up a moral position which already half disposes them to allow its assertions?"

Certainly, my brethren, it must be admitted that the Christian evidences presuppose a certain moral sympathy in an inquirer. They are in fact moral and not mathematical or experimental. They are not of so imperative a character as to impose themselves, as the sensible experience of an earthquake or of an eclipse imposes itself, upon reluctant wills. We do not accept the Apostles' Creed by a mental act identical with that which accepts the conclusion of a proposition in Euclid. For the Creed addresses itself not simply to our capacity for speculative thought, but also by implication to our sense of duty, because we know that if it is true, a great many practical consequences immediately follow. Therefore the evidence in its favour is so adjusted as to be sufficient for those who wish for attested information as to the nature and will of the Author of the law of right and wrong within them, and insufficient for others who, conscious of disloyalty to that inner law, would rather be without such information. In this sense it must be granted that Christianity expects to be met—if not half way, yet to a certain point—by the yearnings of human nature; by desire based upon a clear discernment of its need of knowledge and of its need of strength. If the evidences for Christianity were of such a character that no honest and educated man could possibly reject them without intellectual folly, whatever his moral condition or history might be, then Christian belief would be like a university degree, a certificate of a certain sort of mental capacity, but it would be no criterion whatever of a man's past or present relation to God. St. Paul makes faith such a criterion; because faith is a moral as much as an intellectual act; because it combines our sense of moral want with our perception of the bearings of moral evidence. Thus a margin of deficiency, mathematically speaking, is even necessary in the Christian evidences as a whole, in order to leave room for the exercise of faith; that vital, emphatic act of the whole soul, by which the soul throws itself on the invisible, and thus secures the proper moral objects of Christianity itself.

III.

It would be easy to show how intimately our prospects of improvement in all departments of human activity and life must depend upon our faith in the continuous fulfilment of the words of the Magnificat. The temper which is there foredoomed is in reality the great obstacle to the attainment of our best hopes for the future.

What is the master passion of many of the noblest men who have ever lived? It is the conquest of speculative truth. And in our day this passion, always energetic, seeks its object more eagerly than before in the experimental sciences. Every Christian must admit that a physical fact is just as much a part of God's truth, although not possibly as necessary for all men to know, as is any fact of the Christian creed. Religious men have been slow to own this. The Church of Rome made a signal mistake in the case of Galileo, and no candid person would affirm that a mistake of that sort was, either two centuries ago or since, likely to be peculiar to the Church of Rome. All ascertained facts are parts of a perfectly harmonious whole, and must be welcomed by any sincere workman who is employed in any corner, spiritual or natural, of the great temple of Truth. But religion has two complaints to make against some representatives of modern physics. It complains, that the submission of Christian intellect is again and again peremptorily demanded not for facts, but for some hypothesis, which, if we are to judge from the past, may be presently discredited and abandoned. It complains further, that there is, on the part of some scientific men, a strange indisposition, which at least rivals any private theological prejudice in its irrational tenacity, to admit facts of a different order from their own. No *a priori* doctrine about the absolute invariability of natural law will persuade us Christians that Jesus Christ did not really rise from the dead. The Resurrection rests upon adequate testimony, and a really comprehensive science will recognise and account for it, whether by supposing the intervention of a higher law or otherwise. It is irrational to demand that Christians shall forget the great fact which sustains their faith because science has formulated a doctrine of invariable law; Christianity may be denounced as unprogressive or reactionary, but Christians will keep their eyes on the evidence which has sustained the highest minds and the noblest efforts for eighteen centuries, and will repeat their own "E pur se muove." Surely there are yet mists of intellectual assumption to be scattered, forms of thought to be put down from their seat; surely there is a simple hungering after all truth to be encouraged, in more quarters of the world of thought than one, if our common object, to know all that we can of the Will and ways of God, is to be successfully attained.

What is the most earnest aspiration of every Christian soul in its best moments? Is it not spiritual improvement? And why is it that the main source of this, the study of the Bible, is so often unproductive? Because men only study the surface of the Bible, or at best the mind of the Bible. They do not study its heart. Doubtless the Bible, more than any other book, is a centre of interest; philological, historical, philosophical, moral. The man of letters was right who said, that if he must have the companionship of only one book to the end of his days, he would choose the Bible. But to see in Holy Scripture the most interesting history, the strongest and most pathetic poetry, the most searching moral teaching known among men, is to do less than justice to the true majesty and power of the sacred volume. We learn all these things from the Bible as its critics; but there is something beyond to be learned from it only when we have the grace to be simply learners, anxious that it should speak to our inmost souls. And its power of doing this is best realized when the great moral barrier of self-complacency has been removed, and the soul hungers to be filled with the good things of spiritual truth. Here it is that we often see the illuminative office of sorrow: sorrow forces us on our knees; sorrow disperses our prejudices; sorrow casts down our mental idols; sorrow sharpens our appetite for the unseen and the eternal. There are psalms, there are passages in the Gospels and in St. Paul, which no man can understand without the preparatory discipline of mental pain; and thousands of Christians have learned to say, with the Psalmist, "It is good for me that I have been in trouble, that I may learn Thy statutes."[1]

And what is the prayer which Christians must most frequently use for the distracted Church of Christ? Must it not be, that "all they that do confess His Holy Name may agree in the truth of His Holy Word, and live in unity and godly love?" Must it not be the earthly echo of that

[1] Ps. cxix. 71.

intercession, begun in the supper-chamber and continued in heaven from century to century, that "they all may be one, as Thou, Father, art in Me, and I in Thee, that they also may be one in Us: that the world may believe that Thou hast sent Me"?[1] Who, indeed, can have any moderate acquaintance with the unbelieving thought of our time without knowing that it appeals to no fact more frequently or with more force than that of the divisions among Christians, when it would justify its rejection of our Master's claims? Doubtless there are real differences of principle underlying our divisions. On the one side the unwarranted claims of Rome, on the other the Puritan denial of what our Lord has revealed as to the structure of His Church, and the grace and power of His sacraments, make separation necessary, until He Who rules the hearts of men as well as the course of events, shall bring about, in whatever way, an understanding between those who sincerely confess His Name. But meanwhile, how different would the situation be if the still inevitable separation were not so often embittered by social and political antagonisms, by accumulations of prejudice and passion which overlay the real points at issue, and which make the angel-chant of peace on earth and goodwill amongst men sound from the heavens, Christmas after Christmas, like a hideous sarcasm! There is enough in some recent circumstances almost to provoke despair; and yet, as Christians, we may be sure that the forces which will ultimately reunite the Church of God and secure its triumph are not really in abeyance. The Conference which was held at Bonn two months ago [2] under the presidency of the first of Church historians, may have achieved less than its more sanguine wellwishers had hoped. But at least it has proved how petty and trivial are some of the misunderstandings which have contributed to produce the

[1] St. John xvii. 21.   [2] In August 1874.

widest chasms in Christendom; it has helped to dissipate, at any rate within a certain area, the moral obstacles to concord between disconnected Churches; it has even seemed to foreshadow, not indistinctly, the advent of a happier day than ours, when a wide unity may be enjoyed without confiscating truth; when truth will be acknowledged, in no half-hearted or indifferentist spirit, at a less costly sacrifice than that of outward and inward unity.

It is encouraging to reflect that we can all work for great and noble ends like this, by learning the moral lesson which is the traditional subject of to-day's sermon in this pulpit. Some assumptions to dissipate, some mental idols to depose, some truth and goodness to hunger after, there must be for all of us. And, as a great living analyst of human nature has lately reminded us, "The growing good of the world is partly dependent on unhistoric acts; and that things are not so ill with you and me as they might have been is half owing to the number who have lived faithfully a hidden life, and rest in unvisited tombs."

SERMON XII.

THE FALL OF JERICHO.

HEB. xi. 30.

By faith the walls of Jericho fell down, after they were compassed about seven days.

FEW events in the history of the Old Testament possess a more varied interest than the fall of Jericho. It marks the first decisive step towards the real conquest of Canaan, and the conquest of Canaan forms an epoch in the history of Israel and of the world. The fall of Jericho sounds the knell of an old civilization: it marks the succession, if not the birthday, of the new. The true Lord of the land has come to take possession, and the tenant, who has so ill discharged his trust, must at last give account of it. The historian is concerned to note how at this epoch a body of social and political truth, which the greatest of human lawgivers had delivered to his rude countrymen, is passing the frontier of desert life, in order to take up a settled place and home among the nations of the world. The moralist dwells upon the tragic collapse of races endowed with some fine natural qualities, but the willing victims of an incurable corruption, which had sapped the best elements of healthy national life, long ere the invader appeared on the hills of Bashan; he bends before that sterner side of the Divine Justice, upon which no sinner can gaze without apprehension, but which no serious Theist can presume to question. And the theologian, who knows what was the real mission of Israel as the preserver and herald of a message from above, sees in the fall of Jericho a decisive step towards the formal establishment of the theocracy; he here welcomes the presage of a triumph which the Gospel would one day win over a prouder and stronger world. In the New Testament, however, the event is noticed, not for its wide historical, or ethical, or theocratic interest, but simply as a victory of faith. Under that aspect let us regard it to-day. The ground, the difficulties, above all the power of faith, may well engage some attention on a festival, when Christians endeavour steadily to contemplate faith's highest Object; when "by the confession of a true faith we acknowledge the glory of the Eternal Trinity, and in the power of the Divine Majesty worship the Unity."[1] Nor is the subject much less appropriate on an occasion consecrated by the custom of the University to considering the extension of the Church of Christ in the dependencies of this great Empire. There are many other reasons for wishing well to such a cause besides those which faith suggests; but faith alone can undertake to promote it with any hope of serious and lasting success.

I.

"By faith the walls of Jericho fell down." Whose faith? The faith, not of a single leader merely, but of a people; the faith, not only of Joshua, but of Israel. And in whom was this faith reposed? In Him Who, as Israel believed, had spoken to the ancestors of the race, had contracted with them a covenant of grace and service, had taught their descendants His Law, and had made them, alone among the nations, its depositaries and guardians.

[1] Collect for Trinity Sunday.

To Israel, He was a living King, ever at hand to teach, to rebuke, to judge, to bless. It was Israel's faith which realized His Presence, as a substantial fact; Israel's was a faith which, needing no daily proof of that which it could not see, was itself the evidence of the truth of its object. It was in short a new sense, a second sight. It was not without relations to reason and conscience, to preceding mental information and to moral life, but it was really an intuitive perception, which habitually pierced the veil of sense, and rested on the Invisible. And its main object, as has been said, was the Personal God. A singular paradox has lately been projected, to the effect that Israel did not believe in a Person at all, but only in some power or stream of tendency, not ourselves, making for righteousness.[1] The object of this theory is to eliminate, if possible, from the earliest records of the faith of Israel, from the primitive religion of the Bible, the last trace of a metaphysical element. The author is clear-sighted enough to see that if you say that God is a Person, you make an assertion which is just as metaphysical as any one of the propositions in St. John's Gospel, or in the Nicene or Athanasian Creeds; and he wishes to relieve the primitive religion of Israel from what he conceives to be a damaging imputation. So Israel, he maintains, knew nothing of a personal God; Israel assigned the name God to conduct or righteousness, contemplated for the time being with deep emotion; or if to something not in any sense ourselves, then to a power, a tendency, conceived of very indefinitely, but moral in its general drift. Now, certainly the God of Israel is not stated in terms to be a Person, since the Hebrew language contains no word to express the idea of Person in the sense of a self-conscious and self-determining being. The idea of Personality, as it has been elaborated by modern philosophy, is not in that elaborated form recognised in

[1] *Literature and Dogma*, by Matthew Arnold.

Scripture; orthodoxy is not concerned to invert the history of thought. And the particular sense[1] in which the word Person is applied by the Church to Each of the Divine Three, Who yet are One in the Indivisible Substance of the Godhead, is not here in question. But if by Person be meant a union of consciousness, will, and character, then who will say that the God of the Patriarchs, the God of the Psalter, the God of Israel in the desert, or of Israel in Canaan, was conceived of as impersonal, or as lacking any one of these ingredients of personality. Insert the definition, "an eternal power or stream of tendency, not ourselves, making for righteousness," wherever you read the words God or Lord in the Psalter, and see what will be, I do not say the religious, but the intellectual outcome. Suppose for a moment that He Whom Israel owned as God was not believed to be endowed with consciousness or will; how are we to explain the love and worship of which He was the object? A power or tendency might provoke fear: it is so with the powers of the physical world. If such a power were believed to be mind, it might, as in Hindostan, attract long and earnest meditation. But love and worship are offered only to a Being Who is presumed to be conscious of the offering, to be willing to receive it, to be of a certain character, which is the earnest of His Will. As Strauss has recently observed, there can be no doubt of the intention of the Old Testament to represent God as a Personal Being;[2] the history of Israel and the devotions of Israel are alike conclusive on the subject.

Yes, it was this Unseen, Almighty Friend,—the Friend of their departed ancestors Abraham, Isaac, and Jacob,—the Inspirer and Guide of the Great Lawgiver who had led them forth from the furnace of Egyptian slavery,—the

---

[1] This would perhaps be most accurately expressed by *subsistentia*.
[2] *Der Alte und der Neue Glaube*, p. 104.

Gracious and Awful Being Whom they had alternately loved and feared, neglected and served, sought and forgotten, Who was, the men of Israel believed, still with them. They were entering on a new tract of their history; they were face to face with the resources of a comparatively ancient and settled civilization, with which their rude experience of the desert ill enabled them to cope. The walls and gates of Jericho, the key of a country which they believed was to become their own, frowned down on their anxieties; and they could but turn upwards to Him Who had made them what they were. In the words of one of the later retrospective Psalms, He had "divided the Red Sea in two parts, because His mercy endureth for ever." He had led His people through the wilderness; He had smitten great kings; He would give their land to be an heritage unto Israel His servant.[1] He, at once the Creator of the world, and the Captain and Patron of Israel, was still with them even before the walls of Jericho: He—His Presence, His Power, His Loving-kindness—was the object of their faith.

Certainly the word faith is used vaguely enough in these days; and men talk of faith in their destiny, faith in the future, faith in a cause or principle, faith in progress, faith in humanity. If these phrases are taken to pieces, they will be found to mean faith in a will that can bring to pass what men variously conceive to be the highest good in the coming years. We Christians enjoy a wider horizon than any of those which are determined by the limits of sense or the limits of time. We are concerned not merely with the fortunes of our race on this planet, but with the destiny of its individual members in an Eternal World. For us the Personal God, Who has revealed Himself as Threefold in His Absolute and Unchanging Being, Who, as Father, Son, and Holy Ghost, has disclosed His

[1] Ps. cxxxvi. 13, 16, 17, 21, 22.

deepest and most important relations to ourselves, is the object of all that deserves the name of faith. His word, when once we are sure that it is His, commands our unhesitating submission. If we, in our fashion and measure, have any hopes for the advance of truth and goodness, if, amid the many sinister appearances which darken the higher prospects of man, we still cling to the faith that in the end the walls of Jericho will fall, it is because He, as we rejoice to know and believe, is with us.

II.

"By faith the walls of Jericho fell down." What was the connection between Israel's faith in his Lord and the fall of the walls of Jericho? Simply this: that that event depended upon Israel's obedience to the command of God. In some way or other God speaks to us all. He speaks to one generation by specific and external communications, to another by the pressure of its recognised principles or of its conscience, as questions of conduct successively arise. Most assuredly, whether to instruct or rebuke, whether to sustain or to test us, He leaves not Himself without witness. At that moment of solemn anxiety, Joshua was encouraged and instructed by the appearance of a heavenly Guide in the precincts of the camp at Gilgal.[1] The sacred narrative will not bear the gloss that this appearance was a purely internal or subjective one; a visible phenomenon of some kind was the accredited language, so to call it, in which these primitive generations of men looked for, and discovered what they knew of, the Will of God. "There stood a man over against him with his sword drawn in his hand."[2] What the sight of the Burning Bush had been to Moses at Horeb, that the vision of the Captain of the hosts of the Lord was to Joshua at Gilgal. In each

[1] Josh. v. 13-15.   [2] Josh. v. 13.

case the specific character of the vision was in sympathy with the circumstances of the time. The furnace of the Egyptian bondage and the warlike preparations for the approaching campaign, are reflected in the forms of the respective apparitions. This is to be explained, not by supposing that men externalize and divinize their own hopes or fears, clothing them in the garb which their thoughts or circumstances suggest; but by the simpler and truer consideration that God speaks to His creatures in all ages, through sights and sympathies which they most readily understand. Was the mysterious Being, the Malaach Adonai, Who appears so constantly in the early history of Israel, and Who here is the Prince of the Army of the Lord, a created Angel, like the Michael of the Book of Daniel? Or was He One Who, before He entered by an Incarnation into time, had been already the instrument of communications between the invisible God and the world of men? Not to enter on this difficult question, we may remark that upon either supposition the communication was from God: and that it made a serious demand upon the faith of Israel. For seven days the soldiers of Israel were to march in procession round the city, with the ark of the covenant, and with seven priests blowing trumpets before the ark. They were to complete the circuit of the city once in every day until the seventh.[1] On the seventh day they were to march round Jericho seven times; the priests were to blow a long blast; the people were to raise a loud shout of war; the walls of the city would fall, and its capture follow.

Now these directions would have tested the faith of Israel in two particulars more especially.

They suggest, first of all, an entire inadequacy, in human judgment, of means to ends. We can trace no relation between the means prescribed and the end proposed. What

[1] Josh. vi. 3, 4.

was the end proposed? The capture of Jericho; a town strongly fortified after the fashion of that age. What were the prescribed means? A daily procession with trumpets round the walls for seven days, repeated seven times on the seventh. Attempts have indeed been made to assign a military value to this procession with trumpets. Thus Rosenmüller[1] suggests that it was an invitation or challenge to the terrified citizens to make a sally, and so to endeavour to take the besiegers at a disadvantage. But this opinion has no warrant in the narrative, and it would be condemned by ordinary military prudence. Nor can we suppose that Joshua's design was to lull the men of Jericho into a false security, and then to surprise them. The walls of Jericho were not first mined and then carried by storm; and the security of the besieged, if it ever could have been fostered by such a method, would surely have been disturbed by the sevenfold repetition of the procession on the seventh day of the siege. It is clear that the procession was not a military measure; its meaning was altogether religious. The Book of Numbers had already assigned a specific religious value to the use of the trumpet by the people of the theocracy:[2] it was a symbolical Kyrie Eleison, by which Israel claimed the mercy and the aid of God. The purpose of the proceedings before Jericho was to repeat the lesson which had been taught so vividly by the circumstances of the Exodus; to check the habit, so deeply rooted in the race, of trusting in the visible and the material, in what the Scriptures call "an arm of flesh;" to throw them back upon their Gracious and Unseen Protector, and to convince them, by the very form of their triumph, that the work was His.

The apparent disproportion or absence of any traceable relations between means and ends in the kingdom of God has in all ages proved a serious trial of faith. Think

---

[1] *Scholia in Vet. Test.* pars undecima, p. 82.   [2] Numb. x. 9.

steadily of the magnificent object which the Church of God sets before herself; it is not merely the instruction and elevation of the human race, but the eternal salvation of souls. Yet how feeble and unworthy seems her machinery for effecting it! The "foolishness of preaching" does not less accurately express the opinion of a large section of the modern world than it did that of the Corinthian critics who discussed St. Paul.[1] How, men ask, can the perpetual repetition and enforcement of a few doctrines, of a few precepts, of a Great Example, effect the result of lifting the world off its axis, and giving a new direction to the lives of men? How should the Christian Sacraments achieve more than any other picturesque and affectionate memorials of the past? How can a few drops of water, or a little bread and wine, be the channels or the veils of a Heavenly Gift warranted to cleanse the sinful and to reinvigorate the weak? Or to what hands has the burden of the Apostolical charge been again and again committed in all ages of the Church; to what hands, it may indeed well be asked, when the drift and purpose of the commission is considered? "Side by side," it has been said, "with the Cyprians, the Augustines, the Chrysostoms, the Gregories,—side by side with an Andrewes, a Ken, a Wilson,—the Church has witnessed an Episcopate presenting the most various moral complexions; the Papacy alone has exhibited every gradation of moral life, from angelic holiness to outrageous wickedness; and the typical prelates of our Revolution and of the early Hanoverian period had their prototypes among courtly and selfish ecclesiastics who once cringed on the steps of the throne of Constantinople."

This trial to faith is probably as old as Christianity; but it is only one department of a larger perplexity suggested by the whole action and bearing of the Church of Christ.

[1] 1 Cor. i. 21.

As she moves through the centuries, on her errand of truth and mercy, yet maimed through internal divisions, or weighed down to the very dust by worldliness and corruptions, men ask if this can be the Divine Society which, for eighteen centuries, has been attempting to regenerate the world, and which has not altogether failed in her mission. What is the historical manifestation of Christianity but one long procession around the walls of Jericho, in which the means employed seem to be altogether unequal to achieving that which nevertheless they do in a measure achieve? What is it but a prolonged contrast between the ideal and the actual, between the anticipated and the real? That traceable order and proportion of cause and effect, that array of powerful influences and of commanding personages who achieve striking and magnificent results in the field of secular history, seems constantly to be wanting in the history of the Church, which thus presents us with a continual paradox, that we may look for its explanation beyond the realm of sense. Yes; now, as at the first, "God hath chosen the foolish things of the world to confound the wise: and God hath chosen the weak things of the world to confound the things that are mighty: and base things of the world, and things that are despised, hath God chosen, yea, and things which are not, to bring to nought things which are:" and why? "That no flesh should glory in His presence."[1]

Besides this, the faith of Israel was tried by the delay which was to be interposed between the first procession around the city and its final capture. If such a plan of operations were adopted, why should it not take effect at once? The walls would not really be more shaken by the procession on the seventh day than by the procession on the first. Meanwhile, how difficult it would be to carry out such instructions for six days without any result. It does

[1] 1 Cor. i. 27-29.

not seem long for us; but, depend upon it, for men who were face to face with an uncertain future and a great peril, the days, the hours, the minutes did seem long. When the second day had passed, and the third, and the fourth, and the fifth, and still the walls of Jericho stood as they had stood for years, do you suppose that there was no additional temptation to question the wisdom of the method which had been prescribed to Joshua? You cannot suppose it.

This delay of expected and warranted results, when the conditions which ought to ensure them have been complied with, even though it be a delay which is itself predicted, is to many minds one of the sorest trials that faith has to encounter. Not to go further for illustrations, did those three centuries, think you, which intervened between Pentecost and the Edict of Milan seem a short interval to the generations who lived and died, one after another, in the belief that when persecution had done its worst, the meek would inherit the earth, and would be refreshed in the multitude of peace?[1] Did the cry "How long, O Lord, how long?" never under the stress of persecution shade off into "Thou hast abhorred and forsaken Thine Anointed, and art displeased at him: Thou hast broken the covenant of Thy servant, and cast his crown to the ground?"[2] Was the old temptation of Israel never repeated, never yielded to in the heart of Christendom; the temptation to think that God had forgotten to be gracious, and had shut up His loving-kindness in displeasure;[3] that the Church had been led out to die in a social wilderness, and had better turn back to Egypt? How many of Christ's early worshippers may, like Demas, have failed under that temptation, One only knows. It is not for us to underrate trials which, through God's mercy, we have never experienced; but the delay of Christ's triumph must have

[1] Ps. xxxvii. 11.   [2] Rev. vi. 11. Ps. lxxxix. 37, 38.   [3] Ps. lxxvii. 9.

weighed heavily on our forefathers in the faith. Again and again the walls of the old heathen society were nodding to their fall; again and again it seemed as if Jericho must presently capitulate,—when lo! the hope proved an illusion. After Philip the Arabian came Decius; after Probus, Diocletian. "Hope deferred maketh the heart sick;"[1] and one of faith's highest and hardest duties is to sustain hope when its fulfilment is delayed, even though in accordance with previous intimations.

III.

"By faith the walls of Jericho fell down." Faith, then, is a power. She plants her foot upon a sure foundation; she grapples with her difficulties, and, in the end, she conquers. It is not to be imagined that the faith of Israel exercised over the material walls of Jericho any compulsion of a magnetic character which they could not but obey. If the triumphs claimed for faith in removing human disease or suffering should hereafter be explained by reference to some unsuspected natural law, which faith has only brought into active play, we need not fear to welcome the discovery. But at least the fall of the walls of Jericho, and a large proportion of the Gospel miracles, would be totally unaffected by it. Again, there is no ground for supposing that the walls were mined, and that they fell at a preconcerted signal. It is possible that their fall was due to the shock of an earthquake. But if this be assumed, we still have to account for the occurrence of the catastrophe at a predicted point of time, and at the apparent escape of the buildings within the city from the effects of the shock. Upon any supposition, the agency of faith on this occasion was limited to its determined reliance and hold upon the unseen agency of God, Who, whether

[1] Prov. xiii. 12.

through some natural law or independently, effected the downfall of the walls. The power of faith is the same; if it does not itself act, it accepts the conditions of action which are prescribed by the real Agent; it thereby, we may dare to say it, puts His Arm in motion; it acts—but through Him.

There is another reason for the power of faith. It is the parent of two of the greatest forces that can move the human soul; it produces hope and trust. The man who believes can trust: his faith sees God, and that sight creates confidence. The man who trusts can ignore or resist present and visible danger, through his clear perception of an Unseen Protector; and his trust is, of itself, a force, whether for purposes of action or purposes of resistance. It has been said that the strength of an army is more than doubled when it has general confidence in its commander. To trust in a great power is to share its strength. The success of every enterprise depends mainly on the belief that it will be achieved: and when the present offers nothing but materials for discouragement, hope comes to the aid of trust, and transfigures the present before our eyes with the enthusiasms of the future. And thus out of weakness men and women are made strong; and many a feeble Christian has felt, in the strength of this moral invigoration, of which faith is the source, as he resolutely takes the difficult line of painful or unwelcome duty, that

> "Si fractus illabatur orbis
> Impavidum ferient ruinæ."

For to him it has been said, "If thou canst believe, all things are possible to him that believeth,"[1] even through these magnificent endowments of hope and trust; and he, in his consciousness of mingled strength and weakness, cannot

[1] St. Mark ix. 23.

but answer, "I will not trust in my bow; it is not my sword that shall help me; but it is Thou that savest us from our enemies, and puttest them to confusion that hate us."[1]

Yes; faith is power. And we of this day who have so largely impaired or lost it must feel that we are weaker and poorer for the loss. It may be that the scepticism which has played so relentlessly over the Creed of our fathers, and whose brilliant sallies have seldom been held in check by any profound moral seriousness, has left us with keener wits than we might otherwise have possessed. But it has also left us weaker. We are not the men we might have been, or the men we were. Do you say that it is the jaundiced eye of theology which thus reads the moral symptoms of the time. Listen, then, to a great writer who has lately passed from among us, and who will not be suspected of any undue tenderness for the Christian Creed. "Energetic characters," says Mr. Mill, "on any large scale are becoming merely traditional. There is now scarcely any outlet for energy in this country, except business. The energy expended in this may still be regarded as considerable. What little is left from that employment is expended on some hobby; which may be a useful, even a philanthropic hobby, but is always some one thing, and generally a thing of small dimensions. The greatness of England is now all collective: individually small, we only appear capable of anything great by our habit of combining; and with this," he adds, not quite accurately, "our moral and religious philanthropists are perfectly contented. But it was men of another stamp than this that made England what it has been; and men of another stamp will be needed to prevent its decline."[2] The writer of course has his own way of accounting for what he thus describes: with him it is only the sacrifice of all marked

---

[1] Ps. xliv. 7, 8.   [2] *On Liberty*, pp. 125, 126.

individuality to the ever-encroaching tyranny of society and its conventionalisms. But why is there not force enough in individuals to resist the encroachment? Is it not because the secret and parent of the highest force has been so largely forfeited? The men who made England what it has been were men of faith. The great Plantagenet kings and statesmen had a faith, which, if, as we hold, not free from error, was at least clear and strong. The Puritans of the seventeenth century had a faith,— narrow, it is true, mutilated, distorted; but it too was clear and strong. Yet not a few of the men who would now mould the thought and destinies of England plainly say that they have no faith—only views and aspirations. "We laugh," says the author of the "Enigmas of Life," "at the scholastic nonsense of Irenæus, and are disgusted at the unseemly violence of Tertullian; but these men were ready to die for their opinions, and *we are not*."[1] Yes, the scepticism of our day, speaking through its most accomplished representatives, betrays a consciousness of its impoverishment: it knows and feels that God, in His Mercy and in His Justice, has stricken it with moral paralysis. And yet we are moving on towards a period when the strongest moral energies will be at least as necessary as they have ever been in the past. The European revolutions of the beginning of the century turned chiefly, although not solely, upon the structure of government; the revolutionary movements of its close, we need no prophet to tell us, will be animated by those fiercer passions which are kindled by questions of social right. All the devotion, the unselfishness, the intrepidity, that could be forthcoming under the most favourable circumstances will be needed in order to surmount these perils with safety and honour; the walls of Jericho will not fall down at the bidding of sentiment which has lost all moral nerve, and has forfeited

[1] *Enigmas of Life*, by W. R. Greg, p. 163.

all right to the name of faith. And it lies with you, my younger brethren, to decide whether the productive cause of the highest moral force shall be there, and equal to the emergency.

IV.

In dealing with the particular subject of to-day's sermon, missionary statistics are less likely to be useful than a restatement of principles on which missions must rely for success. We live in days when the duty of extending the Church of Christ is vehemently disputed; when the difficulties of extending it are greatly exaggerated; when the final failure of our attempts to Christianize the greatest of our dependencies is confidently predicted.

The duty of extending the Church of Christ cannot be a serious question between Christian and Christian; it can only be a question between Christianity and unbelief. It is part of that larger problem, whether Christianity is worth the trouble and expense which its propagation entails; whether it is really what, in the writings of St. Paul especially, it claims to be, the absolute and therefore the universal Religion needed by man, of whatever race, or in whatever stage of civilization; and needed in order to enable man to realize the true idea and end of his existence. We are not to-day discussing that vital question: we take the Christian solution of it for granted. Only let those who dispute our conclusion mark well the premiss on which it rests, and which must be set aside in order to dispute it successfully. My brethren, if it be true that God has so loved the world that He gave His Only Begotten Son, that whosoever believeth on Him should not perish, but have everlasting life; if Jesus our Lord is not merely a literary study, but a living Being; if His Holy Incarnation, His Atoning Death, His Perpetual Intercession, His Gifts of

Grace, are real things upon which we have staked our deepest hopes and our best activities,—there can be no doubt as to the practical interest which we must take in the extension of His Church. To every Christian, Christ gives a commission to do what he can, in his sphere and measure, for the spread of the Faith. To Englishmen He has given the responsibilities of empire, and among them its highest responsibility—that of doing the best thing that can be done for the largest possible number of human beings. Colonists who have left a Christian home and friends; and heathens, who have been brought under the sway of a power which owns, however inconsistently, the Name of Christ, have alike a claim on His Church which she cannot disown. The true Captain of the Lord's Host, revealing Himself amid the providences of our national history, appears once more to true hearts in Israel near the camp at Gilgal, and points to the duties which await them beneath the walls of Jericho.

To make the Church of Christ co-extensive with the dependencies of this Empire may appear, at first sight, a hopeless enterprise. Doubtless much may be done in those colonies to which our civilization has been transplanted from home almost in its integrity; or where we come into contact with pagan religions of such low, embryonic, unformed, and fluctuating types, that no more serious resistance is offered to the advance of the Church than to other features of European thought and life. In South Africa, for instance, as beyond the Atlantic, and in Australia, the difficulties of the Church, in the main, are those which she encounters at home; they arise from the divisions of Christians, or from the godlessness and indifference of large sections of a commercial and materialized community. But in India it is far otherwise. There we meet with religions which were ancient in days when Christianity was not yet born; with religions which, like Brahminism, have lost and

regained their empire, or which, like Islam, have wrenched
from the Church of Christ her most ancient home, the
hallowed centre of her most cherished memories, the scenes
of her earliest triumphs. And too often our missionaries
have represented not our strength but our weakness, as
they have gone forth to grapple with these mighty
traditions of error, embodied in vast literatures, defended
and propagated by immense organizations, pressing a subtle
philosophy, or all that is popular and concrete in human
superstition, into their service; and we naturally marvel
at an enterprise which seems, at first sight, to be so
hopelessly out of proportion to the proposed results. Something, indeed, may be done—is being done—to diminish the
interval. Christian missionaries, who, with the learning
and frankness of the Alexandrian teachers of old, can recognise in ancient religions those stray elements of truth
which in fact constitute their strength, will find that one
great barrier has disappeared. And Christian bishops, who
should organize a native ministry, and with it a vernacular
liturgy of Indian growth, would probably demolish another.
If the object be to extend the Church of Christ, with all
that is really essential to the tradition of the Faith and the
Sacraments, but not necessarily with all the forms and
associations which for a thousand years have encrusted
that tradition in Western Christendom, then sooner or later
this problem must be considered. Certainly it is improbable that a liturgy which is so dear to ourselves, because
it is the outgrowth of our spiritual and national history,
and which bears on its front not a few traces of our Saxon
temper, should ever be regarded, on the banks of the Indus
and the Ganges, at least by the people at large, as other
than an exotic. Points like these may safely be left
in the hands of the prelates who now rule the Indian
Church, and who have brought to their work a union
of religious fervour and philosophical insight from which

the happiest results may be expected.¹ Surely the efforts of such men might be reinforced more largely than they are, not merely by clergy, but by the many laymen who, whether in the civil service or in the army, pass the best years of their life in India, and who prepare for those years not unfrequently at Oxford. If I am speaking to any such, I would beg them to remember that Christianity is judged in India as in Europe, not so much by the arguments of its professional advocates, as by the lives of the great mass of its professed adherents; that laymen have it in their power to raise barriers to its advance among the heathen, which no clerical or missionary zeal can hope to surmount; and that laymen have it also in their power to recommend Christianity, by word and example, with a success which too often is denied to clergymen, however earnest or instructed. A layman has not to struggle against the rooted suspicion which is so often fatal to clerical enterprise, and which constitutes the only serious "clerical disability;"—the suspicion that what he says for Jesus Christ our Lord is only the language of professional propriety, and not that of personal conviction. It would be wrong to pretend that this suspicion is invincible, or that it is not counterbalanced by the immense religious opportunities of clerical service. Yet those of you who have not to encounter it should know your strength.

When all have done what they may, no doubt it will still seem that we are making a procession with trumpets; that the means at our disposal are unequal, on every ordinary principle of calculation, to achieving the end proposed. Jericho will still seem inaccessible to our efforts; and those efforts will be criticised almost in the terms in which some recent writers comment on the text of Joshua. The Church of Christ can never expect to escape such criticism: let

---

[1] The allusion is especially to the late Dr. Milman, Bishop of Calcutta, and Dr. Douglas, Bishop of Bombay.

her never fear it. She may be unable to trace the process by which ultimate success will be secured; but does this matter, if He be near to Whom the coming centuries are already present, and Whose word is sure? She may have to encounter many disappointments, much delay, abundant presages of failure. But he that believeth will not make haste:[1] a Christian knows his portion, and is not disheartened by anything but his own unfaithfulness. God, he knows, is patient, as being Eternal: duties are imperative; results are in wise and strong Hands; we can afford to wait. "The vision is yet for an appointed time; but at the end it shall speak and not lie: though it tarry, wait for it; because it will surely come, it will not tarry."[2]

[1] Isa. xxviii. 16.   [2] Hab. ii. 3.

SERMON XIII.

THE COURAGE OF FAITH.

Rom. i. 16.

I am not ashamed of the Gospel of Christ; for it is the power of God unto salvation to every one that believeth.

IN days that have passed away, such a subject as "the extension of the Church throughout the colonies and dependencies of the British Empire" would probably have suggested questions of one kind only. It would have been generally agreed that such an extension is desirable; and any possible discussion would have turned upon the best means of carrying it out. In these latter days, as we know, it is somewhat otherwise. Propose to propagate the Gospel, and to extend its concrete embodiment, the Church, and you raise in certain minds the previous inquiry, whether the Gospel or the Church are worth the effort. In former days, it was a question of the minor premiss alone, now it is a question of the major. Then men asked how they could do least wrong to a great conviction; whereas now, some of us seem to doubt whether or not, in the Apostle's language, to be "ashamed" of it.

St. Paul is led to use this expression by an association of ideas which it is easy to trace. He is writing to a Church, founded by other hands than his, founded, it would seem, some years before, but by no Apostle or Apostolic man. As befits an Apostle, he yearns to visit this Church

that he may impart to it some spiritual gift.[1] He has
desired to visit it long ere now; but again and again
he has been hindered.[2] He still hopes some day to
carry out this purpose.[3] For he has in his keeping a
truth, which, as he believes, belongs by right to every
human being, although as yet only a few members of the
great human family have claimed it as their own. He,
for his part, is, in his own words, a debtor until all rights
are satisfied; and his creditors comprise the world. "I
am a debtor," he exclaims, "both to the Greeks and to the
Barbarians, both to the philosophers and the unintelligent."[4]
Therefore he must do what he may do, always and everywhere. Therefore he will add, "As much as in me is, I am
ready to preach the Gospel to you that are in Rome also."[5]

In Rome also! It might seem as if a word had escaped
him which, even for an Apostle, had some disturbing—
I had almost dared to say—some magic power. For
here, suddenly, his thought takes a new direction and a
wider range. In Rome also! The little half-organized
Church disappears from view, and before the imagination
and mind of Paul there rises—indistinct, no doubt, but
oppressively vast—the imperial form of the mistress of
the world. And this vision of Rome, thus for the moment
present to the Apostle's mind, produces in it a momentary
recoil; so that, like a man whose onward course has been
sharply checked, he falls back to consider the resources at his
disposal. He falls back upon himself, upon the faith that is
in him, upon the Author and Object of that faith. There is
a moment's pause, and then he writes, "I am not ashamed."
If he were speaking he might almost seem to falter in his
tone; "I am not ashamed of the Gospel of Christ."

He is not ashamed of the Gospel. We are struck at
first by the reserved and negative phrase; it seems to fall
below the requirements of the occasion, and the character

[1] Rom. i. 11. [2] Rom. i. 13. [3] Rom. i. 15. [4] Rom. i. 14. [5] Rom. i. 15.

of the man. Is this, we ask, the language of passionate feeling, so strong that it shrinks from the attempt to say what it is, and ventures only to say what it is not? Or is there some subtle irony, flavouring the phrase that seems thus to disappoint us? No, this cannot be. Putting other considerations aside, this mood is inconsistent with what those who know him best would anticipate from the simplicity, the sincerity of the Apostle's literary manner. And yet, if we understand him literally, how is this mere negative state of feeling equal to the desire which burns within him, or worthy of his past and present relations to the Gospel of his Lord and Master?

Certainly, brethren, elsewhere the Apostle uses very different language from this. He loves to call the Gospel, as the Jews called their law, his " boast." Consider only one sentence, in his Epistle to the Philippians, in which he states positively what the Faith of Jesus Christ was to him. " I count all things but loss for the excellency of the knowledge of Christ Jesus my Lord, for Whom I have suffered the loss of all things, and do count them but dung, that I may win Christ, and be found in Him."[1]

And yet, ten years later, quite at the close of his great career, when he now knows Rome well, by a first and a second imprisonment, when the last scenes are now almost in view—the tyrant's throne, the accusation and the defence, the solemn travesty of justice, and the sharp suffering beyond—he writes to a disciple, " I am not ashamed: for I know Whom I have believed, and am persuaded that He is able to keep that which I have committed unto Him against that day."[2]

The truth is that the Apostle is not using a rhetorical figure; his negative and measured phrase is imposed on him by the thoughts which rise before him. He is confronted by the idea of Pagan Rome; he is making head

[1] Phil. iii. 8, 9.   [2] 2 Tim. i. 12.

against and resisting a feeling which threatens to overawe him; and it is in this travail of protest and disavowal that he cries, "I am not ashamed of the Gospel of Christ."

Why, we may ask, should he be ashamed of it? What was there in the prospect of a missionary visit to Rome which could, even for a moment, suggest any feeling of the kind to such a soul as St. Paul's?

I.

Would not a man have been struck first of all by the apparent insignificance of the Gospel, when viewed relatively to the great world of thought and action represented by and embodied in Rome?

That which impressed every subject of the Empire when his thoughts turned towards Rome, was its unrivalled grandeur. The very name of Rome was the symbol of magnificence and power. For Rome was the seat of empire; the city which had conquered and which ruled the world. Rome was the centre of society; she welcomed to her receptions all that was noble and wealthy and distinguished; all the year round her palaces were thronged by dependent kings and princes. Rome was the nurse and patroness of such learning and thought as was tolerated by the political jealousies of the Imperial age; the great days of Athens were already of the past; literature was too much of a courtier to take up its abode contentedly in a conquered province. Nay, Rome was, in a sense, a great religious centre too, or at least a great centre of the current religions. At that date, all that was spiritual, all that was debased and superstitious and grotesque, found a place and a haunt in Rome; with magnificent impartiality, she smiled a welcome to all the truths and all the falsehoods that presented themselves at her gates. She was to ancient civilization what since the Revolution Paris has been to France: everything else was provincial. From her went forth law, and the secrets of administration, and the varied enterprise of a ruling race, and the canons of taste and fashion, and the rewards of honour, and the authoritative opinions which swayed the world. Back to her returned all that the subject peoples could give; their skill, their arts, their wealth, their customs, their philosophies, their religions. Learning might yet linger around the walls of Athens; Jerusalem, we know, was a sacred spot. But, cherished in the imaginations of the men who dwelt on the shores of the Gulf of Salamis, or on the shores of the Lake of Tiberias, there dwelt ever an image of the distant Empire City, in which this world's splendours reached their utmost height; the city which every man who aspired to fame or power dreamt at least of seeing before he died. Truly Rome was the "colluvies gentium;" at once the queen and ruler of the nations, and the sink into which they poured their corruptions and their filth; but we must remember that men who looked at her from a distance, as St. Paul had hitherto done, did not share any such keen political discontent as that of Tacitus, or any such social irritation and disgust as that of Juvenal. Now and then, indeed, as when Philo the Jew, with his four Alexandrian companions, sought to obtain justice at the court of Caligula, the provincials might discover what lay beneath the splendid robe of their imperial mistress. But when Philo is describing that extraordinary interview with the emperor in the gardens of Mœcenas, in which the caprice, and the insolence, and the buffoonery of the master of thirty legions vented themselves on the terrified envoys, he is profoundly impressed with the magnificence of Rome;[1] and it is certain that St. Paul, writing to the Romans eighteen years after Philo's visit, would have been no stranger to a like impression.

[1] Philo Judæus, *Legatio ad Caium.*

And the Gospel—how did it look when placed in juxtaposition with this popular estimate of the greatness of Rome? If it had yet been heard of in the upper circles of the Imperial city, how did men think of it? what did they say of it? Was it not, relatively to everything in the great capital, as far as the natural senses and judgment of man could pierce, poor and insignificant? The best informed, who deigned now and then to bestow a thought upon the morbid fancies of the Eastern world, could have distinguished in it only a rebellious offshoot from the most anti-social and detested religion in the Empire; it was itself an "exitiabilis superstitio;" and it had about it a touch of inconsequence and absurdity from which Judaism was free. The estimate which an average French Academician might be supposed to form of Quakerism is probably not unlike the estimate which approved itself to the most cultivated minds in Rome as due to the religion of St. Paul and St. John. If Christianity meant to propagate itself, where was its organization? how could the government of a few unnoticed congregations enter into any sort of rivalry with the mighty system of the Imperial Rule? To what could it point in the way of literature, at least so far as the literary public knew? how could it compete with the genius of poets and historians who had the ear of the world? What was the capacity of its leading men—at least in public estimation—when set side by side with the accomplished statesmen who had created, and who still from time to time ruled the Empire? Well might it have seemed that Rome, the centre of Imperial life, must bring the infant Church to bay; Rome must teach it to measure itself by other standards than any which could be supplied by a remote Asiatic province; Rome must overawe, by the magnificence of its collective splendours, the pretensions of any system or teacher coming forth from some obscure corner of the Empire on a mission to illuminate and to change the world.

True enough it is that St. Paul had his eye on higher things; but his was too sympathetic a nature not to be alive to what was meant by Rome. Yet, if I have said that his voice might seem for a moment to falter, he at once recovers: the glories of Rome do not overawe him. He is not enslaved by the apparent at the cost of the real. He knows that a civilization which bears a proud front to the world, but is rotten within, is destined to perish. Already, five years before, he has shown in one line of his Second Epistle to the Thessalonians that he foresees the end of all this splendour;[1] already he may have caught some of the accents of that Christian prophecy which, a few years later, on the lips of another Apostle, chanted the doom of the mistress of the world: ". . . She saith in her heart, I sit a queen, and am no widow, and shall see no sorrow. . . . Alas, alas, that great city Babylon, that mighty city! for in one hour is thy judgment come. And the merchants of the earth shall weep and mourn over her; for no man buyeth their merchandise any more: the merchandise of gold, and silver, and precious stones, and of pearls, and fine linen, and purple, and silk, and scarlet, and all thyme wood, and all manner vessels of ivory, and all manner vessels of most precious wood, and of brass, and iron, and marble, and cinnamon, and odours, and ointments, and frankincense, and wine, and oil, and fine flour, and wheat, and beasts, and sheep, and horses, and chariots, and slaves, and souls of men. . . . The merchants of these things, which were made rich by her, shall stand afar off for the fear of her torment, weeping and wailing, and saying, Alas, alas, that great city, that was clothed in fine linen, and purple, and scarlet, and decked with gold, and precious stones, and pearls! For in one hour so great riches is come to nought."[2]

In Christian eyes, Alaric was at the gates of Rome long

---

[1] 2 Thess. ii. 7.   [2] Rev. xviii. 7, 10-13, 15-17.

before his time. The luxury, the ostentation, the lofty confidence and scorn, which were concentrated in the Empire city were doomed. "All that is in the world, the lust of the flesh, and the lust of the eyes, and the pride of life, is not of the Father, but is of the world. And the world passeth away, and the lust thereof; but he that doeth the will of God abideth for ever."[1] Like St. John, St. Paul knew that one man, of no great culture or accomplishments, yet with a clear, practical faith, is more than a match for a brilliant society, which at heart believes in nothing as right and true. St. Paul was well aware of the insignificance of the Gospel, and of the insignificance of the Church, when measured by ordinary human standards: it was his own observation that "not many wise men after the flesh, not many mighty, not many noble," are called to take their places in the Kingdom of the Redemption.[2] But, then, in his estimate of the relative value of the seen and the unseen, of the Divine and the human, of nature and of grace, this very insignificance is power. "God hath chosen the foolish things of the world to confound the wise; and God hath chosen the weak things of the world to confound the things which are mighty; and the base things of the world, and things which are despised, hath God chosen, yea, and things which are not, to bring to nought things that are: that no flesh should glory in His presence."[3] There was nothing in the glories of Rome to arrest the exclamation, "I am not ashamed of the Gospel of Christ."

II.

Another reason might have deterred the Apostle from proclaiming the Gospel in the face of the society and thought of Rome; there was about it a suspicion, if not an appearance, of failure. Had it succeeded as yet in

---

[1] 1 St. John ii. 16, 17.   [2] 1 Cor. i. 26.   [3] 1 Cor. i. 27-29.

achieving all that men might have looked for in a religion which claimed to have come from heaven? It is common, and very natural in us Christians of the latter days, to idealize the Church of the Apostolic age. But, in sober fact, missions working under the eyes of the Apostles were not always prosperous; and Churches, founded and visited by Apostles, were not always united or always pure. If when St. Paul wrote the sentence, "I am not ashamed of the Gospel of Christ," he was thinking of Rome, it is well to remember that he was writing from Corinth. And Corinth, that Church of Corinth, from the midst of which he wrote thus bravely, what was it, at any rate a short year before, in the judgment of the Apostle himself? If it was to be judged from St. Paul's First Epistle to the Corinthians, might not this Church have seemed to be a typical sample of the failure of the Gospel to realize its ideal? Its discipline was forgotten; its unity was rent by schisms; some fundamental articles of the faith were questioned or denied among its members. The Gospel was designed to purify unto Christ a peculiar people zealous of good works. But at Corinth there were scandals, "such as were not even named among the heathen;" and the Corinthian Christians had not on this account felt the impatience and shame which became a Christian Church.[1] The Gospel was based on the truth that Christ died for our sins, and that He was buried, and above all that He rose from the dead the third day, according to the Scriptures.[2] It was based on this last fact so entirely, that if Christ was not risen, then was the preaching of the Apostles vain, and the faith of Christians was also vain.[3] But at Corinth there were men who still maintained some sort of connection with the Christian Church, and who yet "said that there was no resurrection from the dead."[4] Once more, the Gospel had for its motto those words of Jesus

[1] 1 Cor. v. 1, 2.   [2] 1 Cor. xv. 3, 4.   [3] 1 Cor. xv. 14.   [4] 1 Cor. xv. 12.

Christ, "By this shall all men know that ye are My disciples, that ye have love one to another;"[1] Christianity was the religion of those who were "one Body and one Spirit, even as they were called in one hope of their calling."[2] But at Corinth were heard the discordant cries, "I am of Paul, and I of Apollos, and I of Cephas, and I of Christ."[3] It might have been supposed by a looker-on that Christ was divided; or that Paul had been crucified for at least some of the Corinthians; or that they had been baptized in the name of Paul.[4] Of all this the Apostle was sufficiently conscious; he had many enemies keen-sighted and clever enough to make the most of it; and yet with Corinth behind him, and with Rome and its gigantic and unattempted problems before him, he still exclaims, "I am not ashamed of the Gospel of Christ."

The truth is, that in this matter St. Paul distinguished between the Ideal, revealed to man, as it lay in the Mind of his Master, and the Real, embarrassed by the conditions imposed on it by fallen human nature; and he did not expect to see the Heavenly Jerusalem displayed in its unsullied and majestic beauty here upon earth. In his own words, he knew that the treasure of the faith was deposited in earthen vessels, that the excellency of the power might be of God, and not of us.[5] And therefore, when human nature, even though illuminated and invigorated by grace, was still more or less feeble or corrupt; when it sanctioned moral wrong, or denied certain truth, or split up the kingdom of faith and righteousness into fragments—St. Paul was not surprised. The cause of the failure lay not in the gift, but in its recipient; not in the Gospel of Christ, but in the race which had professed it. Men could still believe that there was a Truth abroad differing utterly from all the recent guesses at truth, and from all the

---

[1] St. John xiii. 35.   [2] Eph. iv. 4.   [3] 1 Cor. i. 12.
[4] 1 Cor. i. 13.   [5] 2 Cor. iv. 7.

ancient and popular errors; it was still possible to proclaim that a new power had entered into our fallen world, and that it was not therefore incapable of raising and saving human nature, because it did not rob man of his free will, and crush out his instincts of resistance and mischief. The failures of the Gospel were such as it could afford in view of its successes. They might have been fatal to a mechanical scheme for the improvement of mankind, but they were even to be expected in a moral system which put no force upon the wills and hearts of men, while it invited them to the knowledge and love of God. "I am not ashamed," said St. Paul, when writing from the midst of such failures—"I am not ashamed of the Gospel of Christ."

III.

But might not the Apostle entertain misgivings lest the very substance of the message which he bore would be a bar to its reception? Assuredly he was well aware that there were features of the Christian Creed, and those not outlying or accidental, but of its very core and essence, which were in the highest degree unwelcome to the non-Christian world. Less than this he cannot mean by such an expression as "the offence of the Cross;" or when he speaks of "Christ crucified" as being "foolishness" to the Greeks.[1] How was this Gospel then to make its way to the hearts and convictions of men? How was this mysterious teaching—familiar enough to a generation which has learned from infancy to repeat the Creed of Christendom, but strange beyond all measure to the men who heard it from its first preachers in the towns and villages of heathendom,—how was it to compass acceptance and victory? Between the means employed and the contem-

[1] Gal. v. 11. 1 Cor. i. 18-23.

plated result there must be some kind of correspondence and proportion : what was the weapon by which the Gospel hoped to win the obedience of the world ?

Was it the cogency of the evidence which could be produced in order to show that Jesus Christ was what He claimed to be, and that His Apostles were sent to bear His message to the world? No doubt, much of the earliest preaching of the Apostles was devoted to insisting on the reality and worth of such evidence as this. The fact to which the Apostles pointed as proving the truth of their message to the world was the fact that Jesus Christ had risen from the dead. For them it had been a matter of personal experience. And they were only a small minority of a larger number of persons—" these five hundred brethren at once,"[1] for instance—who had seen the Risen Christ. In those days a man's personal witness was not liable to be set aside as worthless by an *a priori* dogma about the impossibility or the inconceivableness of the supernatural; or by some pedantic criticism of a simple unguarded narrative, which, if generally employed, would be fatal to all ordinary human testimony whatever. The Apostles were strong in knowing that they had in their different ways seen and heard our Risen Lord; and in virtue of this their personal contact with Him, they invited in His Name the faith and obedience of the world.

Certainly the Resurrection of Christ was sufficiently well attested; and yet its witnesses were not believed. For evidence of the truth of an occurrence, although at first hand, is powerless against a strong hostile predisposition of the will. It is a matter of very modern experience that if men of good faith tell the world of some strictly natural occurrence, of fair antecedent probability, they will not be believed, if their narrative should interfere rudely with existing prejudices. The will has various tried devices for protecting

[1] 1 Cor. xv. 6.

itself against the intellectual cogency of unwelcome evidence; and as the will is the soul's centre and stronghold, it is clear that something beyond evidence is needful, if the hearts of men are to be taken captive by such a religion as the Gospel.

And here it is that the Apostle would give his reason for not being ashamed of the Gospel of Christ; for not despairing of its capacity to win a hostile and scornful world. He says that it is "the power of God unto salvation to every one that believeth."[1] There is lodged in it a moral impetus and constraining force, which pours forth from it into the human soul, and quells proud thoughts and lustful passions, and lands it safely on the Eternal Shore. For this is what St. Paul means by salvation; he means a process begun here, and completed, so as to be placed beyond all risk of reversal, hereafter. Observe that St. Paul does not say that the Gospel was an instrument in the Hands of God, which He designed to *make* efficacious. He speaks of it as being itself "the power of God," and this because it is the self-unveiling of God; because in and through it the Eternal Son of God, Incarnate and Crucified for man, speaks and acts; because the truth and grace given to men in the gift of the Gospel are the secrets of true moral force. And by the Gospel he means most assuredly no mere fragment of the Gospel; such as Christian morality without Christian doctrine, or the Atonement without the grace and power of the Sacraments. For all that God has given us in His Blessed Son is really implied in that free, unmerited gift of righteousness which faith receives at the hands of Christ, and which robes human nature in the "garments of salvation." St. Paul knew that this had been his own experience. Since that scene on the road to Damascus he had been another man; he had lived a new life; "old things had passed away, behold all things

[1] Rom. i. 16.

had become new."¹ Now he could do all things Christ, that strengthened him.² And as with himself, with others: the Gospel had made many a man whom he knew utterly unlike his former self. Before it was received, men had been "foolish, disobedient, deceived, serving divers lusts and pleasures, living in malice and envy, hateful and hating one another."³ But now the Gospel was the power of God unto salvation: it had changed the moral scene: it had conferred peace, courage, love, joy, patience, hope, the power of controlling self, the power of assisting others, resignation and trust both in life and death. These things are not natural to human beings; and when we find them in anything like excellence, they show that some new force has entered into human life, and made it what it never could be, if it were left to its own natural resources.

It may be said that this reason for not being ashamed of the Gospel is after all only a subjective reason. It may be satisfactory enough to the individual who has had inward experience of its reality, but it says nothing to the intellect of the world. Doubtless it is true that a personal conviction of the truth of a doctrine, based upon the knowledge of what it has done for the man who holds it, is in a great degree incommunicable. No other man can exactly feel what is felt by the most conscientious exponent of such an experience; others can only take what is stated as to the internal effects of Christian truth more or less upon trust. But St. Paul does not say that the fact that the Gospel is "the power of God unto salvation" is an intellectual evidence of the truth of the Gospel: he merely says that this fact warrants him in not being ashamed of it. With St. Paul, for the moment, it is a question not of a logical weapon, but of moral decision. Why is he to go forward when there is so much to discourage him? Why is he not

[1] 2 Cor. v. 17. [2] Phil. iv. 13. [3] Titus iii. 3.

to be ashamed of Christ's Gospel? Because he knows perfectly what it has been to himself; he knows something of what it has been, within the range of his own observation, to multitudes besides, and he infers that it is the power of God unto salvation to every one that believeth.

Before we pass on, let us observe that the Religion of Jesus Christ is here upon ground peculiarly its own. There are many claimants, in our modern world, for the throne which it has owned for eighteen hundred years in the souls of Christian men. There are metaphysical and physical claimants; names which have won the thinking and the unthinking homage of educated Europe. But whether the eye rests on the masters who have done what they could for mind, or on the masters who have spent themselves in manipulating matter (they are near enough to us, and I need not name them); let me ask what has been achieved by these most distinguished men that could by any defensible use of language be described "as a power of God unto salvation"? No, the deeper aspects of life, and, much more, the grave significance of death, are quite beyond them—

>—"nec quidquam tibi prodest
>Aerias tentasse domos, animoque rotundum,
>Percurrisse polum, morituro."

It is only Jesus Christ Who has thrown light on life and immortality through the Gospel; and because He has done so, and has enabled us by His Atoning Death and Intercession to make the most of this discovery, His Gospel is for all who will a power of God unto salvation.

Yet, even in the case of men to whom St. Paul's language describes their own happy experience, there may be, not indeed shame, but hesitation, in proclaiming it. Those to whom the saving power of Christ's Cross is most intimately certain, as being to them a matter of personal experience, cannot at once, and without difficulty.

bring themselves to say much about it. We do not, any of us, readily talk about that which most nearly touches us. Men have no objection to talk politics in public, even when they feel strongly on political questions; and the reason is, because politics address themselves not to that which is exclusively personal, but only to those common sympathies and judgments which we share with some section of our countrymen. But no man will consent, if he can help it, to discuss his near relations, or a family interest, in public. This is not because the details of private life do not interest other people; every one must know how very far this is from being true. It is because the feelings which they arouse in those concerned are too tender to bear exposure.

And this motive operates not unfrequently in the case of religion. Religion, even in its lower and most imperfect forms, twines itself round the heart like a family affection; it is throned in an inner sanctuary of the soul, the door of which is closed to all except a very few, if not indeed to everybody. Religion has its outward and visible side; its public acts of homage; its recognised obligations. But its real strength and empire is within; it is in regions where spiritual activity neither meets the eye nor commits itself to language. All to whom our Saviour is a real Being know that their souls have had and have relations with Him which belong to the most sacred moments of life. If we may employ a metaphor which Holy Scripture suggests, they hesitate to discuss these relations almost as naturally as a bride would shrink from taking the world into her confidence. The case of each soul is altogether peculiar to itself; the relations of each soul to the Lord of souls are, like the character or the countenance of every man, quite unique. And therefore the best of men are not unfrequently least able to talk freely upon the one subject respecting which they feel most deeply. Especially is this the case with us Englishmen, who are naturally at once sincere and reserved; reserved perhaps, in fact, because sincere. Beyond any other race of men we shrink from the risk of saying more than we feel, or even from the duty of saying as much as we feel, unless it be strictly necessary to do so.

Some of you who hear me, and who look forward to taking your part in that work for which St. Paul lived and died, will one day, if you do not now, understand me. You will understand that often in exact proportion to the reality of a religious experience may be the difficulty of making it public property; and that one of the most trying features in a clergyman's work may consist in his having to make a perfectly sincere proclamation of that which he knows to be true, after actual contact with it in the chambers of his own soul. Doubtless a nature so human and sympathetic as St. Paul's would have felt this difficulty in its full force; yet we know how completely, how generously, he overcame it. In his large, self-forgetting charity, he has made his inmost life—its darkest as well as its brightest passages—the common heritage of the world. If he did not yield to the instinct which would have sealed his lips, this was because he knew that the Gospel of his Lord and Master was not really, like some family secret, a private matter. The Friend of *his* soul, Who knew its wants and weaknesses, Who had healed its diseases, Who was privy to its inmost confidence, was surely the true and much-needed Friend of every human being; and therefore no false reserve could persuade St. Paul to treat the Gospel as if it concerned himself alone, or to shrink from saying with the Psalmist, " Come near, and hearken, all ye that fear God, and I will tell you what He hath done for my soul."[1]

[1] Ps. lxvi. 14.

IV.

St. Paul's mind about the Gospel is the mind of Christ's true servants to the end of time. The pagan Rome of history has perished; and yet that which it represented to the Apostle's eye is still, in a modified form, before us. The vast and complex organization of human life—material, social, mental, moral—which we call civilization, so far as it lies beyond the scope of the Gospel, is substantially what it was of old. The outer aspects of the world, as a thinking and acting force, now, as then, reduce the Church to a relative insignificance. And throughout Christendom the Church confronts the world with a faith in the Unseen, perhaps enfeebled by some false philosophy, perhaps discoloured by superstition; with a unity which is a dream of the past, or of the future; with a message which is treated even less respectfully than it was at the hands of Porphyry and Celsus.

And yet, to any who can take a sober measure of men and things, there are no reasons for being ashamed of Christ's Gospel. The world which confronts us is not really more splendid or more solid than the empire which has long since perished. The religious weakness and disorganization which alarms us in the Church is not different in kind from that which was familiar to St. Paul. The assaults upon the faith, which have been conspicuous features of the mental life of this generation, are not more formidable, and do not cut deeper, than those which he resisted. And the Gospel is now, as it was then, but in a much greater multitude of souls, "the power of God unto salvation." There is no reason whatever for being ashamed of it; it will live with or without our advocacy; it has an inward force that is all its own.

"I am not ashamed of the Gospel of Christ." This is the profession—need I say it—not merely of Christ's great

Apostle, but of the humblest and weakest of Christian ministers. No man who wears Christ's livery can be ashamed of His Gospel without incurring even the scorn of the world. The world itself has no pity for those who voluntarily undertake the championship of a religion which can never flatter the wayward errors or the natural propensities of man, and who yet, like the children of Ephraim of old, " being harnessed and carrying bows, turn themselves back in the day of battle."[1]

" I am not ashamed of the Gospel of Christ." Is not this, too, the rule of every Christian man, of every young man who is entering upon life ? You know, my brethren, what is practically meant by being ashamed of the Gospel. The Creed is best confessed in the life of the believer. The sermon which is lived is the most eloquent of all sermons. The act of loyalty which is not foregone because of a frown or a sneer, seen or anticipated; the act of wrongdoing which is not consented to under the more imperious pressure of a personal friendship, or of a false code of social ethics : these are the victories to which every man among us is invited, in very various degrees, and our equally various ways of meeting the invitation are registered above against the great Hereafter.

" I am not ashamed of the Gospel of Christ." Here, surely, is a fitting motto for a Christian nation ; for a country which owes to Christ's Gospel so great a debt as England has owed it for fourteen hundred years ; for a people which might well say to Him, " Thou, Lord, hast taught me from my youth up until now; therefore will I tell of Thy wondrous works."[2]

They tell us, indeed, that the Gospel is an admirable guide of life for individuals, but that it has no business to venture within the sphere of politics. Political life is said to be beyond its scope; the Gospel must content itself

[1] Ps. lxxviii. 10.   [2] Ps. lxxi. 15.

with the useful career which is open to it in the privacy of the Christian home.

But language of this kind is impossible for a serious believer. If Christianity has really come from heaven, it must renew the whole life of man; it must govern the life of nations no less than that of individuals; it must control a Christian when acting in his public and political capacity as completely as when he is engaged in the duties which belong to him as a member of a family circle. If a religious principle is worth anything, it applies to a million of human beings as truly as to one; and the difficulty of insisting on its wider application does not furnish any proof that it ought not to be so applied. Yet many a man who is exemplary in all the private relations of life, is in his public conduct, and in the political opinions which he professes, too often ashamed of the Gospel of Christ; and this repudiation of the public claims of Christ is by no means confined to any one of our political parties. How is it possible to reconcile any true sense of the value of His Gospel with the support of educational schemes which, if they were carried out to their full results, would virtually banish Him from every infant schoolroom in the country? How can we Englishmen look steadily in the face of the Chinese who asks us whether we mean our Religion of the Cross, when, as a nation, we have forced on him, at the sword's point, a trade in opium, which has involved his countrymen in physical and moral misery unknown to them before? How can we really confess Jesus Christ, if we are ready, for the sake of some material interests, real or hypothetical, to perpetuate the sufferings of millions of human beings, whose chief crime in the eyes of their persecutors is that they own, amid whatever imperfections, Christ's Adorable Name? No, brethren, let us be honest; let us either have the courage not to be ashamed of the Gospel of Christ in any department of life and thought, or let us own that we have adapted the morals of the New Testament to suit a state of feeling and conduct which they were intended gradually to render impossible.

However men may think or feel upon these serious questions, there ought to be no room for controversy among Christians as to the duty of England towards her great dependencies. And that duty, as it affects some among us, may take a practical form.

If, in some respects, there is grave reason for anxiety in the present circumstances of the Church of Christ, there is also ground for thankfulness and hope. And one subject which may warrant this, is the spirit in which Holy Orders are now approached. Time was when young men drifted into ordination, for social and family reasons, almost without any will of their own; and it could not be that they added to the real strength of a society which is nothing if not an aggregate of spiritual convictions. Now, the current of feeling runs the other way; and if a man is ordained at all, it is in virtue of a strong personal conviction. The embittered controversies of the time, the uncertainties of the future, the enemies, many and fierce, who prowl around the camp of the Church,—these things make some men's hearts faint, and their resolves feeble. But what is lost in one direction is probably gained in another. A stirring time, though it be a time of danger, is welcome to every active and generous spirit.

"Per damna per cædes ab ipso,
Ducit opes animumque ferro."

It is not in quiet days that the Apostolic hymn is best understood;—

If we suffer, we shall also reign with Him;
If we deny Him, He also will deny us;
If we believe not, yet He abideth faithful:
He cannot deny Himself.[1]

[1] 2 Tim. ii. 12, 13.

And if any man who hears me is in doubt what to do with his life, one suggestion may be furnished by the subject of to-day's sermon. It will not be hereafter a matter of regret if you should resolve to devote yourselves to Apostolic work in the dependencies of this great Empire, in those cities of America, and Australia, and India, which, before long, must powerfully affect, if they do not even govern, the course of the civilized world. We are not far from the time when Sydney, and Melbourne, and Calcutta, and Cape Town will rank with the old capitals of Europe; already a new world is being created by the colonial enterprise of England. No light privilege is it to have a hand in building up the moral life of these new communities; no common honour surely to help to lay side by side with the foundations of their free political institutions the broad and deep foundations of the Church of God. Often enough it is little that can be done in an old country, where life is ruled by fixed and imperious traditions; while much may be done where all is yet fluid, and where, if religion is sometimes unprotected and unrecognised, she is not embarrassed by influences which deaden or cramp her best energies at home. But wherever we labour, the rule and the profession of the Apostle must be ours; and whatever be our personal mistakes and failures, God grant that our consciences may never accuse us of being ashamed of the Gospel of Christ.

SERMON XIV.

THE CURSE ON MEROZ.

JUDGES v. 23.

Curse ye Meroz, said the angel of the Lord, curse ye bitterly the inhabitants thereof; because they came not to the help of the Lord, to the help of the Lord against the mighty.

ISRAEL'S struggle against the Canaanitish king Jabin closes the first period of the history of the Judges. Of that struggle the central figure is the speaker in the text, Deborah, prophetess and mother in Israel. This extraordinary woman might have ranked, so far as natural strength of character is concerned, with those of her sex who, by splendid examples, whether of energy, or intellect, or sanctity, have from time to time reversed the ordinary relations of men and women, and have left their mark for ever upon the history of the world. She belongs to the same class, in respect of natural ascendency, as Joan of Arc, as Elizabeth of England, as Catharine the Second of Russia, not to mention humbler but, speaking religiously, greater names. She had, besides her natural gifts, the gift of prophecy, as before her had Miriam the sister of the Lawgiver; as had Huldah the wife of Shallum in a later age. Her husband Lapidoth is mentioned; he is mentioned only to be forgotten: Deborah's was a life

shaped by the pursuit of public rather than of domestic
objects. In her song of victory Deborah implies that the
rule of her predecessors, although marked by deeds of
heroism against the oppressors of Israel, had failed altogether to restrain the predatory ravages of the Canaanites.
The public ways were unsafe and deserted; men skulked
from place to place by out-of-the-way paths; there was
no safety for property or life.[1] Especially would the whole
level country of the Kishon valley, and Deborah's native
tribe, have been exposed to the violence of the Canaanitish
tyrant of Hazor and his general Sisera. This may explain
her removal to her southern home. Under a palm-tree of
Benjamin she judged Israel: she heard appeals from the
sentence of lower tribunals, as became the supreme judge
of the nation.[2] Of the actual extent of her influence, of
her relation in particular to the northern tribes, of the cause
which immediately determined her to proclaim a rising
against the Canaanites, we really know nothing. She
summoned Barak, her fellow-tribesman, to advance from
Kedesh, in the extreme north of the country, upon Mount
Tabor, with ten thousand men, in order to attack Sisera.
Barak refused, unless the prophetess would herself accompany him; soldier as he was, he lacked the needful
strength and convictions to brace him for the conflict.
Deborah warned him that he would thus forfeit the
honours of victory. But she joined him at Kedesh. Upon
their reaching Mount Tabor, Sisera brought up the associated Canaanitish forces, and nine hundred chariots of
iron. Barak suddenly rushed from the heights into the
valley; and at Taanach, by the brook Megiddo, a desperate
encounter resulted in the utter defeat of Sisera. The
original word denotes the extraordinary character of the
victory as effected through some unmentioned natural
phenomenon: it even seems to rank Sisera's defeat with

[1] Judges v. 6. [2] Deut. xvii. 8.

the destruction of Pharaoh in the Red Sea, and of the Canaanites at Gibeon.[1] The rout was indeed complete. The host of Sisera was driven in a north-west direction to Harosheth, where Sisera kept a kind of independent court; the waters of the Kishon, then at their height, swept many of the fugitives into the Mediterranean; but ere the last man had been destroyed at Harosheth, Sisera had left his chariot, and had fled on foot towards Lake Merom, where, in the neighbourhood of Kedesh, he met his death in the tent of Jael.

I.

It was in the course of this hot pursuit that Meroz incurred the curse of the Angel of the Lord, who, as the revealer of the Invisible God, fought for Israel, and smote the Canaanites. Meroz, situated, it is probable, on the southern slope of Tabor, would seem to have closed its gates against the conquerors, or at any rate to have refused to take its part in the great struggle against the enemies of the theocracy. Whether it was destroyed at the time, or left to perish through the fear and aversion of all good Israelites for the spot, we know not. It is not mentioned again in Scripture. Deborah heard and uttered its doom on the day of Israel's triumph; and forthwith it disappears from history.

It is in the song of Deborah, rather than in the prose narrative of the sacred writer, that we best understand the exigency of the time, and the spirit, the passion of the leaders of the theocracy. The theocracy was for the moment almost impersonated in Deborah. And Deborah lives in her song; in all the power of her prophetic utterance, in all the penetrating intensity of her womanly feel-

---

[1] Exod. xiv. 24. Josh. x. 10. Cf. Keil's remarks on וַיָּהָם *in loc.*

ing. In her prelude she glances at the great days of Israel, when God was felt to be among His people marching from Sinai;[1] she mourns the period of weakness and degradation that had followed;[2] she does not shrink, through any false modesty, from marking her own arising as the epoch of her country's resurrection.[3] She proclaims her sympathy with the national leaders; with the volunteers from among the people: nobles and people are to reflect on the mighty acts of the Lord—for such indeed they were—as the returning warriors related them among the women watering their flocks.[4] And then, after again rousing herself to the task of minstrelsy, while Barak is leading the captives in procession before her, she repeats the story of the victory: the streaming of the heroes of Israel down from the heights to fight the enemy in the plain of Jezreel; the terrific, never-to-be-forgotten shock of battle at Taanach; the fighting of the very stars in their courses against Sisera, through some storm or other natural phenomenon which increased his difficulties or hastened his discomfiture; the swollen waters of the Kishon, laden with the bodies of the dying and the dead; the wild confused flight of the dreaded chariots of iron before the men of Israel.[5] She ends with the tragic death of the general himself in the tent of Jael, and with the picture suggested by her own woman's heart; the picture of Sisera's mother expecting her son's return, explaining to herself the delay, for which there was, she already instinctively feels, all too surely another explanation. And then the song pauses suddenly with a burst of prayer, that all the enemies of the Lord might perish as did Sisera.

Yet Deborah is not merely a poet: she is a judge; and in the midst of her passion she apportions with discriminating accuracy their exact measure of desert to the

---

[1] Judges v. 4, 5. [2] Judges v. 6, 7. [3] Judges v. 7.
[4] Judges v. 9-11. [5] Judges v. 19-22.

different tribes; to all who had contributed, or who ought to have contributed, to the great victory. The place of honour is reserved for Naphtali and Zebulun: these had been unsparing in self-sacrifice; they had hazarded their lives unto the death upon the high places of the field.[1] Less had been done, but something had been done by Ephraim, by Benjamin, by western Manasseh, by Issachar; they had sent contingents, probably with Deborah herself, to the aid of Barak.[2] Then there came the defaulters. Reuben had felt the agony, the enthusiasm of the moment: there had been all the agitation, it would seem, in this tribe of a prolonged indecision; but at last it was resolved to prefer the comfortable repose of a shepherd's life to taking part in the struggle for God and for Israel.[3] In the same spirit the other tribes beyond the Jordan had remained at home; while on the western side of Palestine commerce proved as enervating as did pastoral interests in the east. Dan and Asher were both too absorbed in the interests of seafaring populations—Dan especially in the growing prosperity of the young port of Joppa and the early Phœnician trade—to have a heart to take part in the national struggle.[4] But the language used as to these tribes is widely different from that which is provoked by, or rather reserved for, Meroz. They were at a distance from the scene of action; they were removed from the sights and sounds which brought the true bearing of the contest in all its anguish before the mind of the inhabitants of the upper Kishon valley. Meroz saw all, knew all, felt all, yet would take no part. To Meroz, even Jael, the Kenite chieftainess, was a reproach. Though it were true that her act fell below the morality of the Law, yet was she "blessed" for the spirit of loyalty which it expressed; while nothing could be said on behalf of the townsmen

[1] Judges v. 18.
[2] Judges v. 14, 15.
[3] Judges v. 15.
[4] Judges v. 17.

who had refused in that moment of unparalleled agony to bring help to the sacred cause of their country, and of their God.

II.

Now, are we to say that the curse of Meroz is a "dark patch of human passion;" that Deborah, in the heat of her exultation and vengeance, was strictly incapable of a balanced moral judgment; that not to have taken part in the pursuit of Sisera was naturally a crime in the eyes of a passionate woman, eager for the emancipation of her race and for the triumph of her cause; but that it is altogether impossible to read history by the light of such excited feelings, and to suppose that Meroz drew on itself, not merely the invectives of Deborah, but also the displeasure and condemnation of a Righteous God?

This way of looking at the language before us ignores one remarkable characteristic of the Jewish theocracy; it ignores what we should term in a secular history its lofty public spirit, its superiority to all that is merely personal and selfish. David and other psalmists especially illustrate this. David reserves his enthusiasms for the friends of God; his aspirations for the success of the cause of God; his anxieties for the risks of God's kingdom; his hatred for the enemies of God's truth and glory: "Whom have I in heaven but Thee? and there is none upon earth that I desire in comparison of Thee."[1] "Do not I hate them, O Lord, that hate Thee? and am not I grieved with them that rise up against Thee? Yea, I hate them right sore; even as though they were mine enemies."[2] So Ezra: "Mine eyes gush out with water, because men keep not Thy law."[3] So a captive in Babylon: "If I forget thee, O Jerusalem, let my right hand forget her cunning. If I do not remember thee, let my tongue cleave to the roof of my

[1] Ps. lxxiii. 24.   [2] Ps. cxxxix. 21, 22.   [3] Ps. cxix. 136.

mouth; yea, if I remember not Jerusalem in my mirth."[1] The language of Deborah was not the expression of a personal, or social, or political spite any more than was the language of David and Ezra. It was not her own cause; not even the cause of her country, as such; it was the cause of the Lord God which she had at heart, which had long since won her love, and now fired and guided her indignation.

Are we to say, then, that if this language be in keeping with the stern spirit of the Law it is out of place in the religion of the Gospel? This, indeed, is often said. But it assumes too hastily that the Gospel repealed not merely the ceremonial but the moral teaching of the Law, not merely its forms of worship but its representation of the Divine attributes, not merely its carnal weapons of warfare but its loyalty to and zeal for truth. In point of fact, the Gospel explained or it enlarged the teaching of the Law. It removed misconceptions which had gathered around that teaching. It did not destroy what God Himself had given.[2] God's earlier Revelation of Himself as a whole, as well as its particular gifts and promises, was, in Apostolic phrase, "without repentance;"[3] it did not admit of repudiation or recall. The Divine attribute of mercy, sufficiently revealed in and insisted on by the Law, acquired under the Gospel a practical and concrete shape in the life and death of our Lord Jesus Christ. The duties of charity, lovingkindness, patience, benevolence, unselfishness, already prescribed by the Law, were elaborated and enforced with a new determination and precision in the Gospel. But the Gospel Revelation did not thereby repeal the earlier Revelation of the Justice of God as a necessary principle of His government; nor did it define the virtue of charity to mean indifference on the subject of moral evil or of

---

[1] Ps. cxxxvii. 5, 6.   [2] St. Matt. v. 17, 18.
[3] Rom. xi. 29, ἀμεταμέλητα.

intellectual falsehood. It prescribed to men the largest consideration for the difficulties, the weaknesses, the failures of others; it taught the doctrine of the relativeness of all responsibility for knowledge of truth and duty, as that doctrine had never been taught before; but it did not slur over the lines which define the boundaries of moral and intellectual truth; it spoke as sternly as did the Law when truth required outspokenness. Why else should our Lord have foretold woe to Chorazin and Bethsaida; why should He have said that Capernaum once exalted to heaven should be cast down to hell;[1] why should He have predicted, with tears of sorrow, the coming desolation of Jerusalem?[2] What was the meaning of the many sayings in which He proclaimed the necessity of accepting, and the danger of rejecting Himself?[3] What is to be said of St. Paul's anathemas against propagating a false faith and against want of love for Christ? "If any man love not the Lord Jesus Christ, let him be anathema maranatha."[4] "If any man preach any other gospel than that which we have preached unto you, let him be accursed."[5] It has been urged that this language of our Lord's and St. Paul's constitutes a foreign element in the New Testament; that it belongs to modes of thinking and speaking which were accepted traditionally from the earlier religion, without being revised. But, not to mention the impossibility of reconciling any such doctrine as this with our Lord's claims to be obeyed as an unerring Teacher of Divine Truth, it proceeds upon a false estimate of the real demands of all religious truth and duty upon man, however partial may be his knowledge of it. It presumes that the acceptance of truth and the performance of duty is really, in the last resort, an affair of

---

[1] St. Matt. xi. 21, 23. St. Luke x. 13.
[2] St. Matt. xxiii. 37. St. Luke xiii. 34.
[3] *E.g.* St. Luke xix. 27. St. Mark viii. 38.
[4] 1 Cor. xvi. 22.   [5] Gal. i. 8, 9.

taste; and it is this vital misconception which makes the sterner language of the Gospel, not less than that of the Law, unwelcome and unintelligible.

III.

What, then, precisely was the sin of Meroz? Meroz was found wanting on a great occasion, as it could not have been found wanting had it been sound at 'heart. Certainly it failed first of all in the duty of patriotism. If we are tempted to think that Deborah's language was unwarrantable, let us consider what we ourselves should say under similar circumstances. Let us suppose that this country had been successfully invaded by a foreign enemy; that during his occupation every form of social and personal misery had been inflicted; that, not to speak of the ruin of our credit, of our trade, of our national character, the exercise of our religion, the sanctity of our homes, the freedom of our persons, had been imperilled or sacrificed; and that at last, under whatever leadership, an organized rising against the invader had been successful, at least within limits, and that he had sustained a decisive reverse. And let us further suppose that at the very crisis of his discomfiture, when everything depended upon making his position untenable, and upon converting a first disaster into irremediable defeat, some single English town, lying in the very valley along which the torrent of war was sweeping, should refuse assistance or even sympathy to the national forces. Do you think that English public men, or English public writers, reviewing the campaign when all was over, would be sparing of denunciation, after their own fashion, of such treachery to the national cause? Would they not insist upon the preciousness, the sanctity of the national life; upon the folly and wickedness of preaching any doctrine which could destroy or impair it;

upon the duty of laying aside all private opinions, grudges, hesitations, in presence of so absorbing, so overwhelming a catastrophe as an invasion? And should it be suggested that in using this language they were only indulging some kind of selfish passion, would they be careful to answer the taunt? Certainly Deborah is passionate; but it is a noble passion which animates her—if it is a true love of her country. Alas! for us Englishmen, if a sickly cosmopolitanism—appealing, not to a pure deep love of humanity at large, but to an unmanly shrinking from exacting efforts and sacrifices, which might be prescribed, I do not say by our historical traditions, but by the position and duties assigned to us in His world by God—should have made us unable to understand her.

Meroz failed, secondly, in a far graver duty, a duty towards its religion. For the cause of Israel against Jabin was not merely the cause of the country; it was the cause of the Church. In Israel Church and State were not "united," for the simple reason that they were one and the same thing. When we Christians use the phrase "Union of Church and State," we imply what is the historical fact, namely, that since the Incarnation, Church and State are fundamentally distinct things; distinct in their origin, in their laws, and in their corporate life; but that under favourable circumstances they may be brought into relations of harmony and interdependence. If the Church were, to use a modern phrase, merely the "expression of the varying religious consciousness of the country," as was really the case with the religions of pagan antiquity, it would be absurd to speak of the "union" of this "expression" with the body politic which alone, moment by moment, produces and sustains it. In Israel Church and State were two aspects of one and the same organization; and hence the politics of an Israelite could not be merely civil; they were always made up of religious principles and opinions. Thus it is that the political language of the Psalter is the natural religious language of the Christian Church. God was in the midst of the Holy State:[1] its prosperity was His glory among men; its failures and humiliations were His dishonour. Meroz was not merely wanting in duty to the race of Abraham and Jacob; to the memories and traditions of Moses and of Joshua; it was undutiful towards the true King of the sacred nation, as yet unrepresented below by any earthly viceroy; the King Who, though He could have done otherwise, had made His honour dependent on the loyalty and affection of His subjects. Meroz would not come "to the help of the Lord against the mighty." Why Meroz failed we know not. It may have been pusillanimity; although this is the less probable explanation at such a moment. It may have been the result of a selfish calculation that the tide of war might yet turn again; that a time might come when Jabin would know how to reward the friends of his adversity. It may have been a fastidious coldness, an isolation of aims and sympathies from those which governed the heart of the sacred nation, a peevish jealousy of the tribes which had taken a lead in the great work of deliverance; it could hardly have had its root in intellectual bewilderment as to the course of duty. Probably it was a strictly analogous case to that of the conduct of the men of Succoth and Penuel towards Gideon in his pursuit of the Midianitish kings.[2] To refuse aid to the sacred cause until it was certain of success, was in a man or a community belonging to the covenanted nation an act of virtual apostasy; and Meroz was not merely politically disfranchised, it was religiously excommunicated.

---

[1] Ps. xlvi. 5; xlviii. 1-8; lx. 6-12.   [2] Judges viii. 13-17.

IV.

Meroz is never unrepresented in history. And the conduct of its representatives has been sometimes explained to imply a faith so strong, and withal so humble, that it cannot venture to offer assistance to One in Whose Power it unreservedly trusts.

God, we are told, will do what He sees best, whether we help Him or not: He can conquer Sisera, at the proper time, without the aid of Meroz. Doubtless He can. But the question is, whether He wills to do so or not; whether, if He wills us to be His agents, we can wisely disobey Him by pleading that we have too much reverence or too much faith to obey. This kind of argument, it must be plain, leaves great room for self-delusion. Men will not argue thus, who know by experience that they are likely to be, at least sometimes, swayed by selfish motives of indolence, or timidity, or self-aggrandizement. The faith in the self-propagating power of Christianity which is so strong that it will not support the cause of Christian missions; the robust faith in the indestructible vitality of the Church which, when occasion permits, would illustrate her life by depriving her of the agencies and resources that ordinarily support it; the faith, in short, in God's power of upholding His own cause in the world, which carefully abstains from contributing anything to serve it, so fearful is it of offering a slight to the Divine Omnipotence; this faith, which would seem to be too vigorous to be in any sense practical, would not yet have been developed in the days of Deborah. It is hardly probable that Meroz declined its part in the great struggle from an excess of trust in the strength of Israel's cause and Israel's God: men had not then discovered that to obey God's will was to incur some risk of dishonouring His attributes.

"Curse ye Meroz." Yes, the words still live. May

they not be heard within the soul when a man has consciously declined that which conscience has recognised as plain duty? Such a man needs no audible voice of the Angel of the Lord or of the prophetess; conscience prophesies within him. The soul becomes inevitably and at once aware of a great moral and spiritual impoverishment. It is a condition of enjoying continued insight into the laws which govern spiritual truth, that we should conform our moral being to that measure of truth which we already see. A deliberate rejection of duty prescribed by already recognised truth, cannot but destroy, or at least impair most seriously, the clearness of our mental vision. Since the affections can only retain their freshness by free expansion towards their highest Object, a refusal to do that which their healthful exercise would imply and prompt reacts upon them in producing coldness, shyness, reserve. Since the will only preserves those qualities of directness and energy in which its excellence consists, by undeviating loyalty to the law of conscience which should guide it, it follows that failure to obey that law on a critical occasion, when the issues are clearly comprehended, means nothing less serious than such grave diseases of the moral constitution as crookedness of purpose and feebleness in resolve. A single act may thus involve grave inward deterioration; it may land the soul upon a lower level of moral life, where there is less light, less warmth, less force; where passion is more imperious and principle is weaker; where a man is less his own master and more readily enslaved to the circumstances and beings around him.

It is a charge against the higher education, as it is pursued in the universities, especially in Oxford, that it has not unfrequently a tendency to unfit men for the battle of life; to make them merely critical or speculative when they ought to be taking an active part on the field of duty. Some very signal instances to the contrary will indeed occur to everybody; but the question is as to a general tendency. Your own experience, brethren, will best decide on the justice of this charge. Have you learned to defer to a standard of taste which is often too fastidious to permit a man to engage in eager action; which is so sensitively alive to the dreaded criticisms of an academical public, that it has no heart to act or to write under the pressure of a sense of duty and in simple forgetfulness of self? Do your studies or your friendships tend to weaken and pulverize, instead of bracing and developing those central convictions, apart from which life resolves itself into a somewhat wearisome game of chance? Refinement and subtlety of intellect have a market value in a literary society which does not belong to them in the world at large. Human life is governed, not by the masters of the abstract sciences or of good taste, but by powerful and glowing enthusiasms which prompt and which imperatively demand action in order to express themselves, in order to live. And therefore, in such proportion as an educational system eats out the core of strong convictions by logical solvents, or paralyzes action by a continuous appeal to some standard of propriety which treats all earnestness as of the nature of vulgarity, it necessarily diminishes capacity for strenuous and heroic action, or even for such modest but praiseworthy efforts as fall far short of being either heroic or strenuous. This is a subject which may be considered from many points of view besides that of religious faith: the curse of Meroz may be the voice of a clearsighted public spirit, as well as of a religious view of life and duty.

Certainly we have been summoned into life at a time when the lesson of the text may have a serious significance for any one of us. The old quiet days when everything was so established as to be almost unchallenged are gone. Sisera is at the head of his wild warriors; and ere we die the life of the nation or the wellbeing of the Church may demand at our hands exceptional sacrifices. Are we prepared for them? There is no single feature of the circumstances of the United States of America upon which the most intelligent and devoted friends of the great Republic look with more unconcealed alarm than the withdrawal from public life of almost the whole of the educated class, and the consequent abandonment of some of the highest and most responsible places in the State to earnest but uncultivated fanatics, or to mere adventurers. It will be an evil day for England if the natural leaders of the people forego their duties because the course of modern politics is unwelcome to them; mistakes of this magnitude are made by an instructed and governing class only once. There are *vestigia nulla retrorsum;* the ground once lost is irrecoverable.

Among the nobler lives which have been lived during the last twenty years in Oxford few can have excelled that of the late Edward Denison. As an undergraduate he determined to qualify himself for combating social mischiefs by close observation and experience. He acted upon the opinion, that in order to represent the poor a man should have had actual companionship with them. And so, at an age when most men in his position would be thinking only of pleasure or of ease, he lived among the poor as one of themselves, in a lodging in a back street at the East end of London. Enough has been published in his letters to disclose something of his real temper and aspirations; but when he was from time to time showing himself at his club, and making his first speeches in the House of Commons, men little knew what kind of life he was leading, and by what principles he was governed. Yet he too had passed through a moment of indecision, when it was doubtful whether he would obey the high ideal of conduct which had been set before him. To miss an opportunity, he said at that time, is not simply to leave undone what you might do: it is too probably to fail to be what you might have been; it is to exchange a higher place in the scale of moral life for a lower one.

But it is Christ's spiritual kingdom against which Satan directs his fiercest assaults, and to which Christians owe their most devoted service. Devotion to the Church should be another name for devotedness to Christ. "Inasmuch as ye have done it unto one of the least of these My brethren, ye have done it unto Me;"—this is the motive and the blessing of all forms of work in the Church of God. It is said that men who would have spent their lives in her service a generation since do not do so now. Some, because they have a higher sense of what such service means than had their predecessors: they may do well. Some who shrink from the manifold annoyances, the controversies, the disappointments, the great and perhaps increasing difficulties of modern clerical life: these must do ill. A great necessity is a great opportunity. Much more is to be done for Truth amid the agitation and turmoil of an age like ours than in the old days of stagnation, when the life of the Church was frostbound and frostbitten, when there was little place for and recognition of heroism and self-devotion. Nothing is really lost by a life of sacrifice: everything is lost by failure to obey God's call. The great struggle of good and evil, of truth and error, which was raging when Deborah judged Israel, rages still. The great laws of the moral world do not vary, however different, under different dispensations, may be the authoritative enunciation of truth, or the means of propagating and defending it. Jabin and Sisera never really die: Deborah is always despairing, triumphing, hoping, judging by turns. And the opportunities of generously serving Jesus Christ are few; perhaps not more than one, in a lifetime. They come, they do not return. The day before Meroz failed there was no warning of its coming trial; the day after there was no reversal of its moral doom. What we do upon a great occasion will probably depend upon what we already are; what we are will be the result of previous years of self-discipline, under the grace of Christ, or of the absence of it. But to most men some opportunity of service is offered, though it be only one. And what that opportunity may be matters much less than whether, when it comes, it is made the most of.

SERMON XV.

THE GOSPEL AND THE POOR.

(WHITSUN-DAY.)

St. Luke iv. 18.

The Spirit of the Lord is upon Me, because He hath anointed Me to preach the Gospel to the poor.

IT is not perhaps too bold to say of this sentence that it is the motto of our Lord's ministry. He had already entered on His public life when He came to Nazareth, "where He had been brought up." As had been His wont, certainly since His thirteenth year, possibly since His fifth or sixth, He was present in the well-known Synagogue on the Sabbath day. The lesson from the Law had been read; the lesson from the Prophets was to follow. He rose, as wishing to read; and a servant of the Synagogue handed Him the roll of Isaiah. There was, no doubt, at that period an appointed lesson for the day; but on this occasion the Reader knew Himself to be Lord of the Synagogue as well as Lord of the Sabbath. He let the roll unwind itself from the cylinder; one after another the great passages describing His Person and His work passed beneath His eye. The first group of Isaiah's writings had gone; the last was rapidly disappearing, when He placed His finger on the passage before us. "The Spirit of the Lord is over Me; because He hath anointed Me to preach good tidings unto the poor; He hath sent Me to bind up the broken-hearted, to proclaim liberty to the captives, and the opening of the prison to them that are fettered; to preach the acceptable year of the Lord."[1]

The passage plainly refers to the year of jubilee, which at somewhat distant intervals came as a season of benevolence and grace to heal the social wounds of Israel. In this happy year the Israelite who had been sold into slavery might recover his freedom; the proprietor whose ancestral lands or houses had been alienated might re-enter on his patrimony on easy terms; the prisoner for debt might obtain his discharge; poverty and distress could put forward their claims, and be sure of a hearing. The blessings of the jubilee were earthly shadows of the blessings of Redemption; and the herald of the jubilee foretold by Isaiah is clearly not the prophet himself, but that Other Figure who is so often before us in Isaiah's later writings; He is the Servant of the Lord, at once distinct from the prophet and greatly raised above him. And thus when, His task being over, Jesus had folded the roll, and had given it to the minister and had sat down, and the eyes of all that were in the Synagogue were fastened on Him, He began to say unto them, "This day is this scripture fulfilled in your ears."[2] There could be no mistake as to His meaning. He Himself was the Preacher Whom Isaiah had foretold; and His message was the predicted announcement of good tidings to the poor.

In Israel the poor did not merely represent that average of failure and destitution which, as it would seem, is the inevitable product of organized human life; they had a more recognised, almost a religious standing in the national system. They were never to cease out of the land;[3] and our Lord's words, "The poor ye have always with you,"[4]

---

[1] Isa. lxi. 1, 2.
[2] St. Luke iv. 19-21.
[3] Deut. xv. 11.
[4] St. Matt. xxvi. 11.

meant this and more. The *anavim* of the Psalter appear both in the earlier and the later psalms: they are not merely poor in circumstances, but poor in spirit. As Gesenius remarks, the word is commonly used with "the added notion of a lowly, pious, and modest mind, which prefers to bear injuries rather than return them."[1] Probably, when our Lord spoke, these religious associations with poverty had somewhat disappeared; His express blessing on the "poor in spirit"[2] might seem to imply this. When He explained Isaiah's words as referring to Himself, He would have been understood to be drawing a distinction between the social condition of the mass of His own hearers and that of other learners in other contemporary schools. The classes who thronged the lectures of the great Rabbis in Jerusalem, and who listened to that compound of occasionally lofty moral maxims and farfetched or grotesque interpretations, which afterwards became the Talmud—these were not the poor. The students of those writers who undertook to establish an understanding between Jewish thought and the outer world of Greek culture and philosophy; the readers of Nicholas of Damascus, of Philo of Alexandria, as later of Josephus; these were not the poor. But the Galilæan peasants, sitting before Jesus in the Synagogue of Nazareth, did answer to the description; and it was that He might announce the good tidings to such as they were that the Spirit of the Lord was upon Him.

That our Lord's ministry was eminently a ministry for the poor is a commonplace which need not be insisted on. His relations were poor people, with the associations, the habits, the feelings of the poor. He passed among men as "the carpenter's son."[3] He spoke, it would appear, in a provincial north-country dialect, at least commonly. His language, His illustrations, His entire method of approach-

---

[1] Ges. s. v. עָנָו.   [2] St. Matt. v. 3.   [3] St. Matt. xiii. 55.

ing the understandings and hearts of men, were suited to the apprehension of the uneducated. When He spoke, the common people heard Him gladly.[1] When He was asked by what signs He could prove His claims, He replied, among other things, "The poor have the Gospel preached to them."[2] His first disciples were poor men; "not many wise men after the flesh, not many mighty, not many noble were called."[3] As they looked back on it, the grace of His example was felt by His disciples and servants to consist pre-eminently in this;—"that though He was rich, yet for our sakes He became poor, that we through His poverty might be rich."[4]

So it was with His earliest Church. The Church of the Apostles was a Church of the poor; of silver and gold it had none.[5] One of the first incidents in its history was an economical experiment for the relief of poverty. Of St. Paul's time and thought a large portion was devoted to organizing collections among the Greek churches for the poor Christians in Palestine. In St. James's short epistle nothing is more remarkable than the apostolic energy with which he upholds the rights, the dignity of the poor, against the insolence of their wealthy neighbours.[6] Here and there, no doubt, there were converts who brought learning, station, wealth, within the fold of the Church. But, upon the whole, it was at once the reproach and the glory of Apostolic Christendom, that it first won its victories, and then lavished its blessings, chiefly among the poor.

I.

This is mere history; it lies upon the surface of the New Testament. But that which may well arrest our

---

[1] St. Mark xii. 37.   [2] St. Matt. xi. 5.   [3] 1 Cor. i. 26.
[4] 2 Cor. viii. 9.   [5] Acts iii. 6.   [6] St. James ii. 1-7; v. 1-6.

attention, on to-day's festival, is the marked connection, in this and other passages, between the preaching of the Gospel to the poor and the gift of the Eternal Spirit. Such a purpose, in so great a gift, looks, at first sight, like an unnecessary expenditure of force. Why, men may ask, should This Almighty Visitor be thus associated with such a humble effort? Why should the Spirit not reserve Himself to dissipate the objections of the intellectual, or the fastidiousness of the highly born, or the pride of the wealthy? Does not Christianity claim to be the religion of the whole human family; and is there not something invidious as well as unaccountable in the primacy of honour thus awarded to poverty by the Unseen Agent Who was to convert the world? Poverty, it is added, is already half-Christian by its very nature; it has everything to gain by a doctrine which makes so little of the present and the visible, and so much of the future and the unseen.

Undoubtedly, my brethren, man needs a heavenly teacher, be his social station or his mental characteristics what they may. Intellect and wealth have dangers all their own, if the wisdom of the one, as it sometimes is, be foolishness with God,[1] and if it be often easier for a rope to pass through the eye of a needle than for the other to enter the kingdom of heaven.[2] But it does not therefore follow that poverty is Christianity in the bud, or a sort of social sacrament, conferring grace, so to phrase it, *ex opere operato*, on all who happen to be poor; or that the mere absence of those specific obstacles to religion which beset the educated and the rich, ensures the virtual presence of religious principles and practice in the poor. The contrary is, in fact, the case. Poverty without a faith and rule of life, poverty without any illuminating principle to turn it to moral account, may well appear to be almost unmitigated misfortune; for poverty does

[1] 1 Cor. iii. 19. [2] St. Matt. xix. 24.

not of itself promote either religion or any of the higher interests of human beings. It may do good to those of us who, through no merit of our own, have entered upon life under very different circumstances, if we forget for a few minutes the ancient East, and contemplate some of the most obvious results of poverty in the lives of many thousands of our countrymen.

A first effect of poverty, then, is the confiscation of a poor man's best time and thought, from sheer necessity, to the task of providing food and clothing for himself and his family. Many men who are far from being poor have to work for a livelihood. But a man can work hard, if he can at will command a holiday. A man can work hard, if his work is also felt to be a source of refinement, of instruction, of discipline, of recreation; if it enlightens his mind, if it purifies his affections. As a rule, a poor man's work is not of this description: it is, from all points of view save that of the wages it yields, unremunerative, because it is more or less mechanical. It cannot be interrupted unless from sheer necessity; the poor man cannot afford to lose a day's wages, and therefore, though feeling depressed or ill, he cannot forego a day's work. As he works he is not thinking of his place in the moral universe, although he is at least as capable of true nobility as is any other human being; he is thinking of the next meal, of the next pay-day, of the next rent-day. The next rent-day is probably his most distant horizon. Rarely can he aspire to win an independence, and so to purchase exemption from the necessity which is laid upon him of supporting existence by incessant toil. Who does not see how this liability must clog and depress the human spirit; how it chokes up the avenues through which even natural light and heat penetrate within the understanding and the heart? Some room must be made for religion amidst the thoughts and occupations of life before it can inspire or control them;

and in the case of the poor man, who has to work hard for his daily bread, and to whom all mental effort is very serious, the difficulty of even getting a hearing for the good tidings which Christ our Lord has brought to earth from heaven is often great indeed.

Another effect of poverty is that it often blights those domestic scenes of happiness which prepare the way of religion in the soul. In the natural course of things, kindliness, courtesy, refinement, are the products of home-life; the home is the centre and the manufactory of these natural graces. It is to his family that a man escapes when his day's toil is over. At home he forgets the passions and the rivalries, be they great or small, of his public life, whatever its sphere or scale of importance; at home the finer side of human nature has a chance of growing, as being sure of its nutriment and its welcome. At home a man knows, if nowhere else, what it is to be interpreted generously, to be trusted, to be loved; here he finds a field for the play of those affections in the exercise of which earthly happiness mainly consists. But for this two things are needed; competency and order. And how often are these wanting in the households of the poor! Many of us must have visited cabins in which a numerous family inhabits a single room; in which the young, the aged, the sick, the hale, the parents and children, herd together by day and by night; in which the mother, who should be a presiding genius of kindliness and of cleanliness, is the representative of ill-humour and of dirt; in which all that protects ordinary intercourse against coarseness, and ordinary tempers against irritation, and average health against disease, and modest efforts to improve against brutal interference, is too often absent; in which all is so crowded that there is no room for delicacy, for reserve, for the charities, for the proprieties of common life. Certainly—

> "Haud facile emergunt, quorum virtutibus obstat
> Res angusta domi."

Worse off, it has been truly said, may be the poor man, whom civilization has made what he is, than was his savage ancestor; for worse his lot who lives in the back lane of a great city, where pure air, and light, and room, and cleanliness are denied him, than that of the man of another time, who roamed in the forest beneath the sky of heaven, and who could at least command, amid whatever disadvantages, the requisites for healthy animal existence, and for the unstinted play of pure affections. Yes! A comfortless home is often even more fatal to character than to health. It chills the affections; it sours the temper; it ends by doing more. Nothing is more common than to hear severe language applied to the poor man's habit of spending his evenings at the public-house. But who of us, when by chance walking at night through the neglected quarters of a great town, has observed how, at more or less frequent intervals, the monotony of dreariness and squalor is broken by the brilliant lights and the ostentatious hospitalities of these establishments, can wonder that the poor man is attracted by the contrast which they present to all that characterizes his home, and that, yielding to their fatal welcome, he essays to drown in an hour of brute half-consciousness the memory of the griefs that too sorely embitter his domestic life? It is the road to ruin, without a doubt. But it is not for those of us who have never felt even the shadow of the troubles which are eating out his heart to cast a stone at him.

The worst result of poverty is that it often destroys self-respect. Self-respect is a different thing, as it is needless to add, from the most venial form of self-complacency. The forfeiture of self-respect does not necessarily take place when a poor man becomes a pensioner on the bounty of others. A man who receives from his fellow-man that assistance which, if their circumstances were reversed, he would gladly bestow, undergoes no moral damage in consequence; he is merely a party to a transaction which effects on a small scale an equitable redistribution of property. If, indeed, he prefers dependence to exertion: if, forgetful of the intrinsic nobleness of work, he attempts to purchase leisure by the servilities of beggary, then, beyond doubt, his manhood is impaired, and he is in a fair way to be and to do much that is fatal to the respect which a good man should entertain for the sanctities of his life. But of itself, dependence does not degrade. Children are not the worse for depending on their parents; servants are not injured by the kindness of their employers; tenants are not humiliated by the considerate liberality of the landlord; nor do we any of us suffer because we are all indebted for all that we are and have to the Eternal Bounty, and He knows us too well, and has too good a care of us, to have ordered anything really inconsistent with our true well-being. No, his dependence does not threaten the poor man's self-respect; but, especially in large centres of life, he is peculiarly exposed to the ravages of a passion which, if yielded to, degrades and brands the soul with a fatal certainty. Certainly, envy is no monopoly of the poor; it makes itself felt in all sections of society: it haunts the court, the library, the barrack-room, even the sanctuary; it is provoked in some unhappy souls by the near neighbourhood of any superior rank or excellence whatever—

> "Pectora felle virent, lingua est suffusa veneno.
> Risus abest; nisi quem visi movere dolores.
> Nec fruitur somno, vigilacibus excita curis:
> Sed videt ingratos, intabescitque videndo
> Successus hominum: carpitque et carpitur una
> Suppliciumque suum est."

But who can marvel if this miserable species of passion, which is stirred even in the prosperous by the achievements, the success, the good fortune of a comrade, finds encouragement amid the hard circumstances of the poor? From their narrow and squalid homes they go abroad to gaze on the mansions of the great and wealthy; at their scanty meals they discuss the splendid banquets which can command every luxury but appetite; as they pursue their daily toil, they see around them men of their own race and age to whom life is made so easy as to become little less than a protracted weariness. Of those unchanging laws which will always create great inequalities in the circumstances of human lives they know little or nothing. Why should things be thus? Why should there be these immense contrasts, this unaccountable caprice —for such it must seem—in the distribution of life's prizes and blessings? These are questions which force themselves naturally enough into a poor man's mind; and the bitter thoughts which they breed lead him from time to time to take part in deeds of violence and blood. The outrage in a foreign capital last Sunday afternoon, which sent a thrill of pain and fear through the civilized world, was the product of social theories created by the passion that finds a ready stimulus in the circumstances of the poor.[1] A writer who has lately sketched with vivid power some of the approaches to the first French Revolution, has analyzed generally with a master hand the explosive forces by which was shattered a social fabric that had lasted already for a thousand years.[2] But he has apparently failed to point out how intimately the moral degradation of the men who trampled the old monarchy in the dust of Paris was due to the pent-up energy of a hidden passion, capable almost beyond any other of brutalizing the human soul.

[1] The second attempt to assassinate the Emperor of Germany, made by Dr. Nobeling, on Sunday, June 2, 1878.
[2] M. Taine.

Poverty of course is and means a great deal more than has thus been stated. But at least let us bear in mind that it involves, very commonly, the exhaustion of life by mechanical work, the degradation of character in the home and in the usual expedients to escape from it, and the loss of self-respect, and of all that that loss implies, through the continued, unappeased, ever-increasing envy of the lot of others. Not that poverty has not produced its heroes, who have vanquished its disadvantages with stern determination. We have here to consider, not the splendid exceptions, but the average result. And that result may, within limits, be counteracted by wise philanthropy and by wise laws. When a sufficient number of regular holidays are secured by law, as in bygone ages the Church did secure them by her festivals for the working poor; when the hours of daily labour are kept within reasonable limits; when homes have been provided for the people on any considerable scale in which the first conditions of healthy living shall be insisted on; when it shall have been made fairly possible for every poor man so to better his condition by work as to escape from poverty into comfort; and when education shall have done all that may be done towards furthering this result, legislation and philanthropy will have achieved what may be fairly required of them. Useful knowledge, practical kindness, and beneficent laws,—these are not the Gospel; but, like philosophy, they are, or may be, its handmaids. They may make its task smooth and grateful; they may associate themselves with its victories, or they may prepare its way.

But for more important results a higher force is needed; nothing less than the Christian faith itself. The faith of Christ reverses the disadvantages of poverty with decisive force. It acts upon poverty not from without, but from within; it begins not with legislation, but with hearts and minds; not with circumstances, but with convictions. When this faith is received, it forthwith transfigures the idea of labour: labour is no longer deemed a curse, but a discipline; work of all kinds is sensibly ennobled by being done with and for Jesus Christ; and by this association it acquires the character of a kind of worship. When this faith is received, it sweetens, consecrates, elevates the affections of the husband, of the father, of the child; it sets the physical difficulties of a pauper household at defiance by referring them to the Holy Home of Nazareth; or it lifts the whole conception of human relationships into an atmosphere where the risks to which they are ordinarily exposed have ceased to exist. When this faith is embraced it changes the estimate of different conditions in life; the first become last, and the last first. The old pagan feeling was that wealth meant character; that—

> "Quantum quisque suâ nummorum servat in arcâ
> Tantum habet et fidei,"

and that poverty was fatal even to human dignity—

> "Nil habet infelix paupertas durius in se
> Quam quod ridiculos homines facit."

But Christian faith knows that wealth means responsibility, and that responsibility may come to mean only heavy arrears of sin; and it knows too His Blessed Name Who worked as the Carpenter's Son in the shop at Nazareth, and Who shed upon the condition and nature which He made His own the glories which belong to the Infinite and the Everlasting. And thus, indeed, it has come to pass in Christendom that the heirs of wealth and station have of their freewill sought lifelong companionship with the ignoble and the poor; and that the poet's words have had a practical meaning of which he little dreamt—

> "Plerumque gratæ divitibus vices;
> Mundæque parvo sub lare pauperum
> Cœnæ, sine aulæis et ostro,
> Sollicitam explicuere frontem."

II.

From what has been said it will have been inferred that the work of preaching the Gospel to the poor is very far from being either commonplace or easy; let us briefly notice two mistakes which have been made in undertaking it.

It has failed sometimes from a lack of sympathy with the mental condition and habits of the poor.

An educated man looks at his religion, not merely as a rule of thought and life, but as a theory or doctrine about the Unseen, about the universe, about human nature. His mind is constantly playing about it, examining its contents, adjusting it with other departments of thought or knowledge, or, as we should say, treating it philosophically. There are more ways than one of doing this, as men conceive themselves to be below truth or above it; the early Gnostics illustrate one method, the Alexandrian fathers another. But between faith and this active intellectual interest in its subject-matter there is no necessary misunderstanding; on the contrary, an interest of this kind is inevitable in every educated and thoughtful Christian. He surveys his creed philosophically, without impairing its authority in thought and life; and the fact that the Christian faith lends itself to this intellectual treatment helps to recommend it to each generation of cultivated men.

But it is not this way of approaching or exhibiting Christianity which wins the poor. In the questions which are debated between Revelation and particular schools of criticism, or mental or physical science, the poor have generally no part. They are not sensitively alive to the logical inconsequence, or to the historical inaccuracy, or to the absence of due method and proportion in the exposition of truth which vex their lettered brethren. For them the whole region of abstract thought and language, which is so natural and so welcome to cultivated men when dealing with sacred subjects, does not even exist. If religion is to reach them, its object must be presented as concrete and personal; so presented as to give the largest amount of satisfaction to the spirit which is compatible with the smallest demands upon the understanding. The poor need religion, not as additional material for speculative enterprise, but as a friend who can help them along the road of life, and through the great change beyond it. For them life is always real. Its hopes, its misgivings, its joys, its heartaches, its catastrophes, its dim sense of the seriousness of being where and what we are, and of the possibilities before us, are quickened by poverty. The poor man, if religious at all, must believe in One Who is not less an Object of affection and obedience, than the most awful and sublime of intellectual truths. And therefore, in order to win the poor, religion must ever study to be such as she was on His lips Who spoke in parables and simple sayings, and Who taught all who listened as they were able to bear it.[1]

There have been times when, in their ministry to the poor, the Christian clergy have failed to forget the schools. And at these times the Church has lost the people. Such a time to a great extent, at least in this country, was the last century. It was indeed the age of Wilson and of Butler. But it was also the arid age in which the Church of England ceased to be the Church of the whole English people. If an educated man is to teach the good tidings which our Master brought from heaven to the poor, he needs a special gift, to which charity and imagination should each contribute. In our day imagination has been withdrawn from the exclusive jurisdiction of the poets; it has been welcomed by a high authority as the pioneer of

---

[1] St. John xvi. 12. St. Mark iv. 33.

even *scientific* venture;[1] it has been bidden, not in vain, to reconstruct out of few and dead materials the once living past of history. Why should not a Christian love of souls enlist the services of this versatile faculty, and bid it enter with sympathy into the mind and life of the poor man, that it may lead him to acknowledge the truths which, after all, are best worth knowing?

The other mistake referred to has lain in an opposite direction. Men who have sympathized warmly with the mental difficulties of the poor have endeavoured to recommend the Christian faith, sometimes by making unwarranted or semi-legendary additions to it, and sometimes by virtually mutilating it.

No impartial student can deny that throughout its history the Roman Church has been the teacher of the poor. It has peculiarly inherited the aspirations and the anxieties of that troubled age when, standing on the ruins of the old Empire, Christendom found itself face to face with the task of converting its barbarian conquerors. The difficulty of that task, perhaps more than any other cause, has resulted in developing some of the popular features of Latin Christianity. If the question, "What is true?" was not forgotten by the evangelists of the seventh and eighth centuries, it was less present to them than the question, "What is edifying?" And this tendency culminated in the active efforts of those great Orders which played so considerable a part in Western Christendom during the ages preceding the Reformation. Like the first preachers of Christianity, they were largely sprung from, and were friends of, the people; the street nomenclature of our old English towns still reminds us that they made their home among the poor. But side by side with their sincere, even passionate devotion to the Person of our Lord, there were other features of their work dictated rather by an

[1] Professor Tyndall.

anxiety to popularize Christianity than by a zeal for God according to knowledge. Hence, for example, a whole family of new devotions, unthought of in early ages, and often inspired by local or temporary enthusiasms; hence a totally new position, disclaimed by scientific theology, but certainly assigned in popular language and thought to Mary; hence such strange outgrowths of the old penitential system of the Church as the system of indulgences, which is in its practical aspects rather a commercial than a theological conception; hence the graceful but baseless legends which sprang from the imagination of the people, and which in turn attracted it, but which, before the sixteenth century had dawned, were already threatening to bring about in Italy a rebellion of educated thought against the whole creed of Christendom.

The Reformation came. It often did its work by tyrannical or rude hands; and sometimes it left behind it crude exaggerations or unsightly ruins. But at least it did effect for a section of the Western Church one signal service: it cut away that coating of legendary and unprimitive matter which, in the course of preaching the Gospel to the poor, had partly overlaid the faith of the Apostles. To many a pious soul, no doubt, the operation was painful; for religious feeling, like the ivy, will often fasten upon the crumbling cement as eagerly and as trustfully as on the rock which defies the storm. But looking to the intrinsic nature and to the permanent interests of Christianity—looking on to the ages of criticism, then looming in the distance, and which are now upon us—it must be felt that this corrective and expurgatory action of the Reformation has been a substantial service to the Christian faith.

On the other hand, in later days warm-hearted men have sought to popularize the Gospel by methods which have involved, however unintentionally, its mutilation. The so-termed Evangelical movement was, in its origin, a serious and noble attempt to reawaken a sense of what was due to their faith in the heart of the English people. No one can read Mr. William Wilberforce's "Practical View of Christianity" without respect for the motives which inspired that remarkable work, and for the movement of which it was a typical expression. Mr. Wilberforce thought that Christianity was dying out, as a practical power, from the thoughts and lives of Englishmen, and that a great effort was needed to reaffirm its claims. In prosecuting this effort its pioneers were largely attracted by an expression of St. Paul. When St. Paul spoke of "the simplicity that is in Christ,"[1] they understood him to sanction a very narrow estimate of the contents of the Christian Creed that would go far to ensure its acceptance by the people. "The simplicity of the Gospel!" That was a phrase by repeating which they made their way; and by "the Gospel" they meant the doctrine of our Lord's atoning death, the justification of the sinner through faith in His merits, and the sanctifying influence of the Holy Spirit. These precious truths are, no doubt, essential features of the good news which is taught in the New Testament. But they are very far indeed from being the whole of it; they are only a fragment of the real creed of St. Paul and St. John. Had such an account of "the Gospel" been exhaustive, some four chapters of the Epistle to the Romans and two of the Epistle to the Galatians would have enabled us to dispense with the rest of the New Testament; the disclosures of the Inner Life of God, the example of our Divine Saviour, the purpose and the grace of the Christian sacraments, the principles and precepts of Christian morality, the nature and structure of the Christian Church, would have been superfluous, or even misleading additions. To such an impoverished estimate of the Gospel as that in

[1] 2 Cor. xi. 3.

question a discriminating criticism and a consistent faith must equally object; it retains too little, unless indeed it includes too much. In truth, like the experiments of an opposite kind which have been noticed, it was the product of unconscious but excessive deference to the empire of a single and generous motive; it sprang from the passion to help the people, from the desire at almost any cost to reach the heart of the poor.

These considerations, then, may lead us to reflect that the connection implied in the text between the presence of the Spirit and the task of evangelizing the poor is not, after all, so surprising. To be sympathetic yet sincere; true to the message which has come from heaven, yet alive to the difficulties of conveying it to untutored minds and hearts; sensible of the facilities which a few unauthorized additions or mutilations would lend to the work in hand, yet resolved to decline them,—this is not easy. For such a work something higher is needed than natural quickness of wit or strength of will, even His aid Who, as on this day, taught the peasants of Galilee in the upper chamber to speak as with tongues of fire, and in languages which men of many nations could understand. And the effort for which He thus equipped them continues still; and His aid, adapted to new circumstances, is present with us as it was with them. Never was that aid, never was this work, more needed than in our own generation. It was a saying of De Tocqueville's that, "if the great questions of the beginning of this century were mainly political, those which will convulse the world at its close will be social." Already there is an uneasy apprehension that this prediction may be realized; and as men look around them for reassurance and protection, they will find it nowhere save in a more sincere and general acceptance, on the part of all classes in society, of that Divine religion which Christ has taught us. Of course piety, even more than charity, must begin at home. But as a Christian patriot, what can a young man do better with his life than offer it to God for the work of preaching the Gospel to the poor? Doubtless the Gospel is preached, indirectly but effectively, by the example of Christian laymen, and especially by the efforts which they make to improve the condition, temporal and spiritual, of their poorer brethren; and the lot of a clergyman, living in a remote agricultural district, or in the back streets of a manufacturing town, is often contrasted disadvantageously with the career of some friend who has made his mark in politics or in literature. But it is more than doubtful whether, when from another state of being we look back upon this life, we shall indorse this judgment. Our brief tenure of earthly existence is best spent in doing what we may for the lasting happiness of others; and it is a sufficient answer to the promptings of natural modesty or timidity, that the Eternal Spirit rests upon Christ's servants to the end of time, to give them the charity, the wisdom, and the courage which are needed by the evangelists of the poor.

SERMON XVI.

CHRIST AND HUMAN LAW.[1]

ST. JOHN xix. 10, 11.

Then saith Pilate unto Him, Speakest Thou not unto me? knowest Thou not that I have power to crucify Thee, and have power to release Thee? Jesus answered, Thou couldest have no power at all against Me, except it were given thee from above: therefore he that delivered Me unto thee hath the greater sin.

NEVER, in the whole course of the world's history, were the forms of justice degraded to serve a purpose which, in point of moral criminality and baseness, can compare with the condemnation of Jesus of Nazareth. Never has the administration of human law received a sanction so authoritative as that which was bestowed on the tribunal of Pilate. Jesus said unto him, "Thou couldest have no power at all against Me, except it were given thee from above." Pilate, agitated by some scruple of which he could not rid himself, and little dreaming of the real scope of his question, had asked our Lord, "Whence art Thou?" In his then frame of mind the Roman judge would probably have regarded the full answer as unintelligible or ridiculous; while our Lord's silence, at once so merciful to His questioner and so majestic in itself, was in correspondence with His rule of withholding spiritual

---

[1] Preached before Mr. Justice Hannen and Mr. Justice Keating, Her Majesty's Judges of Assize, Feb. 28, 1869.

knowledge from minds which are, through indifference, or scornfulness, or some incurable perverseness, unfitted to receive it. But to the Roman judge the silence of Jesus wore the aspect of a sullen contumacy, if not of a studied contempt of court; and in Pilate's next question we observe the spirit of an official, accustomed to revel in the sense of his wielding a fraction of the imperial authority, and irritated at encountering even a momentary resistance to the bias of his personal will. "Speakest Thou not unto me? knowest Thou not that I have power to crucify Thee, and have power to release Thee?" Without noticing this appeal to hopes and fears natural to a prisoner on trial for his life, our Lord replies by pointing to the real source of that authority, the exercise of which appeared to His judge to be within the province of personal caprice. "Thou couldest have no power at all against Me, except it were given thee from above."

Now, in this passage, what is the sense of the emphatic but purposely indefinite word ἄνωθεν? To refer it with Semler to the action of the high Sanhedrin which had actually given Christ into the hands of the Romans, is to make our Lord lay down a very questionable proposition, namely, that He could not have been brought before the Roman lay tribunal unless the Jewish spiritual court had authorized it. To explain ἄνωθεν with another modern critic[1] as an allusion to the higher power of the Roman Cæsar, whose deputy and representative Pilate was, is to suppose that our Lord, in that supreme moment of His moral victory, was capable of making a petty criticism upon the constitution of the Roman Empire, as intrusting too great and too arbitrary a power to the hands of the local magistracy. There is no undercurrent of complaint on this or any like score in these majestic words; since again and again our Lord refers to His Father's counsel

[1] Usteri, quoted by Stier.

and the Divine Providence as determining all the circumstances of His death. Who does not see in this ἄνωθεν a profound glance at Pilate's own question which his Prisoner had left unanswered—"Whence art Thou?"[1] "Thy power," our Lord implies, "is from that higher world with which thy secret irrepressible presentiment associates Me; that world of which I know and proclaim the secrets." This is hinted; it is not said. Our Lord does not expressly say that Pilate's power is "from God." He does not even say that it is "from heaven." He will not open large theological questions before a pagan court. He will not furnish material for blasphemy. He will not give that which is holy to the dogs, or cast pearls before swine. And yet by an expression, deliberately vague, He recognises the indefinite surmises, it may be the dawning convictions, of His judge. Pilate would have felt the force of our Lord's ἄνωθεν, yet it would have raised in him no controversy; our Lord would have used it just as naturally before Cæsar's own tribunal as before the tribunal of Cæsar's deputy. The administration of Roman justice, with all its partialities, with all its personal tyrannies and caprices, was still "from above;" and this particular exercise of the Roman authority over the Divine Prisoner before it was itself a matter of special appointment.[2] The words which follow imply that Pilate's coming use of his authority would be sinful, for other reasons, and as involving the sacrifice of his own sense of justice to popular clamour. Mark the calm of the moral atmosphere which surrounds the Soul of Jesus. Where a strong human feeling would almost naturally exaggerate, Jesus will weigh scrupulously the exact extent of the sin of Pilate. It was less than the sin of Caiaphas and the Jews who had delivered Jesus into the hands of the Romans; but it was a grave sin, especially because it prostituted to pur-

---

[1] Cf. Stier, *Reden Jesu, in loc.*   [2] δεδομένον.

poses of earthly passion the exercise of an authority which had a higher than earthly sanction. "Thou couldest have had no power at all against Me, except it were given thee from above: therefore he that delivered Me unto thee hath the greater sin."

I.

Our Lord's words then teach, first of all, that human law and the authority which wields it are from God. This is the deeper ground of His earlier precept to "render unto Cæsar the things which are Cæsar's," and of His own practice as based upon it.[1] The Apostles repeat the general doctrine under circumstances which tested its application severely. Writing to Roman citizens, when Nero was on the throne, St. Paul bade every soul be "subject to the higher powers," on the ground that "there is no power but of God," and that "the powers that be are ordained of God."[2] Writing to provincials in the Proconsular Asia, on the eve, as it would seem, of an anticipated persecution, St. Peter bids them "submit themselves to every ordinance of man for the Lord's sake, whether to the emperor, as chief of the state, or to his representatives."[3] St. Peter's phrase κτίσις ἀνθρωπίνη marks the fact that civil government, although its original sanctions are divine, is human in its immediate origin. Here civil government differs from that of the Christian Church. The Apostles were immediately appointed by our Lord Himself; whereas civil power is derived from Him only mediately, although really, through the force of events, through dynastic struggles, or through the will of the people.

---

[1] St. Matt. xxii. 21. St. Mark xii. 17. St. Luke xx. 25.
[2] Rom. xiii. 1.
[3] 1 St. Pet. ii. 13, ὑποτάγητε οὖν πάσῃ ἀνθρωπίνῃ κτίσει διὰ τὸν Κύριον, εἴτε βασιλεῖ, ὡς ὑπερέχοντι, εἴτε ἡγεμόσιν, ὡς δι' αὐτοῦ πεμπομένοις.

If we look to the historical influences which have actually enacted human codes, and which have governed their administration, it is at first difficult to understand the sanctity which is thus attributed to the law and its ministers. And if, further, we examine the contents of human codes, and observe how far short they fall of enforcing, even within the limits that must bound all attempts at such enforcement, anything like an absolute morality, this difficulty is not diminished. Between law and equity there is, perhaps there must always be, a considerable interval. Between law and absolute morality there is at times patent contradiction. The undue protection of class interests, the neglect of the interests of large classes; the legislation which consults, chiefly and above all else, the profit of the legislator, whether he be king, or noble, or popular assembly; the legislation which postpones moral to material interests, and which makes havoc of man's highest good in order to gratify his lower instincts, his passing caprice, his unreasoning passion;—all this and much else appears to forbid enthusiasm for human law. The moral element in it is so mixed with alloy, that statute law must often repel a well-trained moral judgment. Who could feel enthusiasm for law as represented by Pilate? If in the case of a Roman provincial governor it was really possible to distinguish between the law and the will of its administrator, certain it is that in Pilate the judge, and not the law, speaks to Jesus; the judge whose will is independent of law, and, as it might seem, of evidence; the judge who feels that his caprice, his irritation, his cowardice, his inertness can make law, as the case proceeds, for the prisoner before him; the judge who can even exult in his sense of power over life and death, apparently without being distressed by any sense of an accompanying responsibility. "Knowest Thou not that I have power to crucify Thee, and have power to release Thee?" And

Pilate is not alone in history. Even English justice is said by popular traditions, still current and strong in the western counties, to have sacrificed the impartial majesty of law to the tyranny of political passion when Judge Jeffreys represented her at Exeter and Taunton.[1] And the question is, How can it be said of courts which habitually administer fear, or prejudice, or contempt, or moral indifference under the forms and in the disguise of law, that a sanction still rests upon them, and should be recognised in them, which has been "given from above"?

The answer to this is to be found in the conditions under which human law is permitted to exist at all. I say "is permitted to exist;" for the restraint which law lays successively upon each one of the individuals who submit to it would be fatal to its permanence, unless there were a general and instinctive conviction of its being altogether necessary. In point of fact, and historically speaking, law is created by and meets a great social want. It satisfies the demand for protection against the passions of anger and desire which are the motive forces in the lives of those multitudes of men who are unchastened, undisciplined by religious influences. These exacting and powerful passions, which make the higher elements of our nature so constantly their slaves, are the incessant revolutionists, against which society, if it would exist, must take due precautions. "From whence come wars and fightings among you? Come they not hence, even of your lusts that war in your members? Ye lust, and have not; ye kill, and desire to have, and cannot obtain."[2] Such is man's nature, until its governing principle has been altogether changed by Christ our Lord; it is an alternation of the passion of desire with the twin passion of irritation, roused at the necessary disappointments which desire must

---

[1] Macaulay, *History of England*, i. 651 (ed. 1856).
[2] St. James iv. 1, 2.

encounter; and hence, from time to time, the propensity to violent outbreaks, of individuals or of multitudes, which are fatal to the security of property, of character, and of life.

Now society cannot protect itself effectually against these foes, who, in varying degrees, have dealings with and a hold upon each of its members—these implacable foes who are ever ready to break it up from within—unless it is prepared to recognise and to put in force at least three great moral laws of God whereon it is itself based. The first business of the legislator is to protect human life against violence; the second, to protect the due transmission of human life; the third, to protect the means whereby human life is supported. In other words, every human code must aim at enforcing more or less perfectly the sixth, seventh, and eighth commandments, if it is to do its work of protecting society against dissolution. The three remaining commandments of the second table of the Decalogue, the law of reverence for parents, the law against detraction, and the law against covetousness, are indeed in a high degree precious as upholding and invigorating the social fabric; reverence for superiors, charity for all men, and contentedness with a man's actual circumstances, are very fair guarantees in their way against indulgence in murder, or adultery, or theft. Of these three commandments, however, the fifth, the ninth, and the tenth, two are, in the letter, more evangelical than the other three; they belong more to the sphere of motive, and less to that of outward acts. And they all provide, in the first instance, for the sanctity and perfection of the individual soul; they may be violated on a large scale, not, indeed, without much social discomfort and distress, but certainly without threatening the actual dissolution of society. It is not thus with the Divine precepts against murder, against adultery, against theft. These prohibitions guard principles which are the main arches on which the social structure rests. Respect for human life, respect for the marriage tie, respect for property;—here are principles which every legislator must keep steadily in view; principles which must be the soul of the most despotic and of the most popular of codes; principles which cannot be defied, which cannot even be trifled with, without tolerating, not merely the serious injury of one man and the grave criminality of another, but a neglect of the vital conditions under which alone organized human life can be maintained. Forms of government may vary, have varied, will vary, to the end of human history. But so long as men shall live together, law must in these main features be invariable. And we cannot too carefully bear in mind, that while the largest licence of political opinion is not merely consistent with the safety, but scarcely other than essential to the wellbeing of society, we no sooner call in question by word or act the great laws to which reference has just now been made, than we do what we can towards bringing about, with all the accompanying ruin and distress, utter social chaos and anarchy.

If, indeed, human law were a matter of infinite caprice; if it were bound to no necessary truths, and bounded by no inexorable conditions; to ascribe to it any heavenly sanction would be impossible. But tied down as it is to the particular work of protecting society, it must enforce the principles which are practically essential to such protection. However imperfectly it may do so; however these fundamental principles may be misapplied, or overlaid by selfish or inefficient legislation; they remain as the heart and core of all human law, while they are themselves Divine. The dream of any voluntary social compact as the basis of government has long since been rejected, if it was ever seriously entertained, by the thought of Europe; whether men believe in God or not, they understand that the central laws which keep society together are not matters of human choice, but are necessary and inevitable. And for those who do believe in a Creator and a Providence, this necessity of such laws is itself eloquent; it tells them of God's mind and will, ay, of the very harmonies of His own moral life, translated into the sphere of creaturely existence; impressed upon that which is not less His gift and work, than are human thought and human language; impressed indelibly upon, indissolubly bound up with, the very being and structure of society.

This, then, was the sense of our Lord's words to Pilate; cruel and cowardly as was the Roman judge, he yet wielded a jurisdiction, he administered a code which was in a sense Divine. He was not free to do his work at all upon the tribunal which he occupied without enforcing, amid whatever grave aberrations, some of the moral laws of God. It mattered not that he was presently about to condemn the absolute Purity Itself; the Truth Which he would condemn Itself proclaimed that the very power which he would abuse in condemning It was given him from above.

II.

But our Lord's words also suggest the grave evil of any discord between the interests of Religion and the enactments or action of civil law. "He that delivered Me unto thee hath the greater sin." Pilate's condemnation of the Just One would be sinful; but a greater sin would lie at the door of those who had given Pilate occasion to try Him. It is the very sacredness of law which makes an antagonism between it and Religion so seriously deplorable. If law were altogether a thing of human device and manufacture, religious men might leave it, without much scruple or anxiety, to encounter the fate which must ultimately await it, when it is engaged in conflict with Revealed Truth. But because law itself embodies primary moral truth of the highest importance; because it is so far derived from the same source as, and can claim like sanctions with Religion herself; a discord between law and Religion is not simply discord between the human and the Divine, but discord between one department of God's moral kingdom and another.

Such a discord may arise when the statute-book contains provisions which are at issue either with natural or revealed morality.

Here it is necessary to guard against a possible exaggeration, based upon the presumption that human law can be made to cover the whole field of personal moral obligations. This has been from time to time the dream, the aspiration, of noble souls, eager to heighten the functions of law, and to give forcible expression to the obligations of morality; longing for their country's sake to make civic virtue, as nearly as might be, a convertible term with absolute virtue, and to see the good man, without further doubt or inquiry, in the good citizen. It is to the honour of Puritanism that, in its earlier days, when it was morally and intellectually stronger than it is now, it cherished this aspiration with a self-denying fervour. And if the legal annals of the New England colonies provoke the indignation or the amusement of the modern historian, this should not prevent our doing justice to a sincere, albeit a mistaken effort, to identify absolutely the interests of religious morality with those of law. Such an effort, indeed, was only possible in a small community; and it has left, we may fear, the almost inevitable legacy of a reaction against the moral ideas which prompted it; a reaction which has not yet died out. As it is, in the old and complex societies of modern Europe, we resign ourselves to a much lower idea of the possible functions of law. Law deals with only so much morality as it is necessary to enforce in order to secure the safety of society; unlike morality, it penetrates into the sphere of motive only incidentally; it measures and judges of the outward and the tangible; its certificate of civil excellence is no certificate whatever of religious excellence; it makes no pretensions to wield any penetrating empire over conduct and conscience, such as is claimed by the precepts of the Gospel, by the law of the Church of Christ.

But if civil law does not attempt to enforce all the obligations of morality upon a Christian man, it may, at least, avoid enactments which are in conflict with the Christian conscience. And if I here proceed to illustrate my meaning, it is not with any wanton desire to provoke or to reanimate controversy; but in the hope that thoughtful men, who love their country and their God, will give to what is indeed a grave matter the needful consideration.

If there be one point more than others stamped upon the very face of our Lord's moral teaching in the Gospels, it is that He raised the law of marriage far above the standard of Gentile or even of Jewish morality.[1] Moses had allowed a bill of divorcement; but Christ reaffirms, without exception, the original law, "What God hath joined together let no man put asunder."[2] In other words, He proclaims the indissolubility of the marriage tie. Alluding to the Jewish law, He rules that if an unacknowledged act of fornication on the part of the woman had preceded the contract, the apparent tie may be dissolved.[3]

---

[1] St. Matt. v. 27-32; xix. 3-9. Deut. xxiv. 1, 2.
[2] St. Matt. xix. 6.
[3] St. Matt. v. 32, παρεκτὸς λόγου πορνείας; xix. 9, εἰ μὴ ἐπὶ πορνείᾳ. "Those who think," says Döllinger, "that in His two statements about marriage, given by Matthew, Christ meant that it was dissolved or dissoluble by adultery on either side, are compelled (1) to maintain, that the word πορνεία may mean adultery, (2) to find a ground for its being used in a crucial passage instead of the ordinary word μοιχεία, (3) to maintain

I say, the apparent tie; because in reality the contract was vitiated from the first; one of the contracting parties was

the principle, that one act of adultery on either side, *ipso facto*, dissolves marriage." Now πορνεία always means incontinence in the unmarried; never incontinence in the married, or adultery. There is no ground for making πορνεία a generic term including adultery. But supposing that πορνεία could be used for *adulterium*, why should the word be used in two passages where it was essential to define accurately the one ground for the dissolution of marriage? Our Lord uses the equivalent to the word μοιχεία more than once in both passages: why should He suddenly substitute πορνεία for it, if He only meant adultery after all?

The theory that an act of adultery, *eo ipso*, destroys marriage, so that the legal pronouncement of divorce *a vinculo matrimonii* is only the natural consequence and recognition of an already accomplished fact, is (1) to forget that God is a party to the marriage contract, and that He ratifies and seals the bond. (2) It makes one sin against the lower and physical side of marriage, destructive of a bond embracing the whole life and all its relations, and of a spiritual fellowship entered into for the common bringing up of Christian children. (3) Thus it degrades the idea of marriage to that of a mere *unitas carnis*, apart from any spiritual bond whatever. (4) Lastly, if adultery does really dissolve the bond of marriage before God, how can he who marries a person divorced on the score of adultery, commit adultery, as our Lord says he does commit it, by doing so? (St. Matt. xix. 9.) He is only marrying an unmarried person, if the adultery has really dissolved the bond. Cf. Döllinger's "First Age of the Church," transl. by Mr. Oxenham, Append. 3, p. 424, 2nd ed.

With this compare Bishop Andrewes' "Discourse against Second Marriage, after Sentence of Divorce with a former match, the party then living, in anno 1601." It is given in the concluding volume of his works, Oxford, 1854, pp. 106-110. Bishop Andrewes argues against the theory that the act of adultery dissolves the bond of marriage, on the broad grounds that, if this were so, (1) "the party offending could not be received again by the innocent to former society of life, without a new solemnizing of marriage, inasmuch as the former marriage is quite dissolved." This, as he observes, is contrary to the practice of all Christian Churches. He observes (2) that, according to this theory, if the innocent husband were to return to the duties of wedded life with a wife who had fallen into sin without remarriage, the husband himself "should in so doing commit adultery, inasmuch as he hath had the use of her that is now none of his. None of his, I say, because their marriage was utterly dissolved by the act precedent of his wife." He further argues (3) that to understand St. Matt. xix. 9 as implicitly sanctioning the theory that adultery does *ipso facto* so dissolve marriage as to allow of the remarriage deceived as to its real terms.¹ Yet, even here, to marry the woman is adulterous; for she knew the terms on of either of the parties during the lifetime of the other, is to put a premium upon the sin of the adulterer or adulteress. "If the committing of adultery do dissolve marriage, then maketh it the persons in the same case they were before they were married; and so may either, as well the guilty as the innocent, marry, which is the very benefit the adulterer propounds to himself." But, as he observes, "it is not our Saviour's will to make the committing of sin gainful or beneficial to any offender." Appeal is sometimes made to 1 Cor. vi. 16 as sanctioning the theory that adultery destroys the original *unitas carnis*, and forms a new one. It has been noticed above, that the essence of marriage lies in the moral force of a contract taken before God, and not in the mere *unitas carnis*. If the latter were the case, every act of sinful intercourse would constitute a fresh marriage-bond.

On the general question see further "An Argument for not proceeding immediately to repeal the Laws which treat the Nuptial Bond as Indissoluble," by the Rev. John Keble, Oxford, Parker, 1857. Also, "Sequel to the Argument against immediately repealing the Laws," etc., Oxford, Parker, 1857.

¹ Döllinger, "First Age," p. 366. The Law punished with stoning a bride who professed to be a virgin and was not. Deut. xxii. 20, 21. With a people who had so strong a feeling of jealousy as the Jews about a bride's virginity, deceit in the matter seemed deserving of death; and if the public conviction and execution ordered by the Law did not actually take place—of which no example is known—it was natural and in order for a man who discovered such treachery to send back the woman who had been disgraced and had dishonoured him to her parents, with a writing of divorce after the Mosaic form. . . . In such cases of divorce there was properly no dissolving of the matrimonial bond, for every marriage took place under the condition recognised by the Law, that the bride should be a maid; and deception in a point so essential to Oriental notions invalidated the whole act, for in such a case the man's consent could not be supposed. It was fair that the man should thus divorce a girl he would never have married had he known of her sin; and he showed forbearance in not getting her put to death. And when Christ added, for the Jews, *who could only thus understand Him*, this one exception, when divorce *was* allowable, His rule, that man may not sever what God has joined, remained wholly unaffected. God only binds those who consent to be bound. . . . . . It is clear how St. Mark, in a narrative designed for Gentile converts, could omit what St. Matthew had said of the exceptional case mentioned by Christ, as something only concerning the Jews, and not affecting the general principle of the indissolubility of marriage. —See the whole passage and note on p. 366.

which she had bound herself. But when a contract is perfect, it is altogether beyond recall, at least before God; a separation from bed and board may subsequently become necessary; but no suspension of the duties or enjoyments of married life can cancel the indissoluble bond itself; and therefore, much more than in the Jewish case referred to, "whoso marrieth her that is" in this sense "divorced, committeth adultery."[1]

It is unnecessary to recite the terms of the Divorce Act, which has become law within this generation. Suffice it to say, that that Act empowers a high officer of the law, sitting in his court, to pronounce, not only separations for a term of years, or, under certain circumstances, for life, divorce *a mensâ et thoro*, but actual dissolution of the marriage tie, divorce *a vinculo matrimonii*. Accordingly it sanctions and makes legal marriages (so termed) of the divorced parties, during the lifetime of the separated wife or husband.[2] Certainly these morally impossible divorces

---

[1] St. Matt. v. 32, ὃς ἐὰν ἀπολελυμένην γαμήσῃ, μοιχᾶται: xix. 9, ὁ ἀπολελυμένην γαμήσας, μοιχᾶται. See Bishop Andrewes, *ubi supra*. The terms of Rom. vii. 2, from which the vow of marriage seems to have been framed, show that the marriage bond is only really broken by death, and that though a woman "become another man's, yet is she not become his wife." Accordingly, in 1 Cor. vii. 11, a woman of herself departing or put away by her husband is commanded either to be reconciled or to remain unmarried. That 1 Cor. vii. 11 must be understood to refer to adultery, and not to other causes of separation, is argued by Bishop Andrewes from the fact that, "were it any other cause but that wherein Christ hath given leave to depart or to put away, the Apostle would not have put it upon either, or upon one, but would simply and absolutely have commanded her to be reconciled, as indeed in all other cases she is bound to seek it, and is not less at liberty."

[2] As showing the sense of the Primitive Church, Bishop Andrewes, *ubi supra*, quotes, among other authorities, Conc. Elib. Can. ix.; Conc. Milev. Can. xvii. : "Placuit ut secundum Evangelicam et Apostolicam disciplinam neque dimissus ab uxore, neque dimissa a marito alteri conjugantur." This was subscribed by St. Augustine and St. Optatus. St. Augustine says expressly that "nullius viri posterioris mulier uxor esse incipit, nisi prioris esse desiverit. Esse autem desinet uxor prioris, si moriatur vir ejus

from the marriage tie had been before enacted by special Parliamentary statutes; and Parliament had learnt its lesson from the practical claim of the Popes, to extend the dispensing power not merely to all ecclesiastical regulations, but to precepts of revealed morality. These unhappy precedents, on a more restricted scale, could not justify our present extension of the mischief to a much larger range of cases;—the contradiction between the pretension to divorce absolutely, and our Lord's plain teaching on the subject, is, to any ordinary reader of the New Testament, sufficiently obvious.

The evil would be grave enough, if no bad results of the measure were traceable. But on this head I may refer to one who was, in former years, a distinguished ornament of the judicial bench, and whose name is held in honour in this his University, and, indeed, wherever the English language is spoken.

"The new law," observes Sir John T. Coleridge, "has, to the present time, had the advantage of being administered by two judges in succession of rare excellency; men who may be equalled, but will scarcely ever be surpassed in their own province; and yet, when I consider the effect on the purity of the public mind of the proceedings of the court, daily circulated among all ages and classes; the collusion between parties, sometimes defeated, but too often, no doubt, successfully practised; and, above all, the fatally strong temptation which its open doors must offer to conjugal infidelity, ... I do not believe that the eminent judges to whom I have referred, could we have the benefit now of their advice, would be disposed to

---

non si fornicetur" (*De Conj. Adult.* ii. 4). St. Jerome puts the case as strongly as possible: "Quamdiu vivit vir, licet adulter sit, licet sodomita, licet flagitiis omnibus coopertus, et ab uxore propter hæc scelera derelictus, maritus ejus reputatur, cui alterum virum accipere non licet" (*Ep.* 52, *ad Amandum*, § 3).

commend the law which they have been called on to administer."[1]

It may be said, that whether it be right or wrong, this legislation is irreversible; that when the current flows so strong in the direction of laxity, we must perforce yield to it; and that it were better to draw a veil over social ulcers, which cannot be healed, than thus to expose them.

But, speaking to young men, many of whom in coming years will have opportunities of serving their country by helping to guide its convictions, perhaps, by moulding its legislation, I cannot resign myself to this despairing view of our actual circumstances. If Christians must be jealous for the honour of their Lord, Englishmen must desire that in days of actual and anticipated change there should be the utmost possible harmony between the various moral forces which sway the action of their country; that, on a subject in which law is still regarded by large numbers of English people as the mouthpiece of religion, religious principles should not be actively contradicted by statute law; that, so far as may be, the verdicts of our Civil Courts of Justice should be accepted without question by the most educated and sensitive conscience of the nation, as being, within the moral sphere to which law necessarily restricts itself, in substantial harmony with the Revealed Mind of the Eternal Judge. To forfeit this harmony is national weakness; to rivet it is national strength.

Another example of the discord between law and religious conscience which I am deprecating may be observed in a legislative anomaly, to which, of late years, attention has been frequently, but not too frequently, directed.

At the English Reformation, as is well known, the supremacy of the Crown in all causes ecclesiastical and civil, was, by the terms of the preamble of the Statute of

[1] *Memoir of the Rev. J. Keble, M.A.*, by the Right Hon. Sir J. T. Coleridge, D.C.L., pp. 417, 418.

Appeals (1533), harmonized with the principle, so unquestionably venerable, and so necessary to the wellbeing of the Christian Church, of deciding spiritual causes by the spirituality.[1] Nor did the creation of the Court of Delegates, by a statute passed in the following year (1534), necessarily conflict with the principle of the Statute of Appeals; because the power to appoint the members of the court resided with the Crown, and the Crown was at least free to exercise its supremacy by appointing a majority of episcopal delegates, so as not to neutralize the principle of the earlier statute.[2] Such, for two hundred and ninety-eight years,[3] was the law of the Church and State of England; but since 1832 it has been otherwise.[4]

---

[1] 24 Hen. VIII. cap. 12. "When any cause of the Law Divine happened to come in question, or of spiritual learning, then it was declared, interpreted, and showed, by that part of the said body politick, called the spirituality, now being usually called the English Church, which always hath been reputed, and also found of that sort, that both for knowledge, integrity, and sufficiency of number, it hath been always thought, and is also at this hour, sufficient and meet of itself, without the intermeddling of any exterior person or persons, to declare and determine all such doubts, and to administer all such offices and duties as to their rooms spiritual doth appertain."

[2] 25 Hen. VIII. cap. 19, sec. 4. "And for lack of justice at or in any of the Courts of the Archbishops of this realm, or in any of the King's dominions, it shall be lawful to the parties grieved to appeal to the King's Majesty in the King's Court of Chancery; and that, upon every such appeal, a Commission shall be directed, under the Great Seal, to such persons as shall be named by the King's Highness, his heirs, or successors, like as in case of appeals from the Admiral's Court, to hear and definitively determine such appeals, and the causes concerning the same."

[3] It should be added that the above-named Acts were repealed by 1 & 2 Ph. and Mary, c. 8, in 1554, and revived by 1 Eliz. c. 1.

[4] By 2 & 3 Will. IV. cap. 92, the whole jurisdiction exercised by the Court of Delegates over the Archiepiscopal Courts was transferred to the whole Privy Council. By 3 & 4 Will. IV. cap. 41, the jurisdiction thus given to the whole Privy Council was transferred to a fixed Committee of that body. On the history of this legislation see "The Civil Power in its Relations to the Church," by James Wayland Joyce, M.A., one of the Clergy-Proctors for the Diocese of Hereford; London, Rivingtons, 1869,

In the words of the eminent authority to whom I have already referred, "a modern statute has placed in the hands of the Judicial Committee of the Privy Council, assisted by two or three of the bishops, not selected for personal fitness as judges, but in virtue of their sees, the final decision of questions touching the doctrine and discipline of the Church. Even if the Committee were necessarily composed of Churchmen, there would be the question whether such matters are properly to be adjudicated on by laymen; but it is well known that among its members may be those who are, conscientiously or otherwise, not only alien from the Church, but opposed to it."[1]

The writer proceeds to point out that the Judicial Committee has by law much more jurisdiction than is necessary to decide on doctrinal points collaterally arising in a particular cause, and only for the purposes of that cause, with a view to its determination. On the contrary, "the Judicial Committee often takes cognizance of doctrine directly, and as the point in issue; it does so in the last resort; its decision binds every court and even itself; so that if it should happen to determine certain propositions not to be contrary to the Articles, or *vice versâ*, however manifestly wrong or dangerous the decision, those propositions might be maintained and preached by any incumbent to his flock with impunity; and to preach propositions logically contradictory of them might subject an incumbent to prosecution and its consequences. It cannot be doubted," concludes this high authority, "that this would practically be very

---

pp. 76 sqq. There seems to be sufficient evidence that the Ecclesiastical Jurisdiction was transferred to the Judicial Committee by a pure accident, due, according to Mr. Joyce, to "that excessive love of verbiage and unnecessary amplification, which appears often to beset those to whom the duty of drafting Acts of Parliament is committed" (p. 79).

[1] *Memoir of the Rev. J. Keble*, by the Right Hon. Sir J. T. Coleridge, p. 467.

much the same as making a new doctrine for the Church."[1]

To this it may be added, that the chief author of the Act alluded to it in language which appears to imply, that to refer doctrinal cases to a court so constituted was nothing less than a legislative blunder. Speaking in his place in Parliament, the late Lord Brougham observed, that "he could not help feeling that the Judicial Committee of Privy Council had been framed without the expectation of [ecclesiastical] questions .... being brought before it. It was created for the consideration of a totally different class of cases, and he had no doubt that if it had been constituted with a view to such cases as the present [the Gorham case], some other arrangement would have been made."[2]

And yet, while within the past week a measure has been brought before the Legislature for the reform of the ecclesiastical courts,[3] it expressly leaves this capital anomaly altogether untouched. It is too much to hope that some effort will be made to remedy so serious and threatening an evil? Is it really impossible to harmonize the historical prerogatives of the Crown, and the just susceptibilities of the guardians of the law, with the immemorial rules, with the governing principles of the Church of Jesus Christ?

It would be easy to dwell for no inconsiderable time upon the grave consequences of the present state of things to the best interests of religion; and those who know anything practically of the difficulties with which the English Church has to contend in a great many quarters at the present moment, know with what urgency and effect this

---

[1] *Memoir of the Rev. J. Keble*, p. 468.

[2] Hansard, 3rd S., vol. cxi. p. 629; quoted by Joyce, *ubi supra*, p. 78. To the same effect, the late Bishop Blomfield: "The contingency of such an appeal came into no one's mind." See Joyce, *ibid.* p. 79.

[3] By the Earl of Shaftesbury.

feature of our actual system is pressed against her. But the question is one of national as well as of religious importance. The strength of Christian States is to be fortified and secured by relations more or less intimate with strong, well-ordered, and loyal Churches, whether they are "established" or not; because such Churches, while training souls for a higher and better world, can, more surely than any other agency, reinforce the pulses of the heart of the nation with constant and abundant and harmonious infusions of moral purpose. And when are Churches strong to do this? Not necessarily when they can command the various influences of station, of wealth, of intellectual culture, of seats in the Legislature; not necessarily when they are invested by the national will with temporal privileges, of which no serious man will think or speak lightly. Churches are strong when their spiritual self-respect is unimpaired; when their deepest life is free to live in accordance with the provisions of that Divine Code which is its first and most imperative law. And it is neither charitable nor wise to neglect wounds in well-instructed and sensitive consciences; wounds which, if untended, will rankle and fester into deadly sores. The Church of God is freer to acknowledge, to uphold, to insist upon the Divine sanctions of the civil law, without suspicion of her motives in doing so, if Cæsar does not touch the things of God; she is better able to proclaim the mission which civil government has received from heaven, if Christian doctrine is not brought, I will not say, before Pilate, but before judges, upon whom high character and position will not of themselves confer the Apostolical power of "sitting on thrones to judge the Twelve Tribes of Israel."

III.

But the subject involves, if somewhat indirectly, a consideration which may have a more immediate and general interest even than the foregoing. What is the responsibility of society at large for the particular crimes which are published in our courts of justice? It was Jewish society which delivered the sinless Christ into the hands of Pilate. It is Christian society which delivers modern criminals into the hands of the officers of the law.

Doubtless it is right—it is necessary—to punish them. And yet how many a criminal may use the words of Christ, in a different yet in a most true and literal sense, when he is placed at the bar for judgment, after being found guilty of robbery or murder: "He that delivereth Me unto thee hath the greater sin." "He that delivereth me!" Not the policeman who arrested me; not the magistrate who committed me for trial; not the witness whose evidence satisfied the jury of my guilt; but society. That vast abstraction, that most real albeit complex agent, society, is the greater criminal. I am but the victim of its heartlessness, the fruit of its neglect, the product and result of its example: "He that delivereth Me unto thee hath the greater sin."

Is this a libel, or is it the voice of truth and justice—of partial truth, at any rate—of some measure of justice? Let us consider.

Many of us are familiar with a modern writer who would answer this question by announcing a doctrine which practically annihilates freewill. He maintains that full knowledge of the antecedents of a moral agent, and of the circumstances which surround him, enable you to predict unerringly how he will act under particular conditions; since his action follows inevitably from a foregoing combination of facts, of which it is the natural product and issue.[1] Obviously, according to this theory, society furnishes a very large contribution indeed towards individual crime. And yet, if freewill do not exist, it is plainly a mistake to describe any act, however horrible its results, as criminal. Upon that supposition a murder and an earthquake must have exactly the same moral significance; and no more *blame* on the score of a social tragedy ought, in fairness, to be attributed to the remote influence of society than to the individual ruffian whose hand is red with his neighbour's blood.

But the immorality of this doctrine should not blind us to the element of truth which it contains, and which is recognised nowhere more fully than in the Christian Scriptures. This truth is, that although no one man is simply what circumstances have made him; although he is what he is primarily in virtue of the secret, self-controlling centre of consciousness and volition, which is himself, and which, by its successive thoughts, emotions, and resolves, has made him what he is; yet society has supplied the mental atmosphere which has encouraged and cherished, or stunted and blighted his moral growth, as the case may be. Society has surrounded him with knowledge or with ignorance, with high moral ideals or with base moral ideals, with encouragements to virtue or with encouragements to vice, with traditions in favour of effort and self-sacrifice or with traditions in favour of sloth and degradation. True, these traditions do not act upon him so irresistibly as to kill his liberty of breaking through them. But they do make virtue easy or difficult; and nothing is more certain than that the responsibility of a moral being, in the eyes of the Eternal Justice, must vary

---

[1] Buckle, *History of Civilization in England*, vol. i. p. 25. "The individual felon only carries into effect what is a necessary consequence of preceding circumstances." Cf. p. 29.

x

in exact proportion to his opportunities. An act of hideous idol-worship at Tyre or Sidon, or an act of debasing vice at Sodom or Gomorrha, implied less moral evil in the agent than did indifference to truth or neglect of opportunities in Chorazin, or Bethsaida, or Capernaum.[1] The Jews were more guilty before God than the Gentiles, because " by the law is the knowledge of sin."[2]

Is this not in harmony with our own experience? When we are with particular persons, or surrounded with particular associations, it seems natural to do right, it seems almost impossible to do wrong. When we are elsewhere or with others, we are, it may be, other men: we think and act without difficulty in ways which, but just now, would have seemed impossible. This variation would not hold good in the case of the extremes in the moral world; it would be true neither of the very bad nor of the consistently holy. In both of these cases, moral habit is sufficiently fixed and strong to defy the pressure and solicitation of circumstance. But of the great mass of men it is true that their moral life depends largely upon the circumstances which surround them; and it is the great mass of men, after all, that is in question.

Undoubtedly the wide difference of opportunities between man and man, class and class, country and country, age and age, is determined by, is a part of the good Providence of God; it is the visible expression of His predestinating will respecting each of His moral creatures; and it thus brings before us one of the most mysterious features of His government of the world. But within this larger aspect of the case we may safely observe a narrower one, and confine our attention to it, since it is practically of the highest importance.

If, for instance, we could trace out the whole personal history of any one of the prisoners who will be convicted

---

[1] St. Matt. xi. 21-23.   St. Luke x. 13-15.   [2] Rom. iii. 20.

of theft or of graver crimes at the forthcoming assizes, we should find that he has enjoyed that particular measure of opportunities which society, that is, the aggregate of men and women living at this present time in this particular part of England, has put before him. Whether or not he has made good use of his opportunities is a matter for his own conscience before God. But whether he has had any good opportunities to make use of is a question for us, as members of society, still more as members of the Church of Christ.

For is not this a matter as to which the great number of educated and well-meaning people in this country habitually deceive themselves? We all of us talk of the duties and the responsibilities of society. But all the while we mean by society an abstract entity, with the action and resolutions of which we have individually as little to do as with those of the English, or it may be of the French Government. Whereas the truth is, that society, or the only part of it with which we have any concern, is but an abstract way of describing a particular relation of other people to ourselves, and of ourselves to other people. And if crime and poverty are upon the increase in England, and this side by side with an increasing concentration of luxury and wealth in the hands of an upper class, it needs no great political discernment to see in this condition of things the elements of grave social danger, which may well demand the earnest attention of the Legislature, but which, in the first instance, make a serious call upon ourselves as individuals.

Now every one of us may individually act on existing crime in three main ways.

First of all, we may do something to prevent it. This chiefly by furthering the Education of the Poor. We may discharge this duty, either through others or by personal labour; either in particular places or by supporting societies with larger fields of operations, whether diocesan or national.[1] By education I mean Christian education. An education in useful knowledge, as it is termed, which leaves God, conscience, the eternal future, the Atoning Blood, the means of grace, out of the question, will not really do much to stay the progress of crime. It will make crime less brutal and stupid; but it will probably deepen its moral complexion. Secular education only arms the brute that is in us all with new weapons of offence, without doing aught to tame his ferocious instincts. But to support *Christian* education is to arrest crime at the fountain-head; it is to cut off the main supplies from the great torrent of national immorality; it is to bring heads and hearts, while nature is yet impressible, under those blessed influences which make crime unwelcome, and which enlist its natural votaries and victims in the cause of virtue.

Secondly, we may do something towards repairing the ravages of crime. There is a great deal of crime which never falls under the hand of the law, or which, after conviction, is unable to recover itself. To help those who have gone wrong, probably through little fault of their own, to return to the paths of virtue, is a privilege which is offered to most men sooner or later in private life. Such opportunities occur almost always under circumstances which do not admit of publicity. In view of this portion of our responsibility towards crime, the support of reformatories and of penitentiaries is of imperative obligation.[2] To give a kindly hand to the many who long to rise, but who cannot rise without it; to inspire hope, the very soul of moral recovery, into those who are still fettered and in darkness, but who hear of a comrade's return to moral light and liberty; this is to do Christ's work in the world, if anything is to do it. And to do it thus in some measure is within the power of every one of us.

[1] Prov. xxii. 6.   [2] Gal. vi. 1.

But, thirdly, it is by honest, unshrinking efforts at inward self-improvement that we can best act upon the great abyss of contemporary crime.[1] Such is the solidarity of this human social world, that the actions, the words, nay, the inward moral and mental habits of each one of us, may powerfully affect for good or for evil human beings whose faces we never saw, but who feel, through contact with others, the pulsations which radiate from our inward life. Our most powerful influence upon others, be it bad or good, is that natural outcome of our hearts and thoughts, which proceeds from us almost without our knowing it; and which penetrates into regions of which we have no suspicion. Especially is this true of those who belong, for the most part, to the higher classes; they have opportunities of making contributions to the world's general stock of bad example and false opinions which are not enjoyed by their poorer brethren.

Beneath our feet a perpetual deposit of moral mischief is accumulating; it is filtered through the thousand avenues of social contact; it forms a subsoil which generates crime as its native product. We may have made more positive contributions to that fund of evil than we think; and on this, as on many other matters, the discoveries of the last Great Day should be anticipated, if they are not to take us by a terrible surprise.

At any rate an assize is a plain call to earnest efforts; to generous efforts for others, to sincere efforts within ourselves. If we are tempted, on reading of such and such a criminal, to any Pharisaic self-complacency, we do well to consider what we individually, being such as we are, should have done if we had been placed in his exact social circumstances; if we had been, perhaps, undisciplined, unrefined, uninstructed, pressed by poverty, uncheered, unaided by friends, unsupported by the many

[1] St. Matt. vii. 5. St. Luke vi. 42. Rom. ii. 21-24.

motives which have power with us, short of that one true motive for a Christian—the love of the Perfect Moral Being, our Lord and God. St. Augustine used to say that, but for God's grace, he should have been capable of committing any crime; and it is when we feel this sincerely, that we are most likely to be really improving, and best able to give assistance to others without moral loss to ourselves.

If it is a duty to punish crime, it is a prior duty, if we can, to save criminals. If it is permitted us to be of moral service, however indirectly, to others, it is safe first of all to place ourselves as penitents at the foot of the Cross of our Lord Jesus Christ, with a prayer which can never be inappropriate to the real circumstances of any human soul: "Enter not into judgment with Thy servant, O Lord; for in Thy sight shall no man living be justified." [1]

[1] Ps. cxliii. 2.

NOTE TO THE SECOND EDITION OF THE FOREGOING SERMON (1869).

PROFESSOR CONINGTON has done me the honour of noticing so much of this Sermon as bears upon Dr. Döllinger's interpretation of our Lord's saying about Divorce.[1] Professor Conington's criticism covers more ground than the argument or the notes of this Sermon; it is, in fact, almost a continuous commentary upon the Third Appendix to Dr. Döllinger's "First Age of the Church." Some acknowledgment is due to a writer of such Christian earnestness and academical eminence, although in the following remarks several of the points which he has raised are unavoidably unnoticed.

Professor Conington admits that philologically Dr. Döllinger "has the advantage of giving a sense to πορνεία, which no one can dispute."

On the other hand, to say the very least, the greatest uncertainty must be allowed to attach to any interpretation of our Lord's words which takes πορνεία to mean adultery with a single paramour. Döllinger proves with unanswerable force the carefully observed distinction between πορνεία and μοιχεία in the New Testament and LXX.; St. Matt. xvi. 19; St. Mark vii. 21; St. John viii. 3; a distinction based upon an earlier and kindred one between the corresponding Hebrew words. As against the view that πορνεία is a generic term including adultery, he observes that when more than the natural sense of the word is meant, either μοιχεία or ἀκαθαρσία are used with it: St. Mark vii. 21; 2 Cor. xii. 21; Gal. v. 19; Eph. v. 3; Col. iii. 5; Heb. xiii. 4. Professor Conington insists upon the ἐν πορνείᾳ ἐμοιχεύθη of Ecclus. xxiii. 23, and rejects Dr. Döllinger's explanation that the two words are put together for emphasis, on the score that this would hardly be the case if one of them was inapplicable. As Ecclesiasticus is beyond doubt an Alexandrian translation from a Hebrew or Aramæan original,[2] is it not probable that this phrase represents an emphatic construction very common in Hebrew, in which the *inf. abs.* is placed before a finite verb of the same stem; and that it would have been rendered literally but harshly ἐν μοιχείᾳ

---

[1] *Contemporary Review*, May 1869, Art. i.
[2] Reusch, *Lehrbuch d. Einl. A. T.* p. 140; Davidson, *Old Test.* iii. p. 418.

ἐμοιχεύθη? If so, it may have been deliberately varied by the translator, partly for the sake of euphony, and partly with the object of hinting that an act, which in any woman would have been at least πορνεία, was in a wife something of a distinct and more serious character, namely, μοιχεία. As to 1 Cor. v. 1, it is at least probable that Döllinger is right in understanding πορνεία to mean incest with a father's widow. The τοῦ ἀδικηθέντος of 2 Cor. vii. 12, as Neander[1] suggests, may very well stand for τοῦ ἀδικήματος; and the Apostle would then mean that he did not write of the sin, considered as an act of social injustice, but considered as an offence against the purity of the Christian life, for which he desired to show his zeal. At any rate we cannot be sufficiently certain that ἀδικηθέντος is masculine and refers to the father of the incestuous person, to ground thereupon a single exception in 1 Cor. v. 1—and it would be no more—to the ordinary New Testament use of πορνεία.

But even if it were clear that πορνεία might, in one or two places, include adultery, there would surely be some risk in insisting upon this rare sense in the case of a practical passage of critical importance. The natural course is to understand the word in that which is confessedly its usual sense. If our Lord had said, "Whosoever shall put away his wife, except for the cause of adultery, causeth her to commit adultery," no question could have been raised as to His meaning. If He meant μοιχεία, why did He say πορνεία? To reply with Professor Conington and others that He meant to include "unchastity before marriage discovered afterwards" is hardly satisfactory, since it assumes that unfaithfulness after marriage would have been primarily understood to be the sense of the expression. To refer to the preference which a modern writer, treating the subject in a similar way, might feel for the generic word "unchastity" as compared with the particular term "adultery," is, as it seems to me, too hastily to attribute a modern sentiment to a sacred speaker in a distant age. In nothing does Holy Scripture differ from writings of our own day more strikingly than in the fearless unreserve and explicitness with which it treats of subjects which cannot be discussed by ordinary persons without grave risk of doing harm to themselves and other people.

Professor Conington would scarcely seem to have done sufficient justice to the admitted and important consideration that St. Matthew had Jewish converts especially in view in the selection of materials for his Gospel.[2] "The solid fact," he says, "that St. Paul, St.

---

[1] Quoted by Alford *in loc.*
[2] Cf. Alford, vol. i., *Prolegomena*, p. 30. Meyer, *Ev. Matthaus, Einl.* p. 20.

Mark, and St. Luke do not mention what St. Matthew does, is, I conceive, to be accounted for simply by the consideration that they were concerned rather with the rule, which, of course, was the thing on which our Lord laid most stress, than with the exception."[1] But is not this language about the rule and the exception misleading? Is it not the case that if our Lord's words in St. Matthew are rightly interpreted, as meaning that divorce *a vinculo matrimonii* may follow upon or is effected by an act of adultery, we have before us in St. Matthew an altogether distinct rule from that which is given by the other sacred writers? "A rule which does not admit an exception is a very different thing from one which does. A law which binds all persons, under all circumstances, is not the same as one which binds only particular classes, or which exempts under certain circumstances from its operation. The difference in such cases is one not of form, but of substance; it makes the rule or the law applicable or inapplicable, according to particular circumstances, and variable in its effects; and upon this applicability or inapplicability depends the responsibility or immunity, moral as well as legal, of those who are within the sphere of its authority; the difference being of course more marked, as well as more important, if the consequences of any violation of the rule or law are made severely penal."[2]

In view of this consideration, the silence of all the other writers of the New Testament on so vital a feature of the Christian Law of Marriage is unintelligible, if our Lord really meant that the Marriage-tie is dissoluble by adultery. It is not too much to say, that upon this supposition, they present us in the Name and words of Christ with a totally different Marriage Law from that given by St. Matthew. There are of course rationalistic accounts of such like differences, but they are generally fatal to the authority of the New Testament altogether. If our Lord did permit divorce on the ground of adultery, the Churches of Corinth and Ephesus would have needed and might have expected to hear of it at least as soon and as fully as the Jewish Churches for whom the first Evangelist especially wrote. Is it not more reasonable as well as more reverent to believe that St. Matthew alone has preserved these words of Christ, because they applied to the case of the Jews alone, and in the sense suggested by Dr. Döllinger?

It is impossible not to sympathize with Professor Conington's unwillingness to recognise any temporary exceptions or references in a discourse meant for all time, such as was the Sermon on the Mount. But may we then admit the Christian and Eucharistic reference (as

[1] *Cont. Rev.* p. 3.
[2] *Considerations on Divorce,* by a Barrister, London, 1857, pp. 5, 6.

distinct from the merely Jewish sacrificial one) of St. Matt. v. 23, 24 ? I rejoice to think so: although Tholuck says, "The Redeemer spoke not to Christians, but to Jews: no wonder, then, if His discourses bear traces of being addressed to those among whom the Jewish worship and ceremonial were still retained."[1] Tholuck's remark may be pushed too far; but its legitimate scope would not appear to be exceeded if we apply it to the two clauses occurring in a single Gospel written confessedly for Jews, which on any other interpretation are inconsistent with the law elsewhere and always stated absolutely of the indissolubility of marriage.

For it cannot be too earnestly repeated that the consistent teaching of the New Testament is in favour of this principle. The Divine precepts, given without any qualification by St. Mark and St. Luke;[2] the Apostolical arguments, Rom. vii. 1-3; 1 Cor. vii. 10, 11; Eph. v. 25-33, all point one way. To take the last: "What more irreconcilable with divorce than the Apostolical precepts, Eph. v. 28-30? If a man can hate his own body, his own self, his own flesh; if the Lord Jesus can hate and forsake His Church; then there may be divorce from the marriage-bond among Christians. Not else."[3] Professor Conington believes that the German Reformed divines are right in saying that the reason why adultery destroys marriage is that the original *unitas carnis* is destroyed, and a new one formed. He appeals to 1 Cor. vi. [16?] But the question is whether the essence of marriage lies in the moral contract *taken before God*, or in the mere *unitas carnis*. If the latter, then every act of adultery or gross indulgence is equivalent to the making of a new marriage-contract,—a conclusion which even Tholuck is apparently driven to accept.[4] If the former, then human unfaithfulness cannot destroy that which has a Divine sanction: man's sin cannot really put asunder what God has joined.

The fatal concessions to which the German Protestant divines are committed do not avail to bridge over the chasm which yawns between the legislation of their country on the subject of marriage and that which they still believe to be the teaching of our Divine Lord. Tholuck remarks, that down to the middle of the eighteenth century no grounds of divorce, save the two allowed by Luther and Calvin, that is to say, adultery and malicious desertion,[5] were generally sanctioned by the statutes of the Protestant Church, the Con-

---

[1] *Bergpred.* in vv. 23, 24.   [2] St. Mark x. 2-12.   St. Luke xvi. 18.
[3] Keble, *An Argument for not proceeding immediately*, &c., p. 42.
[4] *Bergpred. in St. Matt.* v. 32.
[5] So limited in Luther's work, *Von Ehesachen*, 1530: he had specified four grounds of divorce in his *Von Ehelichen Leben*, 1530. Thol., *Bergpred.*

sistories, and the writers on Ecclesiastical law ; although there were some exceptions at Zurich, at Basle, in Wurtemberg and in Prussia. With the period of "Illumination" there came a still laxer code. The civil courts were generally invested with the control of marriage affairs, as being purely *civil* affairs. New reasons for divorce were insisted on, such as, "uncongeniality of disposition," "irreconcilable enmity," and the like. "After the middle of the eighteenth century, the influence of this laxity began to extend even to the law-books. Not crime merely but even misfortune was considered a valid ground for divorce. At last, the Prussian legislation, having arrived at the highest pitch of 'illumination,' sanctioned divorce by mutual consent where the marriage was childless, thus changing it into a matter of contract and private law."[1]

It is instructive to read Olshausen's commentary on the passages in St. Matthew, as exhibiting the struggle of a sincere conscience vainly endeavouring to be loyal at one and the same moment to the teaching of Christ and to the unchristian marriage-law of Protestant Germany. Olshausen abandons the endeavour to observe even that portion of our Lord's teaching upon marriage which he still upholds. And to do this the better, he projects a distinction between an external and an internal Church, which, if it could be accepted, might help us to set aside all Christ's moral precepts that are in any way distasteful to corrupt human nature. "The external Church," he argues, "as a visible institution cannot possibly be regarded as the expressed *ideal* of the kingdom of God. It is rather the mere covering, in which the communion of all the faithful is enswathed, than the kernel in the shell. *Hence* the regulations of the external Church cannot answer to the *ideal* requirements of the βασιλεία ; but as the Church occupies the Old Testament standing-ground in the majority of its members, it must also order its regulations in conformity to the Old Testament. As, then, in the Old Testament God permitted not only divorces, but also the remarriage of the separated persons, so the Church *may* admit modifications of our Lord's law, as expressed in St. Matt. v. 31, 32. Indeed the Church *must* do so."[2] The "external" Church of Christ would, upon this supposition, be defined as a body of professing Christians who cannot be expected to keep the moral precepts of Christ. Is it not plain that some of the best divines of Protestant Germany are fatally influenced by civil laws and a public opinion which they should improve or resist ; the power of a corrupt human tradition blinding them to the requirements of the Word of God ?

May He grant that it be not so among ourselves !

[1] *Bergpredigt, in St. Matt.* v. 32.   [2] *Comm. in St. Matt.* v. 31.

www.ingramcontent.com/pod-product-compliance
Lightning Source LLC
Chambersburg PA
CBHW031853220426
43663CB00006B/600